2-6

Strategies for Elementary Social Science Education

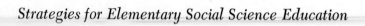

Bruce R. Joyce

The University of Chicago

STRATEGIES
FOR
ELEMENTARY
SOCIAL
SCIENCE
EDUCATION

S R A

Science Research Associates, Inc.

Chicago

To my wife Betsy

PREFACE

The writing of this book grew out of the conviction that we are at the beginning of a new period in the teaching of the social studies—a period that is creating a closer relation between scholars and educators, between the social sciences of the university and the social education of the elementary school. The term *elementary social science education,* appearing in the title of this book, actually expresses the belief that a child best learns a subject discipline by pursuing that discipline in the manner of a scholar. The sophisticated ideas and methods of the social scientist are deemed accessible to the child six to twelve years old—provided they are developed in words and situations that the child is able to handle on his own. In short, a social science education is intended to make the power of mature scholarship available to children. An obvious corollary is that the teacher himself must deepen his own educational background in the social sciences and, in fact, become both a social scientist and an educator if he is to teach proficiently in this new period of rethinking and revising the social studies.

From the outset I attempt in this book to define why it is valuable to instill in the child the approach and outlook of the social scientist. As suggested in Chapter 1, the goals of such an education are not solely intellectual; they are also the development of the child's emotional and personal maturity and of his critical awareness of the responsibilities and possibilities of democratic citizenship. The intellectual and social goals of education complement one another rather than conflict. Such goals, too, are not new, nor are my suggested means of attaining them. A social science education has rational support in educational theory old and new, from John Dewey and Charles A. Beard to Jerome S. Bruner.

A period of change is no time for producing a textbook that describes the social studies as popularly taught and that prescribes methods fitting the present mold. The need, rather, is to prepare teachers to innovate and experiment in curricula and methods of instruction and to help teachers to derive an understanding of what is centrally important in the wealth of knowledge of the social sciences—that is, important for the child's intellectual, civic, and psychological development. Only with such understanding can the aspiring teacher begin to think and teach boldly and inventively; only with some rationale to guide him in selecting materials and methods can he free himself from excessive dependence on the guidelines of prescribed elementary textbooks. For this reason the chapters that follow pay particular—and perhaps unusual—attention to the structure of the social science disciplines and to theories of learning and child development. Chapters 2 through 5, in the section entitled "The Content of Social Science Education," are given over completely to examining the central concepts and methods of the social sciences and relating them to the ends and means of education. Chapters 6 and 7 of the following section, "The Psychology of Social Science Education," describe research in social and cognitive psychology, and relate this research to the concepts and modes of inquiry of the social sciences. All these chapters collectively are intended to help curriculum planners and teachers in their search for rational bases on which to repattern the social studies.

The next section, "Strategies for Teaching the Social Sciences," essays a fresh look at the organization of lessons and curricula. An intensive analysis of the organization of curricula and of the principles on which they are organized would perhaps be unnecessary if one assumed the perpetuation of the traditional curricular patterns. However, if one assumes a period of innovation in the social studies, then analysis would seem imperative; thus in Chapter 9 I have discussed at length several curricular patterns, old and new, and outlined possible strategies for organizing curricula on the basis of principles suggested in the earlier chapters on social science education. In addition, in defining lessons and "depth studies" in Chapters

8 and 10, I have tried to offer the beginning teacher some theoretical and practical guidelines for organizing his children's daily and semestral work. The intention is to offer the teacher the kind of understanding he needs if he is to experiment and strike out on his own.

The content of the next five chapters, grouped under the heading "Materials and Methods for Teaching the Social Sciences," is suggested by the titles and headings listed in the Table of Contents. All varieties of instructional methods and materials are discussed: international exchange programs, field trips, resource persons, textbooks, trade books, pamphlets, documents, testing materials, and audio-visual aids such as filmstrips, slides, motion pictures, television programs, maps, charts, tables, and graphs. However, rather than vainly attempt to dictate specific materials or prescribe recipes for instruction, I have tried to be more general and to point out several criteria for selecting materials, various reference guides such as bibliographies, and countless *examples* of worthwhile materials and methods—all for the purpose of getting the beginning teacher sufficiently grounded so that he can exercise his own inventiveness and learn how to find instructional aids appropriate for his particular classroom needs.

In order that the education student reading this book may have an opportunity to exercise this inventiveness, I have provided at the end of each chapter a list of problems, tasks, or discussion questions under the overall heading "Inquiries." Each inquiry either calls upon the student to apply what he has learned in the chapter to some specific classroom condition or encourages him to do further reading and research on a particular topic. The list of "References and Readings" immediately following the inquiries in each chapter is intended both to acknowledge my personal debt to published materials in the writing of this volume and to serve as a bibliographical aid to the student's further reading.

x

The ideas contained in this book were stimulated by so many colleagues and tested by the reactions of so many education students and elementary school children that I am reluctant to begin naming them. Even the bibliographies only begin to acknowledge the sources of ideas I found in books and journals. To the editors of the college department at Science Research Associates I owe gratitude for the innumerable queries and suggestions that have vastly improved the final product, while permitting me—even encouraging me—to venture into new fields that in my view deserve exploration.

BRUCE R. JOYCE

CONTENTS

THE PURPOSE
OF SOCIAL SCIENCE
EDUCATION

Chapter 1

PURPOSE

Three goals direct the social studies.

Humanistic education is the first goal. The social studies should help the child comprehend his experience and find meaning in life.

Citizenship education is the second goal. Each child must be prepared to participate effectively in the dynamic life of his society. Correspondingly, the society needs active, aware citizens who will work devotedly for its improvement.

Intellectual education is the third goal. Each person needs to acquire the analytic ideas and problem-solving tools that are developed by scholars in the social sciences. With increasing maturity the child should learn to ask fruitful questions and examine critical data in social situations.

The point of view of this book is that these three goals are compatible and that educational activities can be designed to strive for all three goals concurrently—even though, in the past, the activities for the three have often been unrelated and conflicting. American public education has had great difficulty reconciling the schools' traditionally intellectual function with the demands of helping people to find themselves and to prepare for active citizenship. The particular purpose of this book is to set forth a plan for the social studies that resolves these demands and develops a systematic rationale for planning and directing coherent instruction.

The tools for accomplishing the threefold objective reside in the social sciences. As we help the child to learn the tools of social, economic, and political analysis prevailing in the social sciences, we also help him to examine the social world about him, lead him to face social problems, and help him to comprehend his experience. As he grows in ability to apply the concepts of social science to his own experience and to contemporary society, his social world will become more comprehensible to him and he will be better able to participate rationally as a citizen. The simple thesis of this book is that instruction in elementary social studies should be centered on the child's examination of his social world, that he should be helped to examine social topics in such a way that he progressively learns to *apply*—not merely memorize—the intellectual tools of the social sciences.

This thesis is not original. Presently, as the thesis is enlarged and explicated, the many sources from which it is drawn will be cited and placed in context.

In proceeding with the explication, we may keep in mind the advice of Ralph W. Tyler, who has suggested that the task of the person planning instruction is to answer four questions:[1]

1. What objectives are being sought? (What pupil behaviors will we seek to change?)

2. What activities are likely to bring about the selected objectives? (How shall the pupil encounter the environment?)

3. How should we organize instruction? (What comes first? What is appropriate for whom? What important ideas or skills or values will we repeat over and over again, year by year, until learning has continuity and the objectives are achieved?)

4. How can progress be measured? (No easy task in social studies. "Does the learner understand his society more fully this year?" is a hard question to answer.)

The answers to these four questions provide a plan for instruction. Throughout the book we shall be guided by these four questions, trying as we go to develop principles that will help the teacher to make plans and carry them out. However, our first concern is with the purposes of social studies instruction—those purposes dictated by the goals we have listed: humanistic education, citizenship education, and intellectual education. The three goals are considered in turn.

Humanistic Education:
Helping the Child to Comprehend His Life

The first goal of the social studies is to help the child sort out the confusion of the social world so that he can attain personal meaning. This need of the child originates in the central purpose of the democratic state. Reality exists, insofar as we are permitted to know it, in the consciousness of individuals. The fundamental purpose of legal government, the fundamental purpose of public education, is to enhance that consciousness. The net result of the social studies should be that the child is better able to

---

[1] Ralph W. Tyler, *Basic Principles of Curriculum and Instruction* (Chicago: Univ. of Chicago Press, 1950).

think effectively about social phenomena—better able to order his own life in terms of social realities.

Every human being is shaped by the culture that surrounds him. Before he is old enough to resist, his social world moves in on him, teaches him, forms him. As he grows older, the pressure to conform to his social milieu does not lessen. Unless the child learns to examine his own society and to see how it shapes him, he will very likely find himself swallowed up by it. The capacity to resist cultural determinism and to help make a better society depends on the acquisition of the ability to analyze the society and the ways it works to determine us. "To the extent that we are able, by whatever device we choose, to use our critical faculties to interpret existing ideas and institutions, to that extent are we saved from falling into an idolatrous pose before them."[2]

What does it mean to help the child comprehend his social experience? It means he comes to understand the causes of behavior, including his own, and develops tactics for inquiring into social problems. It means he develops values and a critical awareness of his values.

As he experiences social interaction, then, he should increasingly be able to analyze it. He should be able to ask better and better questions about social behavior, get better and better information, and use it more effectively to explain and improve interaction. He should, in short, develop a strategy that he can apply to social problems, a strategy that will help him identify the critical factors that are operating.

— He should also become increasingly aware of the values he is absorbing from the culture and develop ways of modifying and extending his values by rational means. When his values conflict with those of other people, he needs to learn to examine carefully the rationale for his beliefs and the rationale for theirs. Then he should have the humility to compromise when that is indicated, the skill to negotiate when that is reasonable, and the courage to stand and be counted when that is appropriate.

Whence come the ideas that will help the child comprehend his social world? They come from the social sciences.

> Scientific method is the only authentic means at our command for getting at the significance of our everyday experiences of the world in which we live. . . . Scientific method provides a working pattern of the way in which and the conditions under which experiences are used to lead ever onward and outward.[3]

---

[2] Stephen R. Graubard, "Preface to 'Excellence and Leadership in a Democracy,'"*Daedalus*, XC (Fall 1961), 626.

[3] John Dewey, *Experience and Education* (New York: Collier, 1963), p. 88.

The methods and major conclusions of the social sciences are our major intellectual means for helping the child to understand life. As we help him examine his experience, we need to teach him to use the tools and ideas which the social scientist uses. To help the child understand his economic life, we have the tools of economics. To help him comprehend his heritage, we have the tactics of the historian and the anthropologist. And so on.

To help the child to understand, therefore, means to help him to learn and apply to his own experience the fundamental skills and knowledge which scholars have developed for social diagnosis. The following passage is a reporter's description of an election day in New York City. Imagine what a difference it might make if the people described were to look at themselves as the political scientist or the sociologist or the anthropologist might do.

PRIMARY DAY? WHAT PRIMARY?

EXCUSES KEEP MANY FROM POLLS

There were all sorts of good reasons for voting in yesterday's primary elections, but the majority of registered New Yorkers found better reasons not to.

The weather was almost idyllic, the voting precincts numerous, and the choices varied. The polls were open from 3 P.M. until 10 P.M., so most working people could vote. But, for one reason or another, the majority preferred to sit on front steps in the sunshine, take the children to the park, eat pizza beneath sidewalk awnings, or sit at home and watch television.

The 19th Congressional District was a microcosm of the city yesterday. In the 19th, a crescent-shaped territory that runs south from West 86th Street around the tip of Manhattan and up through the Lower East Side to East 20th Street, Leonard Farbstein, the incumbent, and William F. Haddad, the challenger, had been battling for two months.

But a walking tour of the district yesterday revealed little interest in this Democratic campaign or the primary. It also showed that some of those who didn't vote felt guilty about it.

"I voted already," said a middle-aged woman on upper Broadway yesterday morning, several hours before the polls opened. She spoke with all the dignity and pride of someone who really had voted.

"I don't live in this district," said a butcher, apologetically, as he carved a side of beef. "So I can't vote. I live in the Bronx, you see." He had forgotten that there was a primary in the Bronx, too.

Several persons who said they were registered voters made comments that indicated they did not know the difference between a primary and a general election.

One man expressed surprise when asked about the voting. "I thought that was all next November," he said.

South of Bleecker Street, where the 19th takes a turn around the base of Greenwich Village, a large woman with bushy eyebrows sat on a folding chair on the sidewalk outside her apartment.

"They won't help us, so why should we help them?" she said of the politicians.

A grizzled man sat on steps nearby. He cursed his employer for not allowing him time off from work to vote. His working hours, he said, corresponded with those of the polls. He was asked for whom he would vote if he could vote.

"I don't know," he replied. "Who's running?"

In Chelsea, a handsome woman with long, black hair explained why she would not vote. "I am a Puerto Rican," she said, "and therefore I cannot vote."

On the Bowery, which is also part of the district, Tommy McCarthy and Frank Joyce lounged in the shadows of a brick building. The two men said they had failed to remember somehow that this was Primary Day.

But Mr. McCarthy said that if a stranger would just tell him who was running—"Who's the G.I. Joe candidate this time, I always vote for the G.I. Joe candidate"—he would immediately perform his civic duty.

"Well," said the stranger, "in your district the men who are running are Haddad and Farbstein."

"Haddadfarbstein," Mr. McCarthy said. "O.K., I'll vote for him."[4]

> ## Citizenship Education:
> ## Preparing the Child for Social Responsibility

The second goal of the social studies is to prepare citizens who can perpetuate and enhance their society. The passage just quoted should be sufficient to show that comprehending life and finding meaning are closely related to citizenship behavior.

Unquestionably the American public expects its schools to provide a continuing supply of literate, informed citizens. Charles Beard eloquently summed up the requirements of citizenship education in one of the seventeen volumes of the American Historical Association's Commission on Social Studies. The supreme purpose, said he, is

. . . the creation of rich, many-sided personalities, equipped with practical knowledge and inspired by ideals so that they can make their way

---

[4] Fred Powledge, "Primary Day? What Primary? Excuses Keep Many from the Polls," *New York Times*, June 3, 1964. © 1964 by The New York Times Company. Reprinted by permission.

and fulfill their mission in a changing society which is part of a world complex. . . . They are firm of will, for without will nothing great will be accomplished. They are imbued with the highest aspirations of the human race, for without aspiration there is no great motive power for action.[5]

The American public has charged its public schools with the development of citizens who know the heritage of their society and are equipped to participate fully in the political and social life of their time. Yet, as Beard has pointed out, the social world is shifting and changing in a way that prevents the formulation of dogmas that can fix what the citizen should know for any great length of time.

Speaking summarily, we may say that the primary information which social science must supply through the schools to individuals is information concerning the conditioning elements, forces, and ideas of the modern world in which life must be lived. Any representation of them is bound to be partial and out of perspective—such is the frailty of the human mind, but it must be attempted in . . . every possible apparatus for conveying information vividly and realistically to the immature mind.[6]

The citizen needs to acquire informal skills and information not only in order to adapt to his rapidly changing world but also in order to help shape his future society. This is a critical goal in citizenship education. F. H. George has pointed out:

We are at the beginning of the biggest social revolution that the world has ever seen, far greater in size and implication than the industrial revolution, and this time we cannot afford to be ignorant of the facts. . . .

We are building, or are about to build, machines that will change the face of our civilization, and unless we are ready to change ourselves at the same time, and see the reasons for the changes, we may be without a future in which to change at all. . . .

The tendency towards inertia, or even active resistance, when confronted with change, is deep-rooted in the biological make-up of man. Change implies new stimuli to which we may not know how to react, and this is a threat to our feeling of security, a feeling which thrives on the familiar. This basic need for security, through the familiar, is especially deeply ingrained in a society that has been successful to any

---

[5] Charles A Beard, *A Charter for the Social Sciences* (New York: Scribner, 1932), pp. 96–97.
[6] *Ibid.*, pp. 98–99.

extent. This applies to Britain and other countries whose very successful background has encouraged a degree of conservatism that makes it difficult to accept even the smallest modification. We tend to live, like an aged matinee idol, on our past glories.[7]

The development of cybernetics and other devices for viewing machine and man in complement has resulted in reconceptions of man and his ends that call for a citizen who can look with cool objectivity and human compassion on the problems of reshaping his destiny, leaving no thinking at all to the ubiquitous "George."

Citizenship education, then, requires the development of leaders or persons who, in Beard's words, can "formulate, propose, advocate, dare and direct."[8]

> The function of citizenship education, however, is partially to provide stability in the society. If citizens fail to grow to appreciate freedom and the possibilities of justice and equality, then the struggle for the realization of these ideals in the actualities of social life soon falters. The gains of the American Negro in recent years are certainly a reflection not only of education for change but of education to appreciate and deepen the meanings of freedom and equality. It is dedication to the core values of America that has made change possible. To encourage dedication to core ideals that hold us together as a human society is a fundamental responsibility. Perhaps in the future the school may need to be the chief agent of social solidarity. "Whatever the facts are about the truth of religion, there seems little doubt that religion did, to some extent, act as a social cement, and now that it has become less effective, one wonders what, if anything, is going to take its place."[9]

The faster the world changes, the more its social institutions will be shaken as they adapt or, even more radically, as they fail to adapt. In the nineteenth century, education could count on the sure enculturation of the young in the core ideals of the community simply by action of the social pressures operating outside the school setting. Mass man, with his institutions whirling in constant change, may find his formal education is the main stem of his ability to see values and purposes in the unfamiliar situations of his social life.

Citizenship education, then, as Robert J. Havighurst has expressed it, serves a twofold purpose: "First, it is the stabilizer or perpetuator of society, and second, it is an agent for change. As a stabilizer, education

[7] F. H. George, *Automation, Cybernetics, and Society* (New York: Philosophical Library, 1959), pp. 11–13.

[8] Beard, p. 100.

[9] George, p. 29.

mirrors what is already in the society and reflects it into the lives of the next generation. As an agent of change, education acts under the direction of technological or ideological forces to make each generation different from its parent."[10]

It is time to point out that the American society which has charged public education with the development of a reflective citizenry has, over the years, made at least partly taboo the examination in schools of many areas of culture, tabbed by Maurice Hunt and Lawrence Metcalf as "closed areas."[11] Franklin Patterson has made an excellent paraphrase of Hunt and Metcalf's categories:

1. Economics. While "open" to professional economists and many laymen, this field is so affected by taboos, confusion, and emotion that schools tend to avoid it as a subject for rational study.

2. Race and minority-group relations. In recent years this field has become more open to reflective inquiry in schools, but in some places fears, tensions, and confusions continue to make it a closed area.

3. Social class. Here is a "truly closed area" in the writers' judgment, "neatly ignored as a result of the widespread belief, 'There are no social classes in America.' "

4. Sex, courtship, marriage. This area is more open to inquiry than it was a few years ago, but critical analysis of contradictions and problems is not usually encouraged.

5. Religion and morality. Morality is somewhat more open to reflective inquiry than are religious beliefs, but both tend to form a closed area as far as schools are concerned.

6. Nationalism and patriotism. This area is one in which it is difficult to question traditional beliefs, even if they are inconsistent with real behavior or the requirements of national survival.[12]

The development of these areas that have been relatively closed to school debate is but a single symptom of what we referred to earlier as a successful society trying to preserve the patterns that have served it well in the past. The result has been a debilitating one; often communities whose schools are undergoing racial integration will frequently resist discussion of race in their classrooms. In other words, the job of citizenship education

---

[10] Robert J. Havighurst, "How Education Changes Society," *Confluence: An International Forum,* VI (Spring 1957), 86.

[11] Maurice P. Hunt and Lawrence E. Metcalf, *High School Social Studies: Problems in Reflective Thinking and Social Understanding* (New York: Harper, 1955).

[12] Franklin Patterson, "Citizenship and Schools for the American Future," in *Citizenship and a Free Society,* 30th Yearbook of the National Council for the Social Studies (Washington: National Education Assn., 1960), p. 12.

for a changing society runs against the fact that each society has built into it mechanisms for maintaining the status quo. If effective education for citizenship is to take place, "teachers, administrators, and the public at large will have to accept the fact that the social studies are one of the major places in the school curriculum where unpleasant questions are asked and perhaps even unpleasant answers are to be found."[13]

> The taboo areas of social inquiry are exactly those areas into which the social studies, from the elementary grades through the graduate school, must penetrate.[14]

How can we help our future citizens develop the commitment and insight that will help them preserve and improve their culture? Four closely related avenues are open to us.

First, we can operate school and classroom so that the child experiences the kinds of human interaction and the kinds of problems that he will face later on. We can involve him in citizenship activities through which he can learn the commitment to social process and the skills that will make him effective later.

Second, we can expose him to discussion of the serious social movements and problems that are shaping the world in which he is to live, so that he will learn to live in and cope with a changing world.

Third, we can provide him with the tactics that social scientists use to approach social problems. These tools will enhance his effectiveness as a citizen as much as they will enhance his personal quest for meaning.

Fourth, we can help him explore his heritage and the heritage of other peoples. We can help him examine the values he is inheriting and learn their significance.

Intellectual Education: Introducing the Child to the Social Sciences

The third goal of the social studies is to introduce children to the modes of thinking of the social sciences. As will by now be clear, the methods of the social sciences are instrumental in the two other tasks given to the social studies: helping the child to comprehend his world and preparing him for citizenship. However, the social sciences need to be taught

---

[13] Jean O. Grambs, "The Challenge to the Social Studies," in *Citizenship and a Free Society*, 30th Yearbook of the National Council for the Social Studies (Washington: National Education Assn., 1960), p. 281.
[14] *Ibid.* pp. 281-82.

on their own merit. A social studies program concerned only with citizenship or with the current life experience of the child would not completely fulfill the intellectual character of the school.

> Experiences in order to be educative must lead out into an expanding world of subject matter, a subject matter of facts or information or ideas. This condition is satisfied only as the educator views teaching and learning as a continuous process of reconstruction of experience.[15]

The fact is that knowledge is made, not found lying around. Adequate cultivation of the intellect means involvement with the places where the best knowledge is being made, with the minds of wise men and inventive scholars. One of the central purposes of the public school, as José Ortega y Gasset phrased it for the university, is to enable men to live at the level of the best ideas of their time.[16] Insofar as we can find the best ideas about the social world in the social sciences, we need to expose children to them. The social sciences consist of models of the social world, models which have been developed by social scientists. As one learns these models, he comes to possess the most complete description of the social world in which he lives.

The social sciences have also developed effective methods with which to analyze human events and problems. As the child matures, he can learn these methods in progressively more sophisticated form and use them to analyze the affairs of the contemporary world.[17]

Summary and Preview

The three goals of the social studies have been described as (1) *humanistic education,* to help the child to understand his social life; (2) *citizenship education,* to develop his citizenship behavior; and (3) *intellectual education,* to make the tactics of the social scientists available to every citizen.

One of the difficult problems of the teacher is to understand these three target areas of the social studies thoroughly and to conduct instruction so that no conflict exists between them.

In the past, many people have felt that the necessity of helping the child come to understand his life and solve his problems conflicted

---

[15] Dewey, *Experience and Education,* p. 87.

[16] José Ortega y Gasset, *The Mission of the University* (Princeton, N.J.: Princeton Univ. Press, 1944).

[17] See Jerome S. Bruner, *The Process of Education* (Cambridge, Mass.: Harvard Univ. Press, 1960).

with the necessity of teaching him content from the subject disciplines. *The point of view of this volume is that these goals do not conflict. The tactics of the social sciences are taught to the child precisely because they are the best tools we have found for helping him comprehend his life and face his problems.*

In some quarters, particularly among social scientists, there is a belief that the disciplines—economics, anthropology, history, and so on—should be taught in such a way as to preserve the integrity of each. *This volume shares that concern.* However, the preservation of the individual content of the disciplines is often taken to mean that there have to be separate courses for each of the disciplines. Underlying the next four chapters, which deal with the nature of the several social sciences and the means for translating them into forms useful in the education of elementary school children, is the assumption that the social sciences have much content in common and that a curriculum can be organized which emphasizes the unique concepts of each of them but does not establish separate courses for them. It is not possible to teach all the findings of all the social sciences or even a small part of them. It *is* possible to teach their central ideas in such a way that citizens will have them available for attack on social problems, and individuals will have them available for personal problems.

INQUIRIES

1. Select several curriculum guides. Pick some from each region of the United States, and be sure that large and small cities are represented. Examine the sections of the guides that define the goals of the social studies. Compare the statements of goals with each other and with the ideas presented in this chapter.

2. Read Chapters 1 and 2 of *The Process of Education,* in which Jerome S. Bruner defines structure. Look at one of the recent curriculum guides or textbook series in mathematics and see if you can find how the idea of structure is being used in that field.

3. Read the first chapter of Herbert Thelen's *Education and the Human Quest.* What is Thelen's conception of the function of the school? Compare his view with Bruner's and with the one expressed here.

4. Look up some of the research into the effects of social studies instruction on voting habits and on other citizenship behaviors. Note carefully the areas of behavior that do not seem to be affected by instruction. How do you explain them?

5. In a totalitarian state, citizenship education might vary considerably from the education we know. Find what is being done in the Soviet Union and what was done in Nazi Germany to ensure a supply of subservient citizens.

6. Find out about the behavior of the Americans who were prisoners of war in Korea in the early 1950s. There are several books and articles on the subject.[18] What are the implications for American education?

References and Readings

Beard, Charles A. *A Charter for the Social Sciences*. New York: Scribner, 1932.

Bruner, Jerome S. *The Process of Education*. Cambridge, Mass.: Harvard Univ. Press, 1960.

Dewey, John. *The Child and the Curriculum*. Chicago: Univ. of Chicago Press, 1959.

————. *Experience and Education*. New York: Collier, 1963.

George, F. H. *Automation, Cybernetics, and Society*. New York: Philosophical Library, 1959.

Grambs, Jean O. "The Challenge to the Social Studies," in *Citizenship and a Free Society*. (30th Yearbook of the National Council for the Social Studies.) Washington: National Education Assn., 1960.

Graubard, Stephen R. "Preface to 'Excellence and Leadership in a Democracy,'" *Daedalus*, XC (Fall 1961).

Havighurst, Robert J. "How Education Changes Society," *Confluence: An International Forum*, VI (Spring 1957).

Hunt, Maurice P., and Metcalf, Lawrence E. *High School Social Studies: Problems in Reflective Thinking and Social Understanding*. New York: Harper, 1955.

Kinkead, Eugene. *In Every War but One*. New York: Norton, 1959.

Ortega y Gasset, José. *The Mission of the University*. Princeton, N.J.: Princeton Univ. Press, 1944.

---

[18] See, for example, Eugene Kinkead, *In Every War but One* (New York: Norton, 1959).

PASSOW, A. HARRY (ed.). *Education in Depressed Areas*. New York: Teachers College, 1963.

PATTERSON, FRANKLIN (ed.). *Citizenship and a Free Society*. (30th Yearbook of the National Council for the Social Studies.) Washington: National Education Assn., 1960.

PHENIX, PHILIP H. *Realms of Meaning*. New York: McGraw-Hill, 1964.

POWLEDGE, FRED. "Primary Day? What Primary? Excuses Keep Many from the Polls," *New York Times*, June 3, 1964.

RIESMAN, DAVID. *The Lonely Crowd*. Garden City, N.Y.: Doubleday, 1953.

SMITH, HUSTON (ed.). *The Search for America*. Englewood Cliffs, N.J.: Prentice-Hall, 1959.

STONE, TOM. "The Age in Which Our Children Will Live," in *Social Studies for the Middle Grades*, ed. C. W. HUNNICUTT. Washington: National Education Assn., 1960.

THELEN, HERBERT A. *Education and the Human Quest*. New York: Harper, 1960.

TYLER, RALPH W. *Basic Principles of Curriculum and Instruction*. Chicago: Univ. of Chicago Press, 1950.

WHITEHEAD, ALFRED NORTH. *The Aims of Education and Other Essays*. New York: Macmillan, 1929.

WHYTE, WILLIAM H., and others. *The Exploding Metropolis*. Garden City, N.Y.: Doubleday, 1958.

THE CONTENT
OF SOCIAL SCIENCE
EDUCATION

Chapter 2

THE ANALYSIS OF THE SOCIAL SCIENCES

Scholarly knowledge has increased so greatly that today even the advanced specialist is incapable of complete mastery of the factual knowledge in any given field. Thus, more than ever before in the history of education, we need to devise an analytical method of sorting out the truly important material and organizing it in such a way that the relatively few things we are able to teach will have maximum educational effect.

For many years educators have pondered how practicing scholars might identify the central ideas in each scholarly field and how educators might translate these ideas into teachable form so that even the younger pupil could learn up-to-date ideas and ways of thinking. A half century ago John Dewey suggested that, from an educational standpoint, the logical handling of a subject discipline consisted of organizing its main ideas. Going on to reject the notion that these ideas should be presented to children in abstract form (in lectures, for example), Dewey argued that if the scholar and the educator could work together, a means might be derived whereby the learner could be led to construct advanced ideas out of his own experience, at first simply and later, with repetition, in more advanced forms.[1] Some years later Charles Hubbard Judd similarly stated that the specialist should select the significant "lines of thought," which the teacher should organize in a way suitable for presentation to "immature minds."[2] Alfred North Whitehead phrased the suggestion in a slightly different fashion when he proposed that a few especially illuminating ideas be identified and then introduced early and reiterated until the learner can use them with ease:

> Let the main ideas which are introduced into a child's education be few and important, and let them be thrown into every combination

---

[1] John Dewey, *Democracy and Education* (New York: Macmillan, 1916).
[2] Charles Hubbard Judd, *Education and Social Progress* (New York: Harcourt, Brace, 1934), p. 263.

possible. The child should make them his own, and should understand
their application here and now in the circumstances of his actual life.
From the very beginning of his education, the child should experience
the joy of discovery. The discovery which he has to make is that general
ideas give an understanding of that stream of events which pours
through his life, which is his life.[3]

The Nature of Organizing Concepts

What is the character of these ideas—this framework of knowledge—
which social scientists have found in their studies to be significant and
worthy of attention? Charles A. Beard defined the essential character as
follows:

> The social sciences are primarily concerned with those manifesta-
> tions of human activity and those activities occurring within society
> which involve social *consequences* and *relations*—called for convenience
> political, economic, and cultural—and with the *inter-relationships* which
> accompany the functioning of society as a whole in its world setting.[4]

Recently Jerome Bruner has restated and popularized this approach
to the analysis of subject matter.[5] Bruner's formulation rests on the contention that the product of scholarly endeavor is a series of major ideas
about relations which explain the findings of the field. The scholar collects
facts and thinks about them. The relations he sees or thinks he sees
between them are the heart of his knowledge, for it is in light of these
relations that facts are explained and organized—and thus understood.
These relations, when established as working principles, might be called
organizing concepts.[6]

---

[3] Alfred North Whitehead, *The Aims of Education and Other Essays*
(New York: Macmillan, 1929), p. 3.

[4] Charles A. Beard, *The Nature of the Social Sciences* (New York: Scribner, 1934), p. 11.

[5] Jerome S. Bruner, *The Process of Education* (Cambridge, Mass.: Harvard Univ. Press, 1960).

[6] In this book the term *organizing concept* is used in a sense identical
with that of Bruner's word *structure.* Joseph Schwab employs the word
structure interchangeably with the term *principle of enquiry* (see below,
pp. 26–27); and John Honigmann, approaching the question somewhat
differently, has relied on the word *concept* (see below, pp. 48–51). We
have chosen the term *organizing concepts* in order to avoid any possible
misconception that these ideas which explore and define consequences and
relations are static or purely formal in nature; they are, instead, working
concepts—concepts which, as we shall see, one may use daily to encounter
and organize reality.

For an example of the development of a major organizing concept, we might turn to anthropology. That each human society has developed distinctive modes of behavior—or norms—was established early in anthropological research and, as a concept, was recognized from the time of the ancient Greeks. However, the idea that culture conditions the very psychological makeup of individuals awaited the 1930s. Ruth Benedict found that the ways of thinking of the Southwest Pueblos were strikingly different from the ways of thinking of surrounding peoples, even though their physical environment was similar. She reasoned that the difference resulted because each culture, by historical chance or otherwise, has evolved and given to its members a unique "psychological set," or orientation toward reality. Culture, she concluded, affects the very ways that minds work. How an individual "sees" his environment and how he processes information obtained from his environment are conditioned by the psychological set of the culture in which he is enveloped. Benedict, by discovering this relation among the facts of anthropology, thereby made the facts more understandable; and her work prompted a search for more information and relations of the same sort in other cultures.[7]

For another example of the evolution of an organizing concept, we might review some socioeconomic experiments conducted in 1927 at a Western Electric plant in Hawthorne, Illinois. For generations, business managers (and even economists) had assumed that labor was a commodity to be bought and sold—that, specifically, higher wages or longer hours increased total output. If a factory worker's wages were increased, he worked faster and processed more items; if his workday was lengthened, he had time to produce more. The Hawthorne experiments scotched these assumptions. For almost a year, a group of girls assembling telephone relays at the plant were made the subject of experiments which tested their reaction to changes in hours, wages, and rest periods. It was found that throughout the experiment, the girls' output of relays increased—increased surprisingly—regardless of whether their pay and working conditions were bettered or worsened. The scientists conducting the research finally discovered that the experiment itself had introducd the new incentive, with interesting implications. "By putting them in a little friendly society of their own, by consulting them often, the scientists had caused a psychological change in these young women and given them a new sense of their status and value. The girls were no longer cogs in an impersonal,

---

[7] Milton Singer, "A Survey of Culture and Personality Theory and Research," in *Studying Personality Cross-culturally*, ed. Bert Kaplan (Evanston, Ill.: Row, Peterson, 1961), p. 23.

pecuniary machine; they were helping in a small way to direct the machine. So their output went up no matter how conditions were changed under them." The economic implications—the organizing concepts—produced by these results were twofold: first, workers (perhaps all men) can be highly motivated if their interest is engaged and they realize that both they and their work are important; second, a group of workers (or any similar group of allied persons) constitute a microsociety, within which will grow all the customary societal teams, bands, and personal alliances; these must be considered and, if possible, utilized.[8]

The potential utility of organizing concepts in education is very great. Since the social sciences are disciplines with great "explaining power," the learner who understands their concepts will be able to organize information more coherently. Because the organizing concepts are relatively few, they are easier to manage than the mass of facts from which they are drawn. They provide a map for getting through the mass of raw data that bombard us.

Bruner has provided a series of hypotheses concerning the application of organizing concepts to education:

1. In the scholarly disciplines, the major organizing concepts (or structures, to use Bruner's term) are essentially very simple.

2. These concepts can be developed in a form that even young children can discover (in childish terms, at first, and progressively in more sophisticated forms).

3. Organizing concepts can be utilized as focal themes in curricula, to be reiterated and rediscovered in more complex and adequate terms as one advances through the grades.

4. The child who is taught so that he discovers the organizing concepts in disciplines will be advantaged for the following reasons:

  a) Organizing concepts facilitate memory. Learning how things are related makes it easier to remember facts.

  b) Organizing concepts provide intellectual power by ensuring greater comprehension of the area concerned.

  c) Organizing concepts facilitate transfer of learning to new situations and problems.

  d) Organizing concepts are the language of the scholar. By learning these concepts the learner is brought closer to

---

[8] Stuart Chase, *The Proper Study of Mankind* (New York, Harper, 1948), pp. 160–63.

the leading edge of the discipline. He learns to think with the most advanced minds in the field.

These hypotheses are so tantalizing that one might ask why we do not immediately proceed to the experiments necessary to test them. The problem is that finding the major concepts in the social sciences is not easy. When one concentrates on the mathematics curriculum, one can call together mathematicians and educators and they can concentrate their attention on the concepts of a single discipline. It is clear, too, that a portion of the curriculum will be focused on mathematics content alone. The political scientist, asked to contribute to a discussion of the social studies, knows that the content from his discipline will be mixed with that of several others. His ideas have to be placed in context with those of the economist, the historian, and other social scientists. A second, perhaps more serious, problem is that the social sciences have yet to organize a system of concepts as thoroughly as have the natural sciences. The older social sciences lack a tradition of quantitative methods; their concepts have not been expressed in the terms of that mathematical logic which has helped so much to sort out the content of the natural sciences. The new social sciences, on the other hand, although they are built on a tradition of quantitative approaches, are vexed by the problem of newness. Their content is developing at such a rate that their taxonomies, terms, and methods are less distinct and definite than those of the older disciplines. A third problem is that the social world itself is elusive and fluid, and holds still for study less readily than does the physical world. For example, social psychology must define attitude in several ways, because attitudes manifest themselves variously and differ enormously according to numerous conditions. This uncertainty in the social sciences is reflected in the different statistical levels of confidence which are utilized in the social and the natural sciences. The psychologist will accept a proposition at the level of a 5 percent probability of error. Imagine a physicist who reported that we could accept his observation that day is brighter than night, with the probability that he would be correct 19 out of 20 times! But that is the relative uncertainty with which we live in the social sciences.

Eventually, any attempt to define the organizing concepts of the social sciences—for teaching purposes—can succeed only through a long-term effort by social scientists who can build concepts and by educators who combine both an acquaintance with behavioral sciences and the sophistication to translate these concepts into operational constructs that can be handled by children. Let us look further into the nature of organizing concepts and see if we can find some clues about the possible shape of such an inquiry.

Organizing Concepts as Modes of Inquiry

We should begin by looking briefly at some notions concerning the nature of knowledge that should be taught. The contemporary debate over what is useful content dates at least from Comenius' attempt to focus attention on content that is socially useful.[9] This Czech educator (1592–1670) saw education as the process by which the child approaches and solves problems—acquiring, as he does, certain ideas about the nature of the world. His English contemporary John Locke (1632–1704), no foe of independent thought, saw childhood as the time when the child acquires the essential knowledge that prepares him to be a rational thinker. He believed that the ideas of past thinkers should be mastered by the child in preparation for the time when he, too, would be able to be an independent thinker. This view of Locke's was typical of many of the views of subject matter that held sway to the end of the nineteenth century. Once something had been "found out," it took its place as a fact and might be learned by someone.

The pragmatists struck hard at the notion that knowledge was fixed. They emphasized the distinction between physical reality and our *conceptions* of physical reality. Because our conceptions of reality are imperfect and changing, subject matter becomes transient and imperfect—the product of the mind rather than a necessary accurate representation of external reality. Thus John Dewey was able to say:

> All knowledge, as issuing from reflection, is experimental in the literal physical sense of experimental. . . . It involves the explorations by which relevant data are procured and the physical analyses by which they are refined and made precise; it comprises the readings by which information is got hold of, the words which are experimented with, and the calculations by which the significance of entertained conceptions or hypotheses is elaborated.[10]

Prior to the pragmatists, many laymen and schoolteachers thought that knowledge consisted of rather formal and unchanging facts and ideas. The pragmatists turned scholarly ideas into hypotheses. One experiments, and one concludes. The conclusion is a hypothesis which merits further experimentation; it is not a concept that will last forever. The hypothesis is

---

[9] John Amos Comenius, *Selections* (Lausanne, Switzerland: UNESCO, 1957).

[10] John Dewey, *Essays in Experimental Logic* (Chicago: Univ. of Chicago Press, 1916).

expressed in words whose meaning varies with the experience and feelings of the perceptor.

While this view of knowledge accords with what is happening in every scholarly discipline, textbooks and instructional methods have largely concentrated on identifying verbal conclusions which are presumably to be taught to children. To read a social studies text for elementary school, for example, is to find statements of conclusions to be learned. ("The greatest corn-growing region of our country is the north central states. It is called the corn belt." "In most of the Latin-American nations the greatest problems are poverty and lack of education." "The Christian church gave Europe a kind of unity in feudal times.") Most of these books, in fact, cover too many topics too quickly to permit the presentation of data from which the conclusions were deduced. Knowledge, then—at least the conception of knowledge which we frequently teach children—becomes a system of pronouncements. In other words, when we ask children to learn statements as if they represented fixed and unchanging ideas, we are teaching them a conception of the nature of knowledge which is out of line with current scholarly thought.

Organizing Concepts and Certainty

Let us turn again to the question, What is an organizing concept? Bruner, explaining his term *structure*, says that it is "the way things are related." What he means, really, is that an organizing concept formulates the way we *think* things are related. He gives the example of an inchworm crawling up graph paper held at various inclinations. The inchworm varies its angle of progression across the graph paper so that its angle of climb does not exceed a certain proportion. We have discovered a *relation* between slope and climb. Now, one may ask how the identification of that relation helps us select content for the child to learn. It doesn't, very much; but before we make a hasty conclusion let us examine some other living organisms to see if they control their movements in patterns analogous to those of the inchworm. If we look, for example, at movements of the sunflower plant, we find that it reacts to directions and intensity of illumination, turning its blossom to face the light source. We could examine further examples, but the point is clear. We have discovered what we presently call tropism, an innate tendency to react to a stimulus in a definite way. Now the tropistic relation between organisms and stimuli becomes an organizing concept in those sciences which study the physical behavior of living things. A person who discovers the idea of tropism is prepared to investigate similar behavior in other living things.

Bruner suggests that if we can identify major concepts like these we will have identified the organization of the discipline concerned. By teaching these organizing concepts, or by introducing them to the child, we will help him to identify an organization for the things he learns, an organization which will be in accord with the way the scholar organizes the information in his discipline. If we follow these organizing concepts, says Bruner, we will avoid teaching fragmented bits of knowledge from a field, because the organizing concepts are themselves stated relations that have been at least tentatively established. The child will thus have a better comprehension of a scholarly field and an easier time remembering what he has learned, and his learning will be much closer to front-line scholarly thinking. Furthermore, a program of instruction which is centered on organizing concepts will encourage the child to discover relations and hence prepare him to be an independent thinker. Bruner rather carefully stresses that the concepts developed by the child for his own use need not be in the sophisticated form which the scholar would use. The child should discover organizing concepts in a form which he can handle, and then rediscover more and more complex and adequate forms as he advances through the curriculum. Lastly, the practice of revising concepts will teach him to hold them tentatively and prevent him from developing the erroneous notion that present knowledge will last for all time.

Joseph Schwab has approached the idea of organizing concepts (or structures) in a manner similar to Bruner's. Schwab emphasizes the changing views of subject matter which recent scientific discoveries have forced upon us:

> Forty years ago, it was possible for many scientists and most educators to nurse the illusion that science was a matter of patiently seeking the facts of nature and accurately reporting them. The conclusions of science were supposed to be nothing more than the summaries of these facts. . . . By the mid-twenties, the revolution in physics had gone so far that we were faced with the fact that some of the oldest and least questioned of our ideas could no longer be treated as literally true—or literally false. . . . Our old assertions about these matters were changed because physicists agreed to treat them in a new way—neither as self-evident truths nor as matters for immediate empirical verification. They were to be treated, instead, as *principles of enquiry*, conceptual structures which could be revised when necessary in directions dictated by large complexes of theory, diverse bodies of data, and numerous criteria of progress in science.[11]

---

[11] Joseph J. Schwab, *The Teaching of Science* (Cambridge, Mass.: Harvard University Press, 1962). The text printed here is from a speech, with minor changes in wording, given in Washington, D.C., in 1961.

In other words, the scholar looks for new information in terms of ideas which spring from the old. "A fresh line of scientific research has its origin, not in objective facts alone, but in a conception, a construction of the mind. And on this conception, all else depends. It tells us what facts to look for in the research. It tells us what meaning to assign to these facts."[12]

The tentative nature of organizing concepts should be revealed to children as they pursue their inquiries. Imagine, for example, that second-graders are studying an Eskimo family. They find that various family members perform various functions. They learn that when a person does certain things regularly we can refer to his cluster of behaviors as a *role* (one of the organizing concepts shared by sociology and anthropology). Having gotten a notion of what roles are, they then turn to study a Navaho family and soon begin to conclude that the sexes in families are assigned distinct roles—the men doing certain things and the women certain other things. Returning to a study of the American family, they find that the sex roles of Americans are, with respect to household chores, becoming less and less distinct. Males are doing housework, females are earning money, both paint the house and drive the car, and so on.

In the first place, the children learned the idea of "role" as it pertained to the Eskimo. Then, studying the Navaho, they concentrated on the development of ideas about sex roles. Finally, they had to revise their conclusions about sex roles and to see that roles are not always clear or well defined.

These second-graders, engaging in a little sociological exploration, had to develop, test, and revise ideas just as the social scientist does.

In sum, scholarly inquiry results in a series of tentative concepts about the relations between facts. These relations give rise to further inquiry which frequently requires that the concepts be modified or discarded completely. Previous views of scholarship had given us the "impression that the goal of all the sciences was a congeries of well-tested hypotheses"[13] or a series of statements on which we could permanently bank.

Using Organizing Concepts in Education

We are now in a position to make a tentative statement about the function of organizing concepts.

First of all, they are generalizations about the data of a field. They

12 *Ibid.*
13 *Ibid.*

are the classifying ideas which show how things are related in any given sphere of inquiry.

Second, they are the basis for organizing knowledge in a field. Facts are classified according to the way they relate to other facts. In the example of tropism, for example, certain behaviors of animals and plants would be classified together because of their similarity.

Third, organizing concepts guide the search for further knowledge. They do this in two ways. Sometimes knowledge is sought because a relation has been discovered in another place. For instance, when anthropologist Ruth Benedict, studying the Pueblo Indians, hypothesized that a certain cultural difference was the product of what she called a "psychological set," it behooved other anthropologists to see if psychological sets could be detected in other cultures—among the aborigines of northern Australia, for example. At other times, the awareness that an organizing concept is inadequate gives rise to research. Sociology had to invent the idea of "anomie" to explain certain normless behaviors observed in mass societies where norms have usually been thought to be particularly strong. As a guide for research, an organizing concept serves as a kind of tool for a discipline, a map to use when venturing into previously unexplored territory.

Organizing concepts should be thought of as tentative and changing, and they should be discovered by the learner rather than laid out for him. Bruner has suggested that we may be able to identify simple forms of organizing concepts which even young children can discover and apply to their own problems.

Let us assume that we will be able to identify concepts in the social sciences. What will be some of our tasks before they will be useful in education?

First we must be satisfied that they can be discovered in a form useful in citizenship education. The learner must have potential use for the concepts, or they will wither and be of little good to him. Insofar as possible, we want the concepts we present to become part of his permanent intellectual equipment, available as he needs them to attack new problems. In short, they should serve one or more of the following functions:

1. Organizing ideas should illuminate a child's study of some topic, such as American history, which he will meet many times in school and in life. If a concept can illuminate a subject area which will recur, then that concept will get exercise and will become second nature to the child.

2. The organizing concepts should be applicable to the study of social and personal problems making up part of the curriculum. They should help the child as he studies contemporary affairs, or

local government organization and function, or problems of democratic processes in his classroom. The study of economic relations in his own community should, if properly conducted, result in the development of some organizing concepts which the child can apply, for example, to the study of economic relations either in other nations or in other historical periods of American life.

In other words, just as organizing concepts provide the scholar with methods for acquiring knowledge, so should these organizing concepts provide the child with a systematic method of attack on areas where he seeks new knowledge. When the child learns how rainfall and land use are related in the United States, he may consider that relation in examining land use or climate in other nations. As he learns how political beliefs and economic interests were related in Revolutionary times, he may inquire whether the same relation holds true today. If organizing concepts are to be useful educationally, it will be because we have found a method for helping children to learn them and to employ them in pursuing research of their own.

Summary

The social sciences consist of ever changing ideas which describe the past findings of the disciplines and which direct the current efforts of scholars. These ideas may be considered the windows through which the scholar views the social world.

In order to develop social studies curricula for elementary school children, these windows have to be identified, and ways have to be found to introduce them to the young child and to help him apply them to the study of the social world.

The successful curriculum will reveal the organizing ideas of the social sciences as tentative probes—as ideas that change as experience and insight increase.

INQUIRIES

1. Look at an introductory college textbook in one of the social sciences. Does the author make clear the methods and central ideas in the discipline? What are they?

2. Read the third chapter in Herbert Thelen's *Education and the Human Quest*, which suggests that students and teachers learn the subject disciplines by practicing them. What do you think of this view? How is Thelen's suggestion compatible with the view of scholarly knowledge expressed in the chapter you have just read?

3. In *Realms of Meaning* (New York: Harper & Row, 1964), Philip H. Phenix tries to describe scholarly knowledge in terms of a rationale for selecting the essentials of general education (education for all citizens). He points out ways in which the social sciences are and are not like disciplines in other areas. What do you think of his ideas?

4. Bernard Berelson's introduction to the *Social Studies and the Social Sciences* (New York: Harcourt, Brace & World, 1962) indicates that social scientists think their disciplines possess benefits for citizenship education but desire to keep the boundaries of their disciplines distinct. What is your position on this issue?

5. Some people have remarked that if we teach children that knowledge is tentative and changing, they will feel insecure. These people believe that children need certainties to hold on to, even if the certainties have to be manufactured. What do you think of this? If knowledge is seen as changing and tentative, what will the child hold on to?

6. In *The Process of Education*, Jerome Bruner has expressed the feeling that teaching intuitive thinking cannot be divorced from teaching the structures of the disciplines. What are the reasons for his view? Where do you stand with respect to his position?

References and Readings

American Council of Learned Societies and the National Council for the Social Studies. *The Social Studies and the Social Sciences.* New York: Harcourt, Brace & World, 1962.

BEARD, CHARLES A. *The Nature of the Social Sciences.* New York: Scribner, 1934.

BERELSON, BERNARD, and others. *The Behavioral Sciences Today.* New York: Basic Books, 1963.

BRUNER, JEROME S. *The Process of Education.* Cambridge, Mass.: Harvard Univ. Press, 1960.

COMENIUS, JOHN AMOS. *Selections.* Lausanne, Switzerland: UNESCO, 1957.

DEWEY, JOHN. *Democracy and Education.* New York: Macmillan, 1916.

————. *Essays in Experimental Logic.* Chicago: Univ. of Chicago Press, 1916.

————. *Experience and Education.* New York: Mentor, 1961.

HUNT, ERLING M., and others. *High School Social Studies Perspectives.* Boston: Houghton Mifflin, 1962.

JUDD, CHARLES HUBBARD. *Education and Social Progress.* New York: Harcourt, Brace, 1934.

SCHWAB, JOSEPH J. *The Teaching of Science* (Cambridge, Mass.: Harvard Univ. Press, 1962).

SINGER, MILTON. "A Survey of Culture and Personality Theory and Research," in *Studying Personality Cross-culturally,* ed. BERT KAPLAN. Evanston, Ill.: Row, Peterson, 1961.

THELEN, HERBERT A. *Education and the Human Quest.* New York: Harper, 1960.

WHITEHEAD, ALFRED NORTH. *The Aims of Education and Other Essays.* New York: Macmillan, 1929.

Chapter 3

INTRODUCING ORGANIZING CONCEPTS TO CHILDREN

The preceding chapter described knowledge in the social sciences as a network of tentative concepts which can be thought of as the windows through which the scholar looks on the world. As he sees new things, he sometimes puts them into previously established categories. Frequently, however, he finds it necessary to alter the categories or even to remake the windows through which he peers. The process whereby an organizing concept is formulated in social science is something like the following.[1]

STEPS IN THE DEVELOPMENT OF A CONCEPT IN SOCIAL SCIENCE

Step 1

The social scientist observes social behavior.

Step 2

He formulates a concept which seems to explain the observed behavior.

Step 3

He collects some samples of behavior under controlled conditions.

Step 4

He checks his concept (Step 2) against the observed behavior under controlled conditions.

Step 5

He checks his concept against other concepts dealing with the same kind of behavior.

Step 6

He revises his concept and the concepts in Step 5, and he plans further investigation.

---

[1] Much of the material in this chapter is taken from Bruce R. Joyce and Carl Weinberg, "Using the Strategies of Sociology in Social Education," *The Elementary School Journal*, LXIV (Chicago: University of Chicago Press, 1964), 267–70.

By no means do these steps always occur in the order just given. However, organizing concepts are always being checked and revised. At the same time, existing concepts serve as maps which enable us to explore areas of life. Let us turn briefly to an example of the way in which some concepts about human interaction can guide the study of a phenomenon and some of the ways in which the concepts can be revised.

Let us suppose that a fifth-grade class is embarking on a study designed to help the children discover and revise one of the central concepts of human geography. The aim is to help them formulate a concept and to revise it as they encounter fresh information. The organizing concept we will use for illustration is that *culture and environment interact to affect patterns of human life*. This is one of the most important ideas in human geography because the interaction between culture and environment is the focus of geographic study; it is, in fact, the source of its subject matter.

Our fifth grade begins with the study of Bedouin groups in the Sahara about the turn of the twentieth century. They find that the Bedouins wore white clothing to reflect the heat. They used camels for transport because the camel is such an effective desert carrier. Their tents are constructed to shield the sun, admit the daytime breeze, and keep out the cold night wind. Trails and settlements closely follow the incidence of surface water. Their literature tends to be oral rather than written. One of their main sources of fuel is camel dung, because trees are scarce in the desert and precious for shade and food. The cloth for their tents is made of spun camel hair. They are Moslems, followers of Mohammed, and may take more than one wife.

When guests come, the Bedouin feels honored and prepares a feast. The more guests there are, the more honored he feels.

The wives live together in the harem side of the tent of hair. They sew, cook, weave, and care for the children.

The men herd sheep and camels and grow tobacco. The sheep and camels, with their wool, are traded for money, which is used to buy rice, coffee, pottery, and utensils. Market towns and grazing lands are located near sources of water.

Any of this information, and much more, can be found in encyclopedias, geographies, and trade books like Sonia and Tim Gidal's *Sons of the Desert* (New York: Pantheon, 1964).

Encouraged by fiction, Bible stories, and folklore, the children begin to form ideas about life in the desert:

"Grazing herds, moving from place to place, are the source of food, cloth, fuel, goods to trade."

"Desert people are Moslems."

"They use camels for transportation."

"They wear white flowing robes to keep off the heat."

"The desert is too dry to grow crops. They have to buy rice and tobacco unless they live by a river, like the Nile."

"The sheik, or clan leader, makes the rules."

We encourage them to form these ideas and to point out the information that supports them.

Then we help the children encounter information about other desert dwellers.

They read about Israel, and find that not far from Beersheba, one of the main Bedouin trading villages in the Negev, huge modern air-conditioned apartment houses rise from the desert. A copper refinery operates in the Negev. Dead Sea salts are dug and used for fertilizer and glass. Canals, pipes, and pumps bring water where the desert had prevailed, bringing forth fruit trees and vegetables from the sand. The religion is mostly Jewish, but Druses, Moslems, Greek Catholics, Greek Orthodox, Roman Catholics, Maronites, Circassians, Protestants, Armenian-Gregorians, and Copts are also found.

Fuel includes natural gases, obtained chiefly from a deposit in the Negev.

Some families are banded together in kibbutzim, in which children are raised in common. Others are gathered in extended-family groups. Others form conjugal units that keep to themselves. The people are individualistic and the government republican. Even sheiks are subject to the common law.

Both men and women in Israel receive military training; and most jobs, including high government positions, are open to both sexes. All this information and much more can be found in *Israel*, by Robert St. John and the editors of *Life* (New York: Time Inc., 1962), in encyclopedias, in the Gidals' *My Village in Israel* (New York: Pantheon, 1959), and in other trade books and films.

Now we help our fifth-graders to take another look at the ideas they have formed about life in the desert.

Every idea has to be modified, for in this second desert group, life was quite different indeed.

"Maybe it's got something to do with the history of your people. Maybe history shows how you're going to live."

"The Bedouins seem to live as they did a long time ago. In Israel almost everybody but the Bedouins seems very modern."

The children are beginning to get the idea that environment alone is not the determinant of human life. They are ready, perhaps, to study how culture is passed down and evolves. Perhaps now they can compare a Virginia plantation of colonial times with a modern cotton or tobacco farm, in order to see how things have and have not changed. Or, possibly, they can study the Navaho and the ways and things he has borrowed from others, in order to determine how culture is transmitted from people to people.

They are on their way. They cannot yet define culture. They still lack the depth knowledge of another culture—knowledge they will need in order to see how culture forms and operates.

They have, however, made concepts, found them wanting, and revised them. They are beginning to dovolop the habits of analysis and self-doubt that drive the social sciences. When they study a jungle people, they will not be so likely to say "This is how people live in the jungle."

More likely, they will say "This is how *one* jungle people lives. Let's see how some others manage it."

A Principle of Teaching

Thus should organizing concepts be taught to children—as tentative explanations of behavior, as ideas that very likely will change. By exploring concepts in this way, the child can, hopefully, prepare himself for the lifelong revision of ideas that will enable him to adapt to a changing world.

A principle of teaching that recognizes the changing nature of ideas can now be stated: *Social ideas should be taught as tentative, changing concepts, constantly to be verified as we acquire new evidence.*

Perspectives in the Social Sciences

Each social scientist views the world of human interaction in a slightly different perspective. Each social science emphasizes some facts more than others, and each discipline organizes its facts a little differently than do the other disciplines.

For example, in studying a desert people, the sociologist might not have focused on the physical environment but on the family or the structure of groups. Looking at the same people, the political scientist might have studied their electoral processes or their power relationships with one another and with their leaders. An economist might have examined their roles in production or the ways in which they are consumers. The anthropologist might have been interested in the ways they transmit culture to their children. And so on.

It is important that we help children to see life in all these perspectives and to see how he can use the different points of view of all the social

sciences to comprehend his own life and that of other human beings. A
second principle of teaching can be stated: *The perspectives of all the social
sciences should become available to the child.* Put another way, the child
should learn to see things from more than one point of view.

A Strategy for Teaching the Social Studies

Every strategy for teaching is based on assumptions about the
nature of learning, about the nature of scholarship in the fields concerned,
and about educational goals.

The strategy for teaching that we will repeatedly discuss in this
book can be described as follows. Some of the assumptions have been made
explicit earlier in the book; others will be discussed in later chapters.

1. The learner should be led to examine his own life and the
societal life of others. Social life provides the raw data of the social
studies. This aspect of our teaching strategy derives from our first
two major objectives of social studies: (1) *humanistic education,*
to help the child comprehend his own life and find meanings in
it, and (2) *citizenship education,* to help him understand his society
and prepare him to make active contributions to it.

2. The conduct of this examination should progressively reveal
to him the organizing concepts that advanced social scientists use
to analyze human life. This aspect of our teaching strategy derives
from our third major objective of social studies: *intellectual development,* to help the child learn the major tools employed by advanced social scientists.

3. The child should be led to apply these tools to his study
of social life. This application is necessary so that what he learns
will become part of his active equipment for facing life problems
and improving his society. For example, as he arrives at a gener-
alization about family life in his community, he should test the
concept when he studies other communities. (Conversely, as he
learns about family life in a foreign community, he should apply
what he learns to the study of nearby families.)

4. The child should learn to make inferences and generalizations as he finds more data that necessitate revisions. In fact,
information should be presented to the child in a sequence that
requires him to revise and restate general concepts and causes
him to learn that the present state of anyone's knowledge is tentative. This aspect of our teaching strategy is necessitated by two

factors. The first, detailed in Chapter 2 and again earlier in this chapter, is that knowledge of society is tentative and shifting. The second is that the shifting, changing nature of social life itself demands of us flexible modes of coping with and managing problems. Although our present knowledge of society may be insufficient for the child who will be alive in 2030, the habit of revising our organizing concepts and our ways of attacking problems is not so likely to go out of date.

As we proceed through the book we will extend this teaching strategy in the light of facts about human development, learning theory, and the nature of social processes. In the present chapter and in Chapter 4, however, we will further examine the modes of inquiry of the social sciences and the means of translating them into our teaching strategy.

Translating Social Science Knowledge into a Form Children Can Learn

One of the real difficulties of teaching is that scholarly knowledge is not created in the language of the child, or created for his particular use. The geographer invents concepts that he and other geographers can use to explain things. When he speaks of a *savanna climate* or a *peninsula,* he is using a term deliberately because it has a precise meaning for him, rather than because children will learn it quickly. When the economist speaks of *balance of trade,* he refers to a useful concept, not necessarily an easy one to teach.

Therefore, one of the most difficult tasks facing the educator is to translate scholarly concepts and methods into forms that can be readily taught to children. The following pages introduce the process whereby scholarly ideas can be made accessible to children.

The Organizing Concepts of Sociology

Sociology provides several organizing concepts that the child can arrive at if he is encouraged to draw upon his own experience. Once learned, these concepts can be used almost immediately, because the child can apply them to many other family, school, and community situations with which he is already familiar. By so doing, he can gain fuller insight into the "arrangement" of his life.

Four sociological concepts may be selected for illustration. (These concepts were tested in the classroom by Carl Weinberg and the author, and the questions and responses given in the following pages were those actually recorded in experiments conducted in third- and fifth-grade classes.) These four organizing concepts, even though designed by sociologists to analyze and describe human groups in a sophisticated fashion, can be understood in elementary terms by the immature child:

Norm. A rule that prescribes certain types of action and forbids other types of action.

Sanction. A penalty for unacceptable behavior or a reward for conforming to standards. Sanctions operate in groups to cause group members to conform to norms.

Value. An object of preference by a social group. Frequently values are cited as the reason for norms. A group that values cleanliness may apply _sanctions_ to persons who do not observe the _normative_ behavior of "keeping clean."

Role. A behavior pattern that is assigned to certain individuals, such as a decision-making pattern, an economic pattern, and the like. Wherever differentiation of behavior is found, roles appear. _Values_ are attached to roles, and roles are circumscribed by _norms_. _Sanctions_ may be used to enforce role-linked behavior.

These four organizing concepts should not be taught directly; the teacher should not, for example, attempt to define a _norm_ abstractly and then proceed deductively to list the ways in which norms manifest themselves in everyday life. Rather the manifestations, or "observed forms," of these concepts should be explored first, so that the children come to formulate the concepts just as the social scientist has developed them from _his_ observations. Organizing concepts should be constructed out of the experience of the child—_by_ the child, with the guidance of the teacher. So learned, concepts can be viewed as working ideas which unfold with experience and analysis.

After selecting the organizing concepts to be sought (in this case norms, sanctions, values, and roles), the teacher must next find familiar forms in which the concepts can be observed by the child. The social groups with which the child is obviously most familiar are his _community_, his _family_, his _school_, and his _peer group_. How do norms, sanctions, values, and roles operate in these groups? The following outline illustrates how the teacher might list some observable forms of the concept "norm," the list to be used as his guide to asking questions and directing the inquiry of his pupils.

NORMS AS THEY APPEAR IN FORMS OBSERVABLE BY CHILDREN

In their community:

We greet our neighbors.

We cut our lawns.

We shovel our walks when it snows.

We don't walk into our neighbors' houses without knocking.

We don't make too much noise outside late at night.

We pay our bills.

We go to work or school in the morning.

We dress up for church.

We register to vote.

We do not tell others how to vote.

We help our neighbors when they ask us.

We do not throw food on people's lawns.

We walk on sidewalks and not on people's lawns or flower beds.

In their school:

We read.

We pay attention.

We wear clean clothes to school.

We do our homework.

We do our work in class.

We do not talk without permission.

We do not cheat on exams.

We do not talk back to the teacher.

We come to class on time.

We do not curse in class.

We do not push in line.

We help the teacher.

The teacher does not have pets.

The teacher treats us fairly.

The teacher does not give us more work than we can do.

With their family:

We ask our parents' permission to go out at night or after school.

We clean our room.

We do chores that our parents ask us to do.

We love our parents and our parents love us.

Our parents feed, clothe, and take care of us.

We come home when our parents expect us.

We do not hurt our younger brothers and sisters.

In their peer group:
>We do not push or bully.
>We play fair in games.
>We do not quit.
>We help our classmates with homework on things they cannot do.
>We lend money when we have a lot and when someone who has none asks us.
>We accept the vote of the group.
>We defend boys in our group against outsiders.
>We join in games. (We do not refuse to play.)
>We play safely.

After listing a variety of these simple statements (statements which can be made more sophisticated as one advances through the grades), the teacher must next formulate questions that will lead the children into discovering and identifying the observable forms of the concept "norm." Children cannot be asked to identify norms abstractly before they know what they are concretely. Thus concentration at this stage should be on helping the children to come across observable data. Then when they are led to reason about this data, they will begin to arrive at some idea approximating, at their level, the idea that the scholar has when he uses the term *norm.* The following is a list of some guiding questions which the teacher might ask of students in conversation in order to stimulate inquiry.

GUIDING QUESTIONS FOR DISCOVERING NORMS

In their community:
>What are some things that people on our street do all the time?
>How do people living on our block behave?
>What are some things we never do on the street or in public that we do in our house?
>What are some rules that can help us get along with people in our neighborhood? (What do our neighbors expect of us and what do we expect of them?)

In their school:
>What are some things that our teachers and principal expect us to do and would not like if we didn't do?
>What are some things the teacher does that we would not like if she didn't do?

In their family:

When we are at home, what are some things our parents expect
us to do and would not like if we didn't do?

What are some things we expect our parents to do and would
not like if they didn't do?

In their peer group:

What are some things we expect our friends to do that we
would not like if they didn't do? On the playground? In
class? In games?

By asking children guiding questions, one can stimulate them into
examining examples of the concepts. Carl Weinberg and the author found,
for example, that third- and fifth-grade children found examples of norms
when asked:

"What are some things that you expect each other to do all the
time and you believe others expect of you?"

The children mentioned many examples of classroom behavior that
were expected:

"You expect them to be quiet in class and do their work."

They also mentioned examples of playground behavior:

"Well, when you're playing, you expect them not to knock it
[the ball] out of people's hands and not to come over and catch
it if you're not in the game."

"You expect everyone to let you in their game, let you play with
them, not in the middle, but when they start."

They found examples of norms in the home as well as at school.
They found expectations that were shared by adults and expectations that
were shared only by children.

They were also able to identify evidence for the existence of norms.
Particularly interesting was the evidence they found of observable forms
of *sanctions* that would be applied to individuals who failed to observe the
norms. For example, the following question was asked:

"What are things we do to show others that we are not happy
with what they do? For example, if somebody is not playing fair

or breaking up our game, how could we show them that we don't like it?"

Here are a few of the children's answers:

"You could holler at him."
"You could just move away and not play with him."
"You could tell him that you'll never let him play in any of your games ever again."

The children, following guiding questions, were also able to identify sanctions that might be applied at home for a violation of norms or for obedience to norms.

"They could send you to bed."
"Take away your allowance."
"They could tell you that they were very angry."
"They can say they're proud of you and show that they like it. They can give you compliments."
"When you do something for somebody, just expect a thank-you."

After the teacher has identified organizing concepts from the social sciences and concrete examples of these concepts, he is in a position to develop guiding questions to lead the children into their own discovery of the concepts—on a level they can understand.

Using Organizing Concepts as Tools of Inquiry

After helping the children to find observable forms of norms, sanctions, values, and roles, the teacher should then help the children to apply the guiding questions to other analyses of social behavior. Not only must children, like social scientists, learn to create organizing concepts, they must also learn to use them as tools of inquiry—as means of examining life and classifying information. If the child studies the English family, the Japanese family, the Indian family, and his own family, using the guiding questions, he will be in a position to compare these families in terms of norms, sanctions, values, and roles, which are the very concepts used by the sociologist to analyze the family and other social groups. When the child studies other people in depth, he should have the guiding questions ready. When he studies current events, he can ask, for example, "What is it that these people believe is important?" (The sociologist would say, "What are their *values?*") At first the child will have no idea what norms or sanctions are *by name,* but as his study proceeds through the years he will develop these organizing concepts more completely, precisely, and maturely. There need be no concern about this lack of terminology, at least until the secondary school years, when he can begin to verbalize the concepts in scholarly form.

Are present social studies materials adequate for this task of promoting the discovery of concepts? They are, to the extent that they provide the child with raw data he can analyze. With fifth-graders the author has used an ordinary filmstrip surveying life in Israel and simply asked them the question, "What is important to these people?" That their responses were intelligent, even though based on inferences from the pallid data of the film, is indicated by the following responses.

> "It said that they herd sheep the way their fathers do. Does that mean it is important to them to be just like their fathers?"
> "Well, they are building a lot of dams and growing things you can't grow without irrigation. That doesn't sound like everything has to stay the same."
> "It means water must be important, too, doesn't it?"
> "Yes, and manpower to do all those things. It even said many of the women hold jobs in industry."

To help the child think clearly, however, we undoubtedly need materials that offer raw data rather than conclusions. Much of the present commercial material in the social studies presents the child with too many conclusions to learn, and too little data to permit analysis by means of guiding questions or by any other inductive method.

Summary

In this chapter several principles which can guide our approach to teaching elementary social studies were identified, principles which follow from the characteristics of the social sciences and the central purposes of the social studies:

1. The learner should be led to examine his own life and the social life of others. Social life provides the raw data of the social studies.

2. The conduct of this examination should progressively reveal to the child the organizing concepts which the advanced social scientist uses to analyze human life.

3. The child should learn to apply these tools to an examination of his own life.

4. The child should learn to make generalizations about social behavior and to revise these general ideas as he encounters new evidence, even as ideas in the social sciences are continually reexamined and revised.

INQUIRIES

1. With a child of elementary age, hold a conversation such as the one reported in the last half of this chapter. See whether you get the same results; that is, determine whether the child is able to find norms, values, and sanctions in groups with which he interacts.

2. See whether you can find some examples of social science concepts that have changed as new knowledge or insights have developed. For example, you might look at the changing interpretations of the causes of the American Revolutionary War or at some of the ideas concerning the matter of government manipulation of economic affairs through balancing and unbalancing national budgets. Can you find any concepts that have *not* changed through the years?

3. Read Bernard Berelson and others, *The Social Studies and the Social Sciences,* and see whether the views of the social sciences presented in that book agree with the ones presented here.

4. Imagine that a first-grade class is studying "The Stores in Our Town." How might the sociological concepts described in this chapter be useful to the children? What would be some examples of the concepts that they might encounter in their unit?

5. How would the organizing concepts of sociology help a sixth-grade class studying the implementation of the 1964 civil rights law passed by the United States Congress?

6. Do you think that teaching strategies derived from sociological concepts would be more useful in the upper or the lower grades? Defend your position.

References and Readings

American Council of Learned Societies and the National Council for the Social Studies. *The Social Studies and the Social Sciences.* New York: Harcourt, Brace & World, 1962.

BEARD, CHARLES A. *A Charter for the Social Sciences.* New York: Scribner, 1932.

BERELSON, BERNARD, and others. *The Behavioral Sciences Today.* New York: Basic Books, 1963.

BROEK, JAN O. M. *The Nature and Study of Geography.* Columbus, Ohio: Merrill, 1965.

CHASE, STUART. *The Proper Study of Mankind.* New York: Harper, 1956.

COMMAGER, HENRY STEELE. *The Nature and Study of History.* Columbus, Ohio: Merrill, 1965.

DEWEY, JOHN. *Intelligence in the Modern World.* New York: Modern Library, 1939.

DUVERGER, MAURICE. *An Introduction to the Social Sciences with Special Reference to Their Methods.* New York: Praeger, 1964.

GALLAGHER, JAMES J. "Research on Enhancing Productive Thinking," in *Nurturing Individual Potential.* Washington: Assn. for Supervision and Curriculum Development, 1964.

HANNA, PAUL R., and LEE, JOHN R. "Generalizations from the Social Sciences," in *Social Studies in Elementary Schools.* (32d Yearbook of the National Council for the Social Studies.) Washington: National Education Assn., 1962.

HOMANS, GEORGE C. *The Human Group.* New York: Harcourt, Brace, 1950.

HUNNICUTT, C. W. (ed.). *Social Studies for Middle Grades.* Washington: National Education Assn., 1960.

JOYCE, BRUCE R., and WEINBERG, CARL. "Using the Strategies of Sociology in Social Education," *Elementary School Journal,* LXIV (February 1964), 267–70.

MARTIN, RICHARD, and MILLER, REUBEN G. *The Nature and Study of Economics.* Columbus, Ohio: Merrill, 1965.

PELTO, PERTTI J. *The Nature and Study of Anthropology.* Columbus, Ohio: Merrill, 1965.

Project on the Instructional Program of the Public Schools. *Deciding What to Teach.* Washington: National Education Assn., 1963.

ROSE, CAROLINE B. *The Nature and Study of Sociology.* Columbus, Ohio: Merrill, 1965.

SORAUF, FRANCIS J. *The Nature and Study of Political Science.* Columbus, Ohio: Merrill, 1965.

Chapter 4

THE SOCIAL SCIENCES
AND APPROACHES
TO CONTENT

Having examined the character of the knowledge produced by the social scientist and having briefly explored how some concepts of one social science—sociology—can be translated into a teaching form appropriate for children, we may now delve deeper into the charactertistics of various social sciences—anthropology, political science, economics, geography, and history.

Anthropology and the Three Types of Organizing Concepts

Anthropology "as a discipline . . . studies the whole range of human behavior. . . . For such a total way of life the anthropologist uses the term 'culture' . . . the whole system of interrelated behavior produced" by a people.[1] Although, admittedly, the most important ideas in anthropology, like those of all young disciplines, are in a state of constant modification (even its central concept, "culture," has been used with "over one hundred different meanings"[2]), we can still say that basically the anthropologist studies three kinds of phenomena: the activities of a people, the ideas they share, and the things they produce. Some anthropologists may emphasize one kind of phenomenon more than others. Some, for instance, may specialize in the structure of languages. Others may combine the study of language with the study of mental processes. And still others may emphasize the ways in which the young are indoctrinated into the culture of their

---

[1] John J. Honigmann, *The World of Man* (New York: Harper, 1959), pp. 3–4.

[2] *Ibid.*, p. 10.

people. But whatever their specialty, anthropologists together seek to contribute to a description of the total portrait of each culture.

Some anthropologists believe that each culture is the unique product of forces operating at a particular time and place, while others believe that general "laws" can be discovered that describe the formation of all cultures everywhere. Regardless of one's conception of the scope of the field, however, most would agree that the singular characteristic of the anthropological method is *comparison.* Comparisons are made in either of two ways. Some anthropologists study single cultures through time, observing cultural change and *comparing* various stages of cultural evolution in the life of a people. Lange's study of the New Mexican pueblo Cochiti is an example of a study tracing a culture from prehistory to the present.[3] On the other hand, anthropologists may compare several cultures existing more or less concurrently. An example of this comparison of different peoples is the familiar *Patterns of Culture* (Boston: Houghton Mifflin, 1934), by Ruth Benedict. By so comparing one culture with another and carefully identifying likenesses and differences, anthropologists have developed their chief organizing concepts. Says Margaret Mead: "All cultural analysis is comparative. It is assumed that without comparison culture would be imperceptible to the individual who would not be able to distinguish between cultural behavior and biologically given, unlearned behavior."[4] In other words, by comparing cultures one is able to distinguish between behaviors that are common to the species and apparently biological, and behaviors that are socially learned and modify gradually with the passing generations. Only these latter behaviors are a part of culture.

The comparative method enables us to begin to separate out those behaviors learned in groups and those mechanically caused through biological adaptation. This is especially important for self-understanding. The behaviors which we see about us while we grow up seem, since they have "always been there," to be so natural as to be almost biologically true to the species. The behavior of people who do not adhere to the patterns of the average of our society often seems to us to be "abnormal," or foreign to the species. When we compare the patterns of our culture with those of another, however, we can see that patterns that seem strange within

---

[3] Charles H. Lange, *Cochiti: A New Mexico Pueblo, Past and Present* (Austin: Univ. of Texas Press, 1959).

[4] Margaret Mead and Rhoda Metraux (eds.), *The Study of Culture at a Distance* (Chicago: Univ. of Chicago Press, 1953), p. 26. Anthropologist Meyer F. Nimkoff has defined cultural behavior similarly: "Of central importance in the culture concept is the idea that such behavior is learned from the group and is not inherent or biological." ("Anthropology, Sociology, and Social Psychology," in Erling M. Hunt and others, *High School Social Studies Perspectives* [Boston: Houghton Mifflin, 1962], p. 31.)

our group are quite normal in the context of another group. Hence we can begin to identify those of our characteristics that are socially acquired and to understand better the processes that made us what we are.

The methods of the anthropologist, then, are characterized by two features. First is the focus on the total culture—the entire configuration of political, social, economic, and other behaviors and artifacts that are developed in a society and transmitted from generation to generation. Second, and integral with the first, is the comparative and historical approach.

To help a child imitate the anthropologist, we must be sure he has access to enough information about a human community so that he can begin to see the totality of its culture. And we need to lead him to make comparisons between different cultures, so that he can begin to understand the organizing concepts of anthropology. For instance, studying families of several lands will enable him to see not only how families function in a culture but also how forms of family life differ in various societies. Similarly, as he sees religions in several cultures, he can begin to identify what religion is, from the anthropologist's viewpoint, and what it does.

If we are determined to help the child develop an "anthropological perspective" (an awareness of the extent to which behavior, including his own, is socially inherited), we should arrange the curriculum so that the child continually makes comparisons between cultures. He can compare literature, political behavior, religions, and so forth, noting always how social inheritance influences the patterns of the present generation.

THREE TYPES OF ORGANIZING CONCEPTS. Before we explore how the comparative studies of anthropology might be introduced to children, it may be well to turn once again to the subject of organizing concepts. In Chapter 2 we introduced definitions of organizing concepts, stating that they indicated relations between facts, organized the knowledge of a discipline, and guided research for more knowledge. In Chapter 3 we adduced a few such concepts in sociology—norms, sanctions, values, and roles. Now, entering anthropology, we are prepared to analyze organizing concepts still further, breaking them down into three general types: observed concepts, inferred concepts, and ideal-type concepts. All these concepts are used by social scientists to filter information and organize it. They differ only in that they are applied to three different types of information.

As one travels through life he has innumerable experiences. The people he meets, the objects he sees, the events he participates in, all leave with him memories that crowd his consciousness with the recollection of things past. These recollections, however, are not simply piled up in his mind like grains of sand. The mind sorts them into categorie between them, and gradually forms a system for organiz   experiences. Anyone who is past infancy meets his daily life with predispositions to organize new information in accord with this gradually emerging network of categories. Some new experiences, of course, do not fit into the old categories, so they have to be revised. For example, the young child sees a smile as an expression of joy. Later he may learn that some people use a smile as a cover-up for sadness. So, whereas a smile first meant happiness, the child learns to suspend judgment until he has more evidence.

The organizing concepts of the social sciences can be regarded simply as systems developed by scholars to categorize experience. Taught to the child, they help him form predispositions for processing information from his world so that his processing methods are in line with the analytical thinking of the advanced scholar.

OBSERVED CONCEPTS.[5] An *observed concept* is formed by noting similarities, differences, or relations between objects that can be apprehended directly by the senses, such as verbal statements, physical actions, or objects. Thus one may note in various cultures the similarities and differences in the objects used for child care. The similarities or differences that the social scientists notes are the *concepts* he uses when he thinks about child-rearing utensils. To use another example, one may note that in some cultures the conjugal (husband and wife) unit is the basic economic unit, whereas in others the "extended" family is the basic unit. The social scientist may perceive that nomadic hunters have more weapons and war capacity than tribes that till the soil. Each similarity and difference, each relation between factors, is described by a new category or concept. Usually concepts are named so that they can be referred to easily. Thus families that revolve about the mother are called matriarchies, while those in which the father is central are called patriarchies. These concepts describe forms of family organization that have been found by *observing* family relationships.

If a child is to form such a concept, he has to be able to see similarities or differences in objects that he has perceived directly or that have been described to him so completely that he sees them as very real and detailed.

INFERRED CONCEPTS. An *inferred concept*, on the other hand, "points to unseen events which can only be inferred from some more immediately

---

[5] Although we have altered the nomenclature slightly, the three kinds of concepts discussed here were developed by anthropologist John J. Honigmann in his book *The World of Man* (New York: Harper, 1959). For what we have designated as observed, inferred, and ideal-type concepts, Honigmann used the terms *concept by inspection, concept by postulation,* and *ideal-type concept* respectively.

observed phenomena."[6] This concept is most easily understood by comparison with observed concepts. The observed concept "matriarchy" could be formed through observation of family relationships. The concept "god-fearing" is a little different, because we cannot observe fear directly, nor can we "see" a belief in a deity. If people engage in worship and if they tell us that they do certain things because they fear a god, and if we note that their religion places strictures on behavior, then we may *infer* that they are god-fearing. Thus, when we form concepts such as "atheist," "believer," "fear," and "anxiety," we are inferring that certain actions that we are able to perceive are caused by unseen characteristics that are hidden from us.

In the same vein, while observed concepts are made about things that are seen, inferred concepts are made about things that are not seen directly but are inferred from things that are perceived. Thus, when helping children to form inferred concepts, we need to lead them to information from which they can infer unseen things and then note similarities or differences in these unseen entities. For example, the child cannot see values directly, but by observing actions he may be able to infer "what is important" to people. ("They made the church so big. Their religion must mean a lot to them. But these other people. They have no church, no priests, and they don't pray. Religion probably doesn't mean so much to them.")

IDEAL-TYPE CONCEPTS. A third kind of concept refers to very general classes, called ideal types. Anthropologist John Honigmann gives as examples "large- and small-scale communities . . . hunting and fishing communities."[7] These concepts are created in the same way as observed and inferred concepts. That is, they are made by observing similarities or differences in relations. But they refer to such complex or large-scale phenomena that they are "ideals" that have no perfect representative in reality. Thus we speak of Cannes, Nice, Brighton, and Atlantic City as *resorts*. And they *are* all resorts. But that is not all that they are. There is no place, in fact, that is purely and simply a "resort city." But the concept is still useful, for it enables us to describe some of the common functions of these places and to refer to them in conversation and manipulate them as an idea.

Another example is *theocracy*, which refers to a place where political power is concentrated in the hands of religious leaders. Yet there are few theocracies that do not contain powerful persons who are not religious leaders. *Theocracy* describes a general type of legal governmental condition, an "ideal" of which there may be no perfect example.

---

[6] Honigmann, p. 53.

[7] *Ibid.*, p. 54.

Ideal types are very useful. They enable us to classify large masses of information. We classify nation-states into *technologically developed, technologically underdeveloped,* and so on. We refer to *socialism, nationalism, free enterprise,* and the like, enabling us to describe the characteristics of large-scale events, social movements, and trends that have something in common but may be only loosely related.

To help the child form ideal-type concepts requires that he be led to examples of the concepts and that he be able to see the common characteristics that enable us to abstract the concept from the examples. To form a concept like "democracy," for example, the child needs to study several nation-states in enough detail to be able to identify democratic and nondemocratic characteristics in those nations and thus see what it is that characterizes democracy.

IMPLICATIONS FOR INSTRUCTION. These distinctions between types of concepts used by the social scientist can be useful in planning to teach concepts to elementary school children. In many cases it is less complicated to teach the younger children to identify "observed concepts." Even the youngest can note similarities, differences, and relations between objects he perceives directly. Inferred concepts, however, require an extra step, since they depend on postulating unseen forces or things and then noting similarities, differences, and relations between these unseen entities. Ideal-type concepts are not especially difficult when they refer to small units or groups of things, but they are very difficult when they refer to large events, processes, or trends. It takes a long time to acquire knowledge of such large entities as wars, nations, and social movements in order to be able to form or understand ideal-type concepts. Several years of study about nations are necessary before one has sufficient data about them to be able to handle concepts such as democracy and communism effectively.

ANTHROPOLOGY AND CULTURAL COMPARISON BY CHILDREN. The following description of nine- and ten-year-old children comparing families representing several cultures provides an example of a teaching strategy that uses inferred concepts as its focus. The central concept—values—was identified from sociology, but the comparative approach is more typical of anthropology. The illustration is taken from a research study performed by the author and his wife.[8]

On five successive days, two classes were shown short films, each depicting a family from a different country or culture group going about its

---

[8] Bruce R. and Elizabeth H. Joyce, "Searching for Strategies for Social Education" (unpublished manuscript).

daily activities—Spanish, Eskimo, Navaho, Italian, and French. The teaching strategy was devised to help the children compare different cultural families on a basis of values. Consequently they were asked to identify, in each film, evidence of what was "important" to the family in question. Because values are an inferred concept, it was necessary to teach the children to recognize good evidence of what is important to people.

As each child ventured a hypothesis about something he believed was important to one of the families, he was asked, "What evidence makes you think so?" Then he was led to suggest all the evidence he could pertaining to that hypothesized value and to debate the merits of the evidence. In this way the children were guided to (1) raise hypotheses about the values of the families depicted in the films; (2) describe and debate the evidence from which the values were inferred; (3) cull the films for conflicting evidence; and (4) compare the lists of hypothesized values that were assembled for each family.

At first the children, responding to the question "What is important to these people?" made inferences based on evidence of the *physical* needs of the people. ("The cow was important because she gave them milk." "The horse was important because he pulled the cart.") Also, at first the children had some difficulty balancing their inferences against conflicting ones made by other students; they appeared reluctant to challenge the judgment of others. Gradually, however, the children learned to make inferences on bases unrelated to physical needs and were able to cite other kinds of evidence:

"When they went to the trading store, the man gave the little girl some candy."
"They wouldn't take the wood that the others had taken out of the water and piled on the shore."
"The little girl went to the house of the sick girl so she could give her some water."
"The little girls helped the baby without being asked."

From evidence of this kind, the children made inferences about what was important to each family. Slowly they developed separate classifications of "important things": "things important for food and shelter," "things important because they are fun," "things that show how people feel about each other."

The children, therefore, in comparing the families on the basis of these inferred values, were acting in a very real sense as anthropologists do when they make cultural comparisons using inferred concepts.

The children also made comparisons at the observed-concept level.

For example, with respect to leisure activities:

> "They both played games. The Spanish boys played bullfight.
> The Eskimos played ring-around."
> "Yes, and the Italians played a kind of bowling [*bocce*]."

And with respect to the artifacts of culture:

> "They used oil light."
> "They all used horse carts except the Eskimos."
> "We saw three kinds of houses."

The children also began to identify the kinds of evidence used to build ideal-type concepts describing the economic structure of the community:

> "The Navahos planted corn and squash and herded sheep."
> "The Eskimos hunted for their food."
> "The Italian family was like the Navaho family in raising their food and carrying water to irrigate their garden."

Hence the children had begun to make cultural comparisons based on all three levels of concept used by the anthropologist.

HISTORICAL COMPARISONS. Some of the most interesting and educative teaching units are built around the methods of inquiry used by the scholar. But frequently, in order to accomplish this, the teacher has to adapt adult readings or construct readings and other teaching materials so that the children can acquire sufficient data to see how the scholar reasoned. Excellent secondary sources for making these adaptations are available, however; for example, on the 350th anniversary of Jamestown, Virginia, the U.S. government published a number of pamphlets and books that can be used as sources of data for the teacher to work into suitable fare for children. *Archeological Excavations at Jamestown, Virginia* provides an excellent map of the sites of diggings, with a thorough text describing what was found and what interpretation was placed on the findings. Using this book, the teacher can construct a unit which directs children to learn about the excavations, findings, and interpretations, and which guides them further to check out the interpretations given in history books and in biographies of colonial leaders. Then the picture of colonial life that emerges can be compared with the picture of life in another colony, in another historical period, or perhaps in another culture.

Political Science

Analysts have identified a great variety of approaches to the study of political science, representing as many as five or six schools of thought.[9] However, there is general agreement that "the subject matter of political science is legal government, including its history, agencies, processes, structure, functions, composition, rationale, and influence."[10] Beyond that point of agreement, however, the aspects of topics that political scientists examine differ so markedly that one political scientist has been moved to remark:

> The differences in the kinds of knowledge we seek and the methods of inquiry we pursue account for the statement so often made that in spite of the common terrain for exploration, American political scientists constitute not one discipline but several disciplines.[11]

Nevertheless it is clear that political scientists have increasingly turned their study to the analysis of political *behavior* (as distinct from political structure or law). Thus, although further work is required in order to pull together the thinking of political scientists and to identify the central concepts that should be introduced to children, the following analysis is presented as reasonably true to behaviorism and reasonably clear in its implications for teaching strategies.

Many political scientists agree that their critical concept is power. This *focus on power* may be substantiated by a large number of quotations from authors of widely different views. "Politics means the rise towards participation in power or influence in the distribution of power between states, within states, or within the groups which make up the state" (Max Weber). "Politics is the study of authority relations between individuals and groups and the hierarchy of power which establishes itself within all numerous and complex communities" (Raymond Aron). "A brief definition of the scope of political science is the study of power, in other words with the phenomena of command which appears in a society" (George Vedel).[12]

---

[9] Evron M. Kirkpatrick and Jeane J. Kirkpatrick, "Political Science," in Erling M. Hunt and others, *High School Social Studies Perspectives* (Boston: Houghton Mifflin, 1962). In this essay will be found both a brief summary of the approaches taken by political scientists and a fine introductory bibliography to political science.

[10] *Ibid.*, p. 111.

[11] Charles S. Hyneman, *The Study of Politics: The Present State of American Political Science* (Urbana: Univ. of Illinois Press, 1959), p. 105.

[12] Maurice Duverger, *An Introduction to the Social Sciences with Special Reference to Their Methods* (New York: Praeger, 1964), p. 47.

What, then, is power? In every social group there are, on the one hand, those who give the orders and, on the other, those who obey. The word *power* describes both the governing group and the function that the group fulfills.[13]

The political scientist observes this power from several viewpoints. First, he observes *the activities of life over which legal government exercises control*. He catalogs the life activities that a political body endeavors to regulate. (Is speech and other communication controlled? Are economic activities regulated and to what extent?) Hence he has developed the concept of totalitarianism (a form of government which, relatively speaking, seeks to control the *total* human organism) as contrasted with the concept of democracy (which attempts to organize affairs so as to permit maximum individual liberty in all phases of life).

Second, the political scientist also observes *how the power to make decisions is distributed*. In other words, who exercises power? (Are religious leaders also political leaders, as in the case of the ancient Mayas or the ancient Egyptians? Do industrial leaders tend to have political power? Does the newspaper editor have the power to influence decisions? Are all people entitled to vote, and do they exercise the right?)

Third, political scientists are concerned with *the distribution of power in formal and informal institutions*. In other words, they describe political institutions. (What is the form of the government? Is there a king, president, military dictator? Are there political parties? How are they organized? Who exercises the judicial functions? What are the mechanisms for carrying out the law?) Much of the literature of political science discusses the comparative forms of governments.

As in the case of anthropology, the work of political scientists can also be described in terms of the three levels of concepts they employ: (1) *observed concepts* (which would apply, for example, when the constitutional duties of legislatures in different states are compared); (2) *inferred concepts* (a typical inference being that Supreme Court decisions have changed because sentiments among the American people have changed); and (3) *ideal-type concepts* (which apply when various regimes are compared and categorized—for instance, when the terms *totalitarian* and *democratic* are used as guides to the classification of nation-states).

These various characteristics of political science inquiry may help to determine the approaches we can take to introduce young children to the study of political aspects of society. Because the central concept of political science is "power," the teaching strategy should lead children to examine power in human groups. Because the political scientist studies

---

[13] *Ibid.*

power from the viewpoint of the life activities that are controlled, the ways power is distributed, and the institutions that implement power, so should the teaching strategy lead the child to examine these phases of power.

Let us apply this strategy to a fourth-grade class that is studying the government of its local community. Perhaps the children can interview the mayor, asking him how he plays a part in making decisions and carrying out decisions and what role he plays in a political party. In their conversation the children may find that the chief of police is not formally even a member of a political party or that he has no official place in the law-making process. However, they may later find that the city council sometimes accepts the police chief's recommendations, thus giving him a part in decision making even though he has no vote in that body.

The children may learn that their city charter permits the town council and the school board to assess taxes on real estate, and they may find that the council or a zoning board further invades the real estate domain by making rules about the kind of building or the use of land permitted in various areas of the town. They will find that the right to assemble is protected by the U.S. Constitution but that the number of people who can assemble under one roof is determined by the fire marshal.

In most social studies programs in recent years the chief subject matter has been formal political institutions, such as the executive, legislative, and judicial branches of government—all studied from the viewpoint of their structure or legal setup. More attention should be given to the concepts of power and to the actual behavior of politics and government. Also, it is important that world political movements, such as communism and fascism, be dealt with objectively so that the child can begin to understand the currents that are shaping his time.

Economics

Economics, like political science, has been defined in various ways, and individual economists emphasize different aspects of economic processes. Nonetheless, for working purposes, many economists accept this definition: "Economics is a study of the problem of using the scarce means of a human society to satisfy competing ends as fully as possible."[14] Lawrence Senesh has suggested that a form of this definition should provide the frame of reference for economic education: "All people and all nations are confronted with the conflict between their unlimited wants and

---

[14] Bruce W. Knight and Lawrence G. Hines, *Economics* (New York: Knopf, 1952), p. 6.

limited resources."[15] In his view, the center of economic study is the choice-making process, and three kinds of activity are studied—the production of goods, the exchange of goods, and the consumption of goods, each characterized by special institutions and activities.

At times, study can focus on production. (What is produced? How? What gives it value? What is the organization of people and resources? Who makes the decision to produce something?) Sometimes a study emphasizes exchange. (What relative values are assigned to various goods? How is value determined? What needs give rise to what kinds of valuation? What kinds of institutions are involved in exchange and value setting?) Or study may give prominence to the distribution of goods. (Who gets what, and how is allocation determined? What institutions are involved in distribution?)

Macroeconomics is the study of these activities on a large scale, as on a national level, and includes the role of governmental policies in actively influencing economic affairs. Macroeconomics is frequently involved with normative decisions, such as whether governments should or should not undertake to effect a balance of trade. Most questions on the macrolevel are too difficult for children, because the mass of information is too large and the relations between data too intricate. However, many of the concepts can be studied on a small scale in situations that simulate the national level of activity.

The concepts of economics are amenable to the same three-way classification that was used in anthropology and political science: (1) *Observed concepts.* The economist notes what goods are produced in various regions of the world. He describes factories, banks, and markets. He notes the flow of goods to retail stores and the kinds of advertising that are used to promote sales. (2) *Inferred concepts.* The economist infers relations between the abundance of capital and the development of production facilities. He infers that where demand increases, prices will rise unless production keeps pace. (3) *Ideal-type concepts.* The economic conditions prevailing in different nations are compared and classified. "Free enterprise," "socialism," "underdeveloped economy," and the like are examples of ideal-type concepts.

Senesh has conducted a series of investigations exploring economic education in the elementary school, and in part of his study he has shown how concepts from economics can be translated into forms comprehensible

---

[15] Lawrence Senesh, "The Organic Curriculum: A New Experiment in Economic Education," *The Councilor*, XXI (Chicago: Illinois Council for the Social Studies, 1960), 3. Senesh's approach is being offered in published form as *Our Working World* by Science Research Associates. Volume I, *Families at Work*, appeared in 1964, and Volume II, *Neighborhoods at Work*, is appearing in 1965.

by young children; he has done this through a study of the economics of the home. In the following passage quoted from his study, each section is preceded by the statement of the concept being developed for the children.[16]

A DIVISION OF LABOR TAKES PLACE WITHIN THE FAMILY WHICH INCREASES THE EFFICIENCY OF THE FAMILY.

Curriculum Interpretation: Work in the home is done more efficiently when each member of the family does what he is best fitted to do.

Student Activities: Children draw pictures or tell stories showing how the various members of the family help in the home. The children may play "A Morning at Home," with the mother preparing breakfast and putting up father's lunch, with father getting ready for work and the children getting ready for school. A second scene will show mother preparing dinner, father returning home to do repair jobs about the house, and the children running errands for the parents and feeding their pets. After the play the children discuss or draw pictures about what would happen if everyone in the family tried to cook the meals at the same time: father would be late for work, children late for school, everyone annoyed, repair jobs and errands neglected.

WITHIN THE HOME ALL MEMBERS OF THE FAMILY ARE CONSUMERS, BUT ONLY SOME ARE PRODUCERS.

Curriculum Interpretation: In the home parents, grandparents, children, healthy and sick, young and old, use or consume durable goods, nondurable goods, and services. Only certain members of the family produce inside and outside the home.

Student Activities: The students draw pictures showing the family's consumption needs: food, clothing, shelter, electricity, automobiles, furniture, air, sunshine, water. Another drawing shows those members of the family who are consumers only: the very young and the very old. A third picture shows those members of the family who are producers at home only: mother doing house chores, a retired man working in the garden. In a fourth picture are those members of the family who are producers inside the home as outside the home: father working at the office and also cutting grass at home; mother working in a store, and also at home cooking meals. These drawings can be an outgrowth of a classroom discussion of what the family's needs are and how certain members of the family provide those needs.

ALL PRODUCERS PRODUCE GOODS AND SERVICES IN ORDER TO EARN INCOMES. IN MANY CASES MEMBERS OF THE FAMILY PRODUCE GOODS AND

---

16 *Ibid.,* pp. 7–10.

SERVICES AT HOME FOR THEIR OWN USE IN ORDER TO SAVE MONEY. WITH
EVERY CHOICE ANOTHER OPPORTUNITY IS SACRIFICED.

Curriculum Interpretation: In most families there are breadwinners
who earn incomes by working in factories, offices, stores, fields, mines,
on the ocean, and in the air. Their incomes are earned as a reward
for producing goods and services useful to other people. When members of the family produce goods and services at home, the money
saved is the same as if earned. If the members of the family had not
produced these goods and services for themselves, they would have
had to hire someone else to do the job.

When one works at one job, he cannot work at another at the
same time; therefore, he may not be earning as much as he could at
another job.

Student Activities: Students can find out at home what their
fathers do, and explain to the class the importance of the goods and
services they produce. The class may prepare a mural showing the
role of the father (representing the father of all the children) as a
producer. Picture 1: Father leaves home for work. Picture 2: Father
shown at work. Picture 3: Father returns home with income. Picture
4: Mother goes shopping. Picture 5: The goods which father produced
are shown in big trucks leaving the factory for the stores. Picture 6:
Many people go to the store to buy the goods which father helped
to produce.

Each child may prepare a picture showing father, mother, and
children at work at home, and explain to the class how much the
family may save on each occasion by doing the work themselves.

Sometimes the members of the family do not save money by doing
work at home. When mother is at home doing the cooking and washing,
she cannot be working away from home and earning a salary. Father
may have asked to stay away from his job without pay to paint the
house. The child may carry newspapers to earn money, but he deprives
himself of time for studying and preparing himself for his future. The
children may draw pictures showing how each member of the family
could have other choices of work than those they are doing now.

IN AN AGRICULTURAL ECONOMY, MOST OF THE PRODUCTIVE ACTIVI-
TIES ARE OR WERE PERFORMED ON THE FARM, SATISFYING THE FAMILY'S
NEEDS. IN AN INDUSTRIAL MARKET ECONOMY, THE WORKPLACE HAS
SHIFTED TO OUTSIDE THE HOME AND MOST OF THE PRODUCTION IS FOR
THE MARKET.

Curriculum Interpretation: In pioneer days, members of the family
produced most of the goods they needed and the family grew its own
food, spun its own wool, made its own clothing, built its own home,

and often provided education and recreation. With the development of industries, specialization of labor increased, and people began to produce for other people. Those who produced for others earned income.

Student Activities: From pioneer stories, the children may reconstruct in their own stories or in table models the relative self-sufficiency of family life. As a contrast they may prepare another story or model showing that today the home is served largely by institutions outside the home: churches, schools, factories, barber shops, restaurants, dentists' offices, meat-packing plants, supermarkets, and power plants.

INCOME EARNED BY FAMILIES MAY BE SPENT OR SAVED. DECISIONS TO SPEND OR SAVE AFFECT WHAT AND HOW MUCH OUR ECONOMY WILL PRODUCE OF EACH COMMODITY.

Curriculum Interpretation: Families usually want more goods and services than they can buy with their incomes; therefore, they have to make choices. Any choice they make has an impact on the types of goods and services our industry produces.

Student Activities: Children may act out a family scene and may express all the things they want and then through discussion establish priorities. They will compromise.

If the children in their play decide to give up buying something they have bought in the past, due to change of tastes or high prices, and decide to purchase another thing, the children may draw pictures showing that the shift of demand from one good to another affects the two industries. For example, if they decide to abstain from the purchase of candy to buy ice cream, the teacher may discuss with them what will happen to the business of the candy manufacturer and the ice-cream manufacturer if lots of children should make similar decisions. The drawings could show the following sequence:

1. Lots of children's heads and above each a cloud showing a candy bar canceled out and an ice-cream cone remaining.

2. Children lining up in front of an ice-cream store, and no one at the candy store next door.

3. The ice-cream factory expands and a sign is visible— "Workers Wanted." The candy factory is closed down, and a sign is visible— "Closed"—and unemployed workers are walking out.

The teacher may discuss how the children's savings may help the entire country. This can be shown through drawings. Picture 1: Johnny puts his money in the bank. Picture 2: Ice-cream manufacturer goes to bank to get a loan to build a bigger business. Picture 3: Ice-cream manufacturer with borrowed money purchases building material, hires labor, buys equipment to build a bigger ice-cream factory. Picture 4: Factory produces and sells ice cream to a large group of children lined up in front of the factory. Picture 5: Factory takes money to bank to repay loan with interest.

After discussing these pictures, the teacher may discuss what would happen if the children of this country would decide not to buy either candy or ice cream. The discussion would lead to the recognition that savings would be unused and both candy and ice-cream factories would close down. The same relationship could be developed as it applies to adults.

In the same article, Senesh illustrates how the same concepts can be extended into a discussion of the neighborhood (beyond the confines of the family). It is interesting to note how well these sophisticated economic concepts have been developed and simplified for the lower primary grades. Indeed, the activities described above were intended for the first grade.

Geography

The geographer studies the interaction of man and his physical environment. As George Cressey expresses it:

What geography seeks is no less than an over-all understanding of the personality of place, a correlation of all those phenomena which make one location different from all others. It asks many questions: Why do the people live where they do? What are the potentials of this place or that? How much of what is where?[17]

The critical area of the geographer's study concerns the interaction of human culture with natural environmental factors. He types the several human reactions to deserts and tropical rain forests. He observes how economic institutions vary with environment, and how man alters his milieu and causes it to adapt to him. He looks at population distribution and the factors that relate to it. He examines how land is used and which resources are utilized. He studies how other aspects of culture affect the use of land and natural resources. It should be noted that although many laymen have been conditioned to regional approaches to geography, today many geographers prefer to study environmental phenomena the world around.

The geographer has developed intricate systems for describing and organizing the data with which he works. His concepts for describing the earth and its land forms, climate, and cultural adaptation are extensive.

---

[17] George B. Cressey, "Geography," in Erling M. Hunt and others, *High School Social Studies Perspectives* (Boston: Houghton Mifflin, 1962), p. 85.

As in the other social sciences, these concepts may be analyzed into three types: (1) *Observed concepts.* These are many in geography, which is the descriptive science *par excellence.* Even complex concepts like "population distribution" are actually observed concepts. (2) *Inferred concepts.* Predictions about the effect of damming up a desert river are based on inferences about the relation between water supply and agricultural product, just as predictions about the effect of disease control on population growth are based on past relationships. (3) *Ideal-type concepts.* The geographer uses many categories based on climate and terrain, as when he speaks of "tundras," "rain forests," "alpine meadows." He speaks of cultural adaptation in terms of "nomadic herders" and the like.

For teaching strategies, the geographer suggests that the focus be on the interaction of cultural forms and natural environment—the same interaction he studies. Consequently, although the child should learn how to identify certain climates, vegetation types, and natural resources, he also needs to learn (1) the processes whereby culture conditions man's adaptation to his environment and (2) the cultural features resulting from various kinds of adaptation. In order to see how culture influences adaptation, probably two examples of an environmental type should be studied at the same time (such as two deserts or two rain forests). In Chapter 3 we saw how children could compare Bedouins and Israeli, both desert peoples, and thereby determine the similarities and differences in their adaptation to the same environment.

History

Historians and educators have long collaborated to improve the teaching of history in the public schools, but unfortunately, from the point of view of the elementary school teacher, this collaboration has suffered from two serious defects. Very little of it has been aimed at the elementary school. And almost totally neglected has been any history not directly in the Western tradition. On the other hand, one of the recent yearbooks of the National Council for the Social Studies does provide two dozen excellent articles dealing with the interpretation and teaching of American history.[18] It includes numerous references for the teacher, such as the *Harvard Guide to American History,* which contains excellent bibliographies of primary source materials.[19]

---

[18] William H. Cartwright and Richard L. Watson, Jr. (eds.), *Interpreting and Teaching American History,* 31st Yearbook of the National Council for the Social Studies (Washington: National Education Assn., 1961).

[19] Oscar Handlin and others (eds.), *Harvard Guide to American History* (Cambridge, Mass.: Harvard Univ. Press, 1954).

Very few teacher education programs are able to provide the prospective elementary school teacher with a substantial background in United States history and a balanced understanding of the recorded history of all the important regions of the world. For the foreseeable future, elementary school teachers will have to engage in more or less constant self-education projects and joint inquiries with their students. Hence sources like the *Harvard Guide* become critically important.

The major task of the historian is to identify and describe as precisely as he can the events of the past. But because the historian usually has access only to limited sources, and because the temper of his times influences his approach to these sources, much of the historian's job is interpretive. Some historians emphasize economic factors; others investigate man's desire for freedom and his struggle against those who would control him. Some believe that each historical era is unique—a never-to-be-repeated coincidence of forces. Others, like Arnold Toynbee, look for cycles of events or for a sequential unfolding of man's destiny. Consequently we find that in explaining an event such as the American Revolution, some historians look to those who profited from it economically, others see it related to the French Revolution and other revolutions that attempted to establish the order of the common man, and yet others see it as a step in the promotion (or conservation) of English representative government.

Perhaps it is not *always* profitable to lead young children into a detailed examination of the various interpretations of historic events. In any case, as we shall see when we examine evidence about the mental ability of young children, it appears that children have difficulty developing ideas about the chronological sequence of historical events and eras. Not until the end of the elementary school years do children seem to grasp the notion of chronology with any facility (although, of course, there are differences in ability).

Some study of history is important, however: the child should at least begin to understand his place in time with respect to the evolution of his species; he should begin to learn about those societies from which he has inherited his ideals, tools, and language; and he should become aware of the extent to which historical events have conditioned the lives of various peoples of the world.

History should be taught as the scholar studies it, with a careful attention to sources of information and with a careful development of the facts from which conclusions are drawn. For example, an upper-grade teacher might display U.S. maps showing both the navigable waterways and the areas of settlement in the years 1650, 1700, and 1750. The child, examining these data, can conclude that a distinct relation existed between population distribution and waterways. People lived near water routes.

However, examining more maps from colonial times to the present, he will discover that many large population centers later developed away from water transport, and he can begin his hunt for other operative factors. When history is taught by such methods, the child has to encounter the tentative state of our conclusions about human events, and he has to participate in the process of modifying ideas as new facts come to light. He is engaged in the exciting attempt to explain—to try out ideas and see whether the data confirm them.

Many interesting questions can lead the child to historical inquiry. Why was Williamsburg abandoned as the chief city of Virginia? Why did New York become so large? What led to the founding of our town? What was the economic position of the men who wrote the Constitution?

Biography enables even fairly young children to study individual lives intensively. Through the depth study of a few key individuals, children can engage in an analytical approach that seems saner and more exciting, as well as more faithful to the methods of the historian, than the catalog of historical events and dates that dominates poor approaches to history.

This kind of teaching also avoids the pitfalls confronting a teacher who tries to give conclusive explanations of past events. The hard fact is that we never really know any single explanation. As historian Bernard Weisberger points out:

> The student cannot be taught *the* interpretation of our history. The honest teacher can only state that each era of the past has presented acute problems to its people, and that we can learn profitably only by rejecting dogmatism as we consider the alternatives which bygone generations weighed, examine the choices they made, and assess the results of these choices.[20]

The child's earliest experiences with history should confront him with the complexity of historical events and the difficulty of interpreting them. For example, suppose a class studies the following passages about the Civil War, taken from a centennial publication of the U.S. government.

> Other historians, such as Charles A. Beard and Harold U. Faulkner, have argued that slavery was only the surface issue. The real cause, these men state, was "the economic forces let loose by the Industrial Revolution" then taking place in the North. . . .

---

[20] Bernard A. Weisberger, "United States History," in Erling M. Hunt and others, *High School Social Studies Perspectives* (Boston: Houghton Mifflin, 1962), p. 130.

A third theory advanced by historians is that the threat to states' rights led to war. The conflict of the 1860's was thus a "War between the States. . . ."

Still other writers believe "Southern nationalism" to have been the basic cause of the war. Southerners, they assert, had so strong a desire to preserve their particular way of life that they were willing to fight.[21]

As they read history books, the children can search for evidence about the particular theory held by the authors. Nearly every history book for elementary school and nearly every biography of a Civil War figure contains opinions about the origins of the war that can come under examination.

We need more units designed to help elementary school children explore problems of interpretation. These units need to be planned and carried out carefully, both because of the complexity of the problem and because of the verbal limitations. But they can be successful with a majority of children. A simple guiding rule is to provide the children with specific data and concrete examples of events wherever possible. For example, the following information is clear and easy to reason about.

At the beginning of the Civil War, the North seemed to possess every advantage:

(1) 23 Northern states aligned against only 11 Southern states. . . .

(2) The population of the Northern states was approximately 22,000,000 people. The Southern states had only 9,105,000 people and one-third of them (3,654,000) were slaves. . . .

(3) The North had 110,000 manufacturing plants, as compared with 18,000 in the Confederate States. The North produced 97% of all firearms in America, and it manufactured 96% of the nation's railroad equipment.[22]

After examining the implications of these data and working out an understanding of other relevant economic and human factors, the students can proceed to an examination of the reasons why the war persisted so long.

Historical units are most appropriate for the more verbal upper-grade children. If one finds that he has to oversimplify the teaching of history because of the limitations of the children, then the study should be deferred.

---

[21] James I. Robertson, Jr., *The Civil War* (Washington: U.S. Civil War Centennial Commission, 1963), p. 5.

[22] *Ibid.*, pp. 7–8.

Summary

Each of the social sciences examines certain characteristics of human relationships. Each utilizes numerous concepts describing the past findings of the field and directing present scholarly activity. These concepts can be classified according to the intellectual activity necessary to create them—hence *observed, inferred,* and *ideal-type* concepts.

The nature of the social sciences should be a critical determinant of social studies instruction. Teachers need to consider carefully how children can learn, with increasing sophistication, the methods and analytical questions used by the scholar. The comparative methods of geography and anthropology suggest that the child's curriculum should include much comparative study of culture groups, even in the primary grades. The bulk of this book will deal with means of accomplishing such goals. However, no matter how carefully a teaching method is described, the quality of the instruction that children receive depends on the knowledge of the individual teacher. Each teacher of the social studies needs intensive preparation in the social sciences, and he must study constantly while he teaches.

INQUIRIES

1. Select a historical period or event which is frequently encountered in the elementary school, such as the westward movement or the meetings of the Continental Congress. Make yourself acquainted with the historians who have done the chief work in these subjects. Identify some of the original sources from which they worked. Compare the interpretations of these historians with those given in a popular social studies text for the elementary school.

2. Which of the social sciences other than history would be the greatest help in the study of a historical era? Why?

3. Imagine that you are going to help a third-grade class study a local shoe factory. For use in the study, identify some concepts from economics and from at least one other social science. Then develop a teaching strategy on the basis of those concepts.

4. Develop a plan for helping third-graders to "practice" politi-

cal science with you. Identify the important questions they might learn to ask, some topics they might study, and some ways in which you might help them determine their degree of improvement in using concepts.

5. At the end of Chapter 12 some of the current curriculum projects in the social studies are listed. See if you can locate some of the curricular materials that have been developed for use with children. See if you can find the opportunity to try out some of these materials with children.

6. When the first-grader enters school, he needs to learn to think effectively about school as a society and about his place in this society. How can social science be related to his initial study of the school environment? Develop a teaching strategy for this situation.

References and Readings

CARTWRIGHT, WILLIAM H., and WATSON, RICHARD L., JR. (eds.). *Interpreting and Teaching American History.* (31st Yearbook of the National Council for the Social Studies.) Washington: National Education Assn., 1961.

DUVERGER, MAURICE. *An Introduction to the Social Sciences with Special Reference to Their Methods.* New York: Praeger, 1964.

EBENSTEIN, WILLIAM. *Totalitarianism: New Perspectives.* New York: Holt, Rinehart & Winston, 1962.

HONIGMANN, JOHN J. *The World of Man.* New York: Harper, 1959.

HUNT, ERLING M., and others. *High School Social Studies Perspectives.* Boston: Houghton Mifflin, 1962.

HYNEMAN, CHARLES S. *The Study of Politics.* Urbana: Univ. of Illinois Press, 1959.

JAMES, PRESTON E. (ed.). *New Viewpoints in Geography.* (29th Yearbook of the National Council for the Social Studies.) Washington: National Education Assn., 1959.

KNIGHT, BRUCE WINTON, and HINES, LAWRENCE GREGORY. *Economics.* New York: Knopf, 1952.

MEAD, MARGARET, and METRAUX, RHODA (eds.). *The Study of Culture at a Distance.* Chicago: Univ. of Chicago Press, 1953.

RANNEY, AUSTIN. *The Governing of Men.* New York: Holt, 1958.

SENESH, LAWRENCE. "The Organic Curriculum: A New Experiment in Economic Education," *The Councilor,* XXI (March 1960).

Chapter **5**

BRINGING THE SOCIAL SCIENCES TO THE CHILD'S STUDY OF HUMAN INTERACTION

In preceding chapters we sought to show how organizing concepts function in the social sciences and how teaching strategies might be developed to initiate young children into the use of these ideas. For purposes of illustration we treated each social science individually, but we must now return to a thesis stated earlier (p. 13): the social sciences have much content in common, and a curriculum can be organized which emphasizes the unique concepts of each of them without having separate courses for them. Therefore the problem posed for this chapter is this: to provide a strategy for selecting content which will enable us to bring to the child the potency of the several social sciences but which will not, at the same time, be overbalanced in the direction of any single one of the disciplines.[1]

In the past, most curriculum plans in the social studies have been organized around *topics* to be surveyed or broad social *objectives* to be sought. For example, in regard to topics, it has been generally accepted that the child should become acquainted with the American Revolution as a critical part of his national heritage. Similarly, the Civil War, westward expansion, and the important international wars involving the United States have been assigned through the grades. Some world geography has also been considered essential to an understanding of international affairs. In short, most curriculum guides have listed topics from which the teacher could select and with each topic have indicated generalizations which the child might learn as the product of his study. However, selecting general topics—topics that are so broadly defined—

---

[1] An earlier version of this chapter appeared as an article by Bruce R. Joyce: "Humanizing Social Studies Content," *The Elementary School Journal*, LXIII (Chicago: University of Chicago Press, 1962), 127–31.

by no means ends the job of content identification. For instance, the study of westward expansion in the United States can send us on an anthropological junket, a study of politics, an analysis of economic forces, or a historical review—or in numerous other directions. Simply deciding to plan an inquiry into westward expansion only narrows the possible content. *How* we treat such a topic determines which of all the possible topic elements will finally be specifically included or excluded.

To name the broadest objectives of the social studies also helps surprisingly little in resolving the task of *specific* content selection. For example, one authority has stated that the goals of social education are "to understand the concepts that describe and explain human society and to develop the insights and skills required by democratic citizenship."[2] This statement does provide us with important criteria, for curricula should indeed be organized to meet these crucial objectives. But, obviously, almost all concepts of social science relate in some way to human society or to democratic citizenship. Thus the broad objectives of social education— although they give us a general focus—do not, by themselves, provide us with sufficient guidelines for selecting *specific* content. It is necessary to develop a strategy that will enable us to screen for children the most promising elements of content that are available in the social topics they explore.

Content Selection Affects Thinking

The selection of content may affect not only the factual knowledge which children acquire but also the thinking processes which they develop. For example, if a child is directed to learn chiefly about the natural resources and agricultural products of a nation he studies, he may tend, when approaching another nation, to ask questions about that country's natural and agricultural resources. In other words, *the selection of content determines to some extent the way the student will be taught to think while he is in school.*

In a recent research study conducted by the author, 60 third-grade and 180 fifth-grade children were asked to pose questions dealing with what they would like to know about a country or people they were to study. Responses dealing with the interaction of people and their values, customs,

---

[2] Ralph C. Preston, "The Role of Social Studies in Elementary Education," in *Social Studies in the Elementary School*, 56th Yearbook of the National Society for the Study of Education (Chicago: Univ. of Chicago Press, 1957), p. 4.

and habits actually declined from the third to the fifth grade. About 40 percent of the questions asked by both grades dealt with physical and economic geography. While about 42 percent of the third-graders asked questions about people or customs, only 29 percent of the fifth-graders asked questions in that category. However, questions about history and government increased from about .5 percent to about 13 percent, reflecting the increased attention to those topics in the middle grades of the school.

Apparently, when teachers repeatedly stress certain sides of topics, children come to regard those sides as the important ones, the ones to be looked for in new topics. I have watched a teacher, generally thought to be very skillful, whose instruction exemplified this tendency when she began a unit on Hawaii. For the children she developed a list of questions that were to guide the class activity—questions dealing with population, topography, climate, products, and interesting sights. There were no questions that would lead to a consideration of the rich lives of the people who inhabit Hawaii or the relations between the people of Hawaii and other peoples, past or present. We should ask ourselves: Will not these children, studying in this fashion, tend to be overly concerned with physical facts and lack the understanding of human behavior needed for active citizenship? Furthermore, when history courses emphasize political and military events (as they so often do), will not children, approaching historical topics not previously studied, tend to look for military and political facts rather than, for example, facts about the daily lives of people?

Experience in mathematics may support this contention. For many years computation was the aspect of arithmetic content that was stressed. Students learned to think of arithmetic *as* computation. Now that mathematical understanding and problem solving are stressed by mathematics educators, both parents and teachers constantly ask: "But won't that interfere with teaching number facts?" "It sounds O.K., but isn't the important thing for kids to learn how to add and subtract?" Such questions indicate that the adult, taught to compute rather than to think about numbers, has come to regard computation as a more important aspect of content than the properties of number systems and the techniques for solving problems.

Can we make the assumption, therefore, that *content, when taught, gradually instills in the learner the same thinking processes that directed the teacher to that content?*

If this assumption is valid, then the systems we use to analyze and select content become important not only because they edit the world that we formally present to the child but also because they shape his thinking. If our systems emphasize material products and neglect people, can we be surprised if the child comes to believe that we think products are more important than people? If our history courses neglect aesthetic and cultural life, are we not helping the child to place a low value on that quality of life?

As important as the topics the child studies are the methods he uses to analyze them. If a child is directed merely to memorize facts and conclusions, he will lack the necessary organizing knowledge to tie these facts together and make useful meaning out of what he has learned. Lacking understanding of the modes of inquiry of the social scientist, he will have difficulty managing and interpreting new sets of conditions in a rapidly changing world. To quote Jerome Bruner again:

> . . . the curriculum of a subject should be determined by the most fundamental understanding that can be achieved of the underlying principles which give structure to that subject. Teaching specific topics or skills without making clear their context in the broader fundamental structure of a field of knowledge is uneconomical. . . . such teaching makes it exceedingly difficult for the student to generalize from what he has learned to what he will encounter later, and knowledge one has acquired without sufficient structure to tie it together is knowledge that is likely to be forgotten.[3]

Bruner's words may be taken as a challenge to teachers of social studies to lead children to discover fundamental ideas about human relations. Returning to examples cited earlier, we need to ask: What fundamental ideas can be explored in the study of the local community or of westward expansion? How can we help children to explore those ideas, to see them in as many combinations as possible? What guidelines can we set down when we analyze content so that what we will select will not be trivial, or one-sided, or fragmented?

For selecting social studies content, therefore, we must develop a curricular strategy which will be comprehensive enough to include the human richness of the social world, which will be useful in developing democratic insights and skills, and which will provide a structure that will tie social facts together in meaningful frameworks.

Assumptions for Developing a Strategy

Several considerations determine the kind of strategy we need for selecting content. First, content for elementary social studies needs to be drawn from a number of academic disciplines without our damaging the

---

[3] Jerome S. Bruner, *The Process of Education* (Cambridge, Mass.: Harvard Univ. Press, 1960), p. 31.

identity or separate integrity of any of them. Perhaps someday, if only for teaching purposes, scholars may be able by persistent effort to synthesize the various social sciences into a single discipline—called, say, "behavioral science." At present, however, any strategy for selecting content needs to blend all the social sciences without our pretending that they have fused into a single study.

Second, content should be selected with a view toward providing continuity in the curriculum and growth of ideas through the grades. The strategy for selecting content should be applicable to topics that can be studied by children of all ages. It should focus on fundamental concepts that can be approached by children of limited experience and explored in depth by more sophisticated learners.

Third, in elementary school the strategic emphasis should be on content that relates the child to his community—that is, on content which draws upon the child's own experience and which he may apply to his immediate experience. This aspect of our strategy accords with current theories of learning. Moreover, the ideas that the child uses to view his own life and community will lead him to understandings that he can bring to the study of other communities and cultures.

Fourth, the strategy should allow for a continual study of topics of immediate import—that is, topics dealing with daily happenings in the classroom and with contemporary events on the world scene. In other words, the child should observe the workings of democracy and of human relations as they are actually unfolding. Thus, at the same time that he is learning new organizing concepts and new ways of viewing and analyzing life, he will have the opportunity to apply his concepts to current problems and see whether they test true.

A Central Idea for the Strategy: Human Groups

In the social sciences we are unlikely to find a single idea as illuminating to the child as the distinction in mathematics between quantity and enumeration. However, it may be possible to identify an idea that is common to the several social sciences and can serve as a reference point in selecting content.

The content of the social studies, we are agreed, should focus on human behavior, especially on human relations. The child needs to grow in power to understand the causes and effects of human behavior and the implications of these causes and effects for life in a democratic society.

Human beings relate to one another largely in groups. "Dwelling together in groups is as characteristic of man as the shape of his teeth or his inclination to laugh."[4] The social sciences all focus on groups. Consider for a moment the parent disciplines of the social studies. Recorded history is the history of groups—national groups, religious groups, ethnic groups. Biography usually presents a person in terms of what he has in common with others. Beethoven is thought of as a German, a musician, a deaf man; Alexander as a Macedonian, a Westerner, a conqueror, a general. In both cases the individual is described as a member of groups. *Political science* is the study of political relations—the government of groups and the relations between groups. A political unit is a group, and within it we can discern other groups—hence parties, factions, the Loyal Opposition, the unfranchised. *Sociology* concentrates on the forms and functions of human groups. The mighty culture concept implies that men in a given area develop common attitudes, codes of behavior, beliefs about reality—that they become, through their relations, a group (and then act, as a group, on other human groups). *Anthropology* could not exist if men did not live in groups. *Economics,* dealing with the production, distribution, and consumption of wealth, implies that men are organized for these purposes. Furthermore, men can be identified by their position in the production, distribution, and consumption systems of a society. Producers in a given category can be classed together; they are, even if strangers, members of a group. *Human geography* is essentially the study of the distribution of human life and its variations in terms of environment. Hence human geography views human groups in terms of their similar and differing milieus and adaptations.

The social sciences, then, deal with human society—with groups of men who are alike or different in certain ways. They deal with the idea of community. Therefore, because man lives in groups and because all the social sciences deal with man's relation to his groups (clusters of persons with whom he has something in common), and with the relations of groups to one another, we may test out the idea of the *human group* as a core idea around which we may build our social studies content.

Questions Focusing on the Group

If we accept the thesis that groups are a common focus of study for the social sciences, we must still determine whether the concept of "group" can be used to identify specific content for the social studies. Perhaps we can make this determination by imagining that we are a teacher approaching a general topic listed in a curriculum guide. What questions must this

---

[4] Stuart Chase, *The Proper Study of Mankind* (New York: Harper, 1956), p. 65.

teacher ask himself in order to identify the kinds of content that focus on the "human group"? The four questions that follow would seem valuable for analyzing topics.

1. What human groups can be found in this society, in this region, in this era that we plan to study?

This question forces us to look below the surface of a general topic and identify relationships within the topic. For example, in the study of the local community, one finds that there are different economic groups, different racial groups, and groups that have different political or religious beliefs. The study of a nation, of any inhabited island, of any region, and of any historical period reveals religious, economic, racial, and political groups. Application of this question involves careful analysis of a topic.

As groups are identified, it becomes evident that they are related to one another. For instance, the economic groups in a nation cannot be considered intelligently without considering the climate, the technology, and the organization of the country.

Frequently groups overlap. The racial groups in the Union of South Africa are also groups of economic interest. In the United States, political affiliation is somewhat related to a broad conception of economic interest. In the San Francisco Bay region, several ethnic groups have retained the culture and customs of their native land—customs which have become mixed with the customs of their adopted homeland.

In other words, the teacher can ask himself: What groups would an economist, an anthropologist, or a human geographer identify, were he to study this topic?

This kind of analysis is useful for most topics now included in the curricula of social studies. Topics like "Our Home," "Our Family," and "The Community" yield to this kind of analysis, as do the study of nation states and cultures and the study of bygone ages.

The use of the first question, as described here, leads to the identification and description of the human groups included under the topic concerned. Once human groups have been identified, the second question follows.

2. What relations do these human groups bear to one another?

Consider the American Revolution as a topic of study. Among the Continentals, Whig and Tory were related politically. Sailmaster and farmer bore economic relations to one another. Soldier and civilian were related, as were Hessian mercenaries, British grenadiers, and Virginia sergeants.

Somewhere in the relations of these groups lies what is significant about the human movements of those days and the human pressures on the individuals of the time. It is in the relations between such groups that we find political and social events.

When we ask this question in social studies, we can view topics in the broadest sense of human relations. The question prevents our viewing historical process in terms of military and political events without considering the human groups involved.

Consider a study of the local community. Having identified the political, economic, religious, and ethnic groups in the community, we ask: What relations do these groups bear to one another? We can also ask of the community itself: What are its relations—political, social, and economic—to other similar groups and groups of which it is a part, such as the nation? From here we proceed to the third question.

3. How did these human relations become what they are?

In the study of the English, this question implies certain other questions. How did lords and ladies get their position? How did the government become a representative one? What in human relations made castles develop? Why did London become so large? When children answer questions like these, they find that kings and queens, steel furnaces and fishing boats, beefeaters and Ulstermen are all part of human culture. From these questions can come the human stories on which lasting generalizations can be built.

This third question—How did these human relations become what they are?—requires us to think of causation as a part of content. It enables us to identify ideas which lead children to think of social events in terms of their causes. History, then, is viewed in terms of process. Contemporary society becomes a part of history.

4. What is the future of these group relations?

With this question consider the study of a local community by third-graders. The children have heard opinions about the need for land for recreation. They have learned that the city government can buy and maintain parks, that the American Association of University Women wants a park, and that the Chamber of Commerce opposes it. We can then ask, How will the issue be resolved? Will the businessmen come to see that the parks will benefit their children? Will the American Association of University Women come to believe that the land should be saved for industry? What will sway the voters?

Answering this fourth question keeps us up to date in our world. When I was growing up, I learned that India was part of the British Empire. I did not realize, until the break occurred in 1947, that India was seeking more independent status, even though I was in high school at the time and was actually studying about India. Egypt's quarrel with the British also came as a surprise to many of us, and it is my impression that the African and Asian nationalistic movements have come as a surprise to most U.S. citizens whose education has not been directed toward appraising the possible changes in the relations between peoples of the world.

By means of the analysis proposed here, geography and history become the study of human relations. Content becomes dynamic—viewed as the emergence of relations—so that current happenings are a part of the historical process. As one author wrote, "If the social studies program is not based on a careful analysis of our changing society, the accusation that schools teach for the past half-century and not for the next half-century could become true."[5]

How can the four questions be used? First, they can be used by teachers to identify content that focuses on human relations. When these questions are used, a study of the economic geography of Italy, for example, becomes an attempt to find people with a livelihood in common and compare them with other people who share another economic position.

Second, social studies teachers in the elementary school can use the rationale to develop continuity in their programs. The study of various regions, historical eras, current events, and the local community will have a common thread if the focus is on group relations. The organizing elements for this continuity will emerge in the children's search to find people with something in common and their attempt to compare or contrast these people with others having something else in common.

Finally, the logic of the four questions can be taught to children so that they will develop a useful framework for approaching social studies topics in class and on their own. As children progress through the grades, they can learn to ask the four questions and to structure their research around the questions. As they grow older, they can use the questions to include more types of groups and more complex relations between groups. Used in this way, the questions provide a means of introducing the basic ideas of the social sciences. As we teach students to identify political groups, for example, we have the opportunity to introduce them to the major organ-

---

[5] Stanley E. Dimond, "Current Social Trends and Their Implications for the Social Studies Program," in *Social Studies in the Elementary School*, 56th Yearbook of the National Society for the Study of Education (Chicago: Univ. of Chicago Press, 1957), p. 75.

izing concepts of political science.

What are the limitations of the four questions? First, a strategy such as this, imposed on topics without regard for the maturity of the learners involved, could result in the identification of unteachable content. The fact that there are several races in a neighborhood, for example, does not mean that first-graders are capable of exploring theories about race relations objectively and maturely.

Second, the strategy provides a means of focusing the social studies but does not include all desirable content. Should a study of Paris omit the Eiffel Tower and the Louvre because the content analysis does not include touristic or artistic relations?

Third, although the strategy could produce an analysis of the ideals and loyalties that people possess in common and although it could be used to identify dynamic elements in democratic groups, it does not provide for the development of desirable attitudes. It provides for an analysis of political power but does not judge whether justice is being done. The four questions can identify groups that share values, but it leaves the implications of those values to be developed by the teacher.

Fourth, while the strategy does not seem to violate the integrity of any of the separate social sciences, it does not ensure development of the basic concepts of these sciences. An untutored person could use the four questions to identify political relations that the political scientist would not recognize as valid.

Finally, although human relations are certainly based on group relations, the essential element in society is the individual. The test of understanding in the social studies is the ability to project oneself into the shoes of a person whose characteristics, group memberships, environment, or desires differ from one's own. If the focus on groups became such that individuals were ignored or groups were perceived to be more important than individuals, then the social studies would be dehumanizing.

Organizing a Teaching Strategy

There would be little point in introducing young children to the central concepts of all the social sciences simultaneously. Learning to use the organizing concepts of just a single social science is alone quite complicated. However, if the focus of social studies is on the human group, instruction can be patterned so that successive units gradually reveal more and more of the tactics used by the several social sciences. Studies in the early grades can introduce some organizing concepts, while those of the later grades expand the number and show how the concepts relate to one another.

Through the grades, units can be arranged so that the analysis of human groups becomes progressively many-sided; questions from more and more social sciences can be added to the children's repertoire. The continual focus on the group, the continual analysis of the reasons for human behavior, and the constant prediction of events keep the analysis from becoming dry and insignificant. By continually expanding social science inquiry, we encourage an intellectual deepening of inquiry.

Summary

Using its own unique perspective, each of the social sciences focuses on human groups. Consequently, it is possible to teach children the organizing concepts of the social sciences while they study human groups in their own culture, in other cultures, and in historical eras.

In this chapter a strategy was explained for unifying the study of the social sciences through a concentration on human group interaction. The child can learn the social sciences by using their concepts to identify human groups, to explain group origins and relations, and to make predictions about the future of groups. By employing the perspective of first one social science and then another to study group interaction, the child can learn the concepts of all the social sciences. Gradually these concepts will become natural to him; he will become able to think like the social scientist —and eventually he will invent his own mature organizing concepts.

INQUIRIES

1. Apply the rationale developed in this chapter to some group of people with whom you are quite familiar—perhaps the university or college community. Select a social science perspective and see what human groups you find and how they relate to one another.

2. How could a topic like "Transportation and Communication in Our City" be approached by fourth- or fifth-graders if they were to concentrate on human groups and view their subject from the vantage point of one of the social sciences?

3. How could a teaching strategy focusing on groups be developed for first-graders who were asked to compare life in their neighborhood with life in an Indian pueblo?

4. Identify the advantages and disadvantages of concentrating on groups in order to introduce children to the organizing concepts of one of the social sciences.

References and Readings

BEARD, CHARLES A. *A Charter for the Social Sciences*. New York: Scribner, 1932.

BERELSON, BERNARD, and others. *The Behavioral Sciences Today*. New York: Basic Books, 1963.

BRUNER, JEROME S. *The Process of Education*. Cambridge, Mass.: Harvard Univ. Press, 1960.

CHASE, STUART. *The Proper Study of Mankind*. New York: Harper, 1956.

DALTON, ROBERT H. *Personality and Social Interaction*. Boston: Heath, 1961.

DIMOND, STANLEY E. "Current Social Trends and Their Implications for the Social Studies Program," in *Social Studies in the Elementary School*. (56th Yearbook of the National Society for the Study of Education.) Chicago: Univ. of Chicago Press, 1957.

HODGKINSON, HAROLD L. *Education in Social and Cultural Perspectives*, Englewood Cliffs, N.J.: Prentice-Hall, 1962.

HOMANS, GEORGE C. *The Human Group*. New York: Harcourt, Brace, 1950.

JOYCE, BRUCE R. "Humanizing Social Studies Content," *Elementary School Journal*, LXIII (December 1962), 127–31.

PRESTON, RALPH C. "The Role of Social Studies in Elementary Education," in *Social Studies in the Elementary School*. (56th Yearbook of the National Society for the Study of Education.) Chicago: Univ. of Chicago Press, 1957.

THE PSYCHOLOGY
OF SOCIAL SCIENCE
EDUCATION

6

DEVELOPING OPEN MINDS

Thus far we have viewed teaching strategies in terms of the social sciences. Concluding that knowledge in the social sciences is vast and ever changing and that we cannot possibly teach children everything, we set out to determine what is durably useful and should be taught. We looked at knowledge from the perspective of the modern social scientist—as a conception of reality that is imperfect, changing, experimental. Organizing concepts were viewed both as the framework of this knowledge and as guides to social science research.

In this chapter and the next we shall consider the social studies from the point of view of psychology and social psychology. Teaching strategies cannot be based solely on a consideration of the nature of the academic disciplines. We must also consider the nature of the child, the nature of learning and the conditions that encourage learning, and the nature of the society in which the child is growing up.

In this chapter we shall discuss the development of the child's mind and personality and the conditions that seem likely to affect the ways he will process information and relate to other human beings. In Chapter 7 we shall examine some of the evidence about intellectual growth and the development of social attitudes.

Conceptual Styles: The Open Mind

In the last few years psychologists have developed some new ideas about learning and thinking processes, ideas that can be extremely useful to educators. In experiments conducted by Jerome Bruner, Jacqueline Goodnow, and George Austin, for example, several persons were studied in terms of the ways in which they handled a concept-formation task, and it was found that there were several different "styles" of approach to the

identification of the same concept.[1] The results of such research suggest
that people, when given a problem, can be distinguished both by the unique
modes they use to search for information and by the patterns they apply in
searching for relations between pieces of information. Faced by a problem,
some people, on grasping a few bits of information, immediately hazard a
quick judgment about what is central to the issue. Others want to gather
a good deal of information before venturing a hypothesis. In processing
information, some people try out two ideas at once, while others are more
single-minded. Some become attached to the first idea they think of and
resist letting it go, while others hold their ideas more loosely and change
them more easily as new evidence appears. This manner in which a person
faces problems, or this disposition or system for processing information, can
be characterized as his *conceptual style*.

The ways a person learns to break down the world into understandable parts and the ways he organizes these parts may be as critical a product
of education as ever takes place. In fact, the information that a child
absorbs while he is in school may have a much less lasting effect on his
life than the characteristic modes of processing information, the *conceptual
style*, that he develops. This is much the point made in earlier chapters
when the organizing concepts of the social sciences were under consideration. These concepts are actually complicated systems for approaching
problems and for processing information. They govern what data the scientist will consider and what categories he will use to classify information he
encounters. Hence, when we teach these concepts to children, we are asking
them to process information in a different way than they did before; we are
asking them to take on the "style" of the social scientist.

A related line of inquiry, conducted by Milton Rokeach and his
associates, has centered on the ways in which people organize their beliefs,
especially with respect to whether their systems of belief are "open" or
"closed."[2] Rokeach's studies appear to indicate that belief systems can
validly be described in terms of the extent to which contrary beliefs are
rejected out of hand ("People who oppose this idea must be Communists"),
the extent to which a person keeps his beliefs separated or compartmental-
ized, resulting in unrecognized inconsistencies ("I believe in equality for
all men"; "Those immigrants should know their place and keep it"), the
extent to which he either distinguishes between friendly ideas or tends to
lump them all together, and the extent to which he distinguishes between
ideas he regards as unfriendly to his system. The belief systems of some

---

[1] Jerome S. Bruner, Jacqueline Goodnow, and George A. Austin, *A Study
of Thinking* (New York: Wiley, 1956).
[2] Milton Rokeach, *The Open and Closed Mind* (New York: Basic Books,
1960).

people are such that they perceive the world as generally hostile; these people tend to be less receptive to new information and ideas. Other people regard the world as a friendly place; they are better able to examine new beliefs and to see the positions of others.

The more closed-minded tend to regard authority as absolute and tend to accept or reject other people according to their tendency to agree with or yield to authority figures.[3] Closed persons have more difficulty handling information that does not confirm their beliefs and have less capacity to be objective about their beliefs.[4] Closed persons tend to tolerate confusion badly and have greater difficulty suspending judgment pending sufficient information. They are unhappy when in doubt and tend to resolve uncertainty in favor of stereotyped solutions. The more open-minded individual, on the other hand, tends to regard authority and values with a greater sense of relativeness.

In other words, as human beings acquire knowledge they acquire sets toward that knowledge which greatly affect their ability to take in and incorporate new information.

Belief Systems Start Early

From birth the human organism begins to absorb the values and patterns of action that he finds in the people around him. In fact, the human personality becomes made up of the characteristics of the people in the immediate environment.

Although human individuals must learn their own core of species behavior through their experience with other members of their group, they must also make of themselves the skills, rules and symbols of their outer cultural world.[5]

Gradually a modal self emerges:

The self thus established (as George Mead, Jean Piaget, and others have pointed out) is largely a private replica of the outer social world (or some part of it) of which the individual is a part; its social relations are mere continuations of those already existing within the group.[6]

---

[3] T. W. Adorno and others, *The Authoritarian Personality* (New York: Harper, 1950).

[4] Leon Festinger, *A Theory of Cognitive Dissonance* (Evanston, Ill.: Row, Peterson, 1957).

[5] W. Lloyd Warner, *American Life: Dream and Reality* (Chicago: Univ. of Chicago Press, 1953), p. 208.

[6] *Ibid.*, p. 209.

These processes of socialization are well along by middle childhood and pervade every phase of life:

> In the world of the eleven- and twelve-year-old child, the same general status values are operating as in adult life. Most of the lower-class children feel, and in fact, are, rejected, whereas most of the higher-placed ones feel, and in fact, are, approved of and accepted.[7]

Bernice Neugarten's study of fourth-grade youngsters is a dramatic illustration of the extent to which internalization of values affects the judgment of the child. Asked to judge their classmates according to cleanliness and leadership qualities, her group of children tended to rate both characteristics according to social-class origins. The higher the economic status of the parents, the "cleaner" was the rating of the child. Careful investigation revealed that there was in fact no relation between economic status and cleanliness. The children apparently had internalized the judgments of the adults about them, learned to judge economic background without having any idea what it was from a sociological point of view, and made their judgments of classmates on the basis of class-linked values.

> The finding that social-class differences in friendship and reputation are so well established by the time children reach the fifth grade may be of some importance to the psychologist. . . . Perhaps one of the reasons the child of lower class is so often a "behavior problem" in school is that he finds himself rejected by his classmates and enjoys such an unenviable reputation.[8]

Stated differently, the child apparently begins to form his system of values at a very early age and as a direct response to his environment. He tends to take on and employ the ways of thinking and feeling that are used by his elders.

Studies of prejudice support this conclusion. Prejudice is now regarded as an act of conformity to one's social group and develops early, although it does not become fully differentiated according to race and ethnic background until the later elementary school years. Allport contends that prejudice arises in the school years of six to sixteen, which, incidentally, is the time of the most active formal social education.[9]

---

[7] *Ibid.*, p. 216.

[8] Bernice Neugarten, "Social Class and Friendship Among School Children," *American Journal of Sociology*, LI (1946), 313.

[9] Gordon W. Allport, *The Nature of Prejudice* (Reading, Mass.: Addison-Wesley, 1954).

Anthropologists have observed that in every society the culture gradually takes possession of the child's mind.

In every society the socialization process may be said to be successful to the extent that the values of the society become internalized in the form of sentiments, and the individual develops an inner monitor or "conscience." He is then able to think, feel, and act as the society requires with a minimum of external controls. Where a culture is stable and relatively simple, the cultural expectations tend to be clear-cut and predictable. In modern urban society, the problem is more difficult, for the child is exposed to a confused image and contradictory expectations.[10]

The result of the fact that the young child is so susceptible to the influences of the adults about him is that the environment begins very early to shape his mind, including the rigidity and flexibility of his belief systems.

The Conceptual System

In order to cope with a confusing world, the human being develops categories or mental pigeonholes into which he separates and stores information and ideas. The organizing concepts of social science which were discussed earlier are just such a system of categories for organizing information. As the developing organism interacts with his world, he develops a very complicated system of concepts, but as we have pointed out, this system of concepts is heavily influenced by the social environment.

Gradually, as the system of concepts develops, it takes on various characteristics which distinguish the individual. Some conceptual systems contain rather few concepts and these are comparatively fixed, with fewer alternative possibilities for handling information. In such cases the individual tends to regard the world in somewhat stereotyped or black-and-white terms. Other individuals develop a greater number of alternative ways to deal with the world. Their responses are less stereotyped and more flexible. They are able to tolerate more differences of opinion and can seek information from people they do not especially like and see mistakes on the part of people they like a good deal. These two styles are probably unrelated to specific beliefs. Two persons may have similar beliefs, but one may hold them concretely and rigidly and may be unable to cope with

[10] Ina Corrine Brown, *Understanding Other Cultures* (Englewood Cliffs, N.J.: Prentice-Hall, 1963), p. 54.

conflicting evidence, while the other holds the beliefs flexibly and can weigh conflicting evidence without discomfort.

> Let us consider the cases of an avid atheist and a zealous believer in God: in terms of many behavioral criteria or attitudinal classifications, these two persons might be viewed as opposites. . . . If they were considered according to . . . their ways of relating to God, the atheist and the zealous believer might be seen as very similar to each other, more similar in fact than either would be to a person to whom the object, God, has little personal relevance.[11]

Once a person's system of concepts begins to develop, it influences all subsequent development. Once rigid categories begin to appear, the tendency is for subsequent information to be bent, in a psychological sense, until it fits into those categories. Thus, a person who learns to accept authorities without question tends to see rules as rigid and to feel uncomfortable when authority is questioned or rules are challenged. The individual with the more flexible conceptual system sees rules as modifiable and authority as reasonably fallible.

O. J. Harvey, David Hunt, and Harold Schroder have suggested that there are several stages of conceptual development through which the maturing organism passes, although an individual may become arrested at one of the stages.

UNILATERAL DEPENDENCE. This is the most rigid stage. The organism tends to use a few simple criteria received from authority figures or from his social milieu. He tends to submit to authority and carefully adhere to the norms of his groups. Probably the infant needs to go through this stage of development, for he is dependent on the direction of his parents and their nourishment for his very existence. The individual who does not develop beyond this stage, however, becomes a good subject for a totalitarian regime. The immature organism *has* to depend on authorities for its culture and for its physical survival. If the mature person does not learn to stand on his own "psychological" feet, but remains dependent on authoritarian control, then we say that he has been arrested at the stage of unilateral dependence. Research indicates that even in the United States many adults, including a surprising number of teachers, manifest the characteristics of this stage.[12]

---

[11] O. J. Harvey, David E. Hunt, and Harold M. Schroder, *Conceptual Systems and Personality Organization* (New York: Wiley, 1961), p. 3.

[12] Bruce R. Joyce, Joan Sieber, and Howard Lamb, "Conceptual Systems and Information Processing: A Study of Teachers" (unpublished manuscript).

NEGATIVE INDEPENDENCE. This stage might be described as a reaction against the conformity of the first stage. During negative independence the individual rejects external control and is less submissive, although he still tends to see things in blacks and whites; his concepts are still few and rigid. It may be that this stage is necessary for progression from extreme dependence. The rebellions of adolescence may be in part the manifestation of the struggle of the organism to free himself from the considerable dependence of childhood. The person thus reacts with hostility to attempts to control him. It can be seen that a person who did not develop beyond this stage would be unhappy, with a considerable amount of interpersonal trouble.[13]

CONDITIONAL DEPENDENCE AND MUTUALITY. The person who manages to overcome the hostility of the second stage and to establish relations with other people on an independent basis is likely to become preoccupied with interpersonal relations and to take other people's wishes and points of view more into account. He tends to develop more complex concepts and more flexible ones, and can deal with confusing and stressful situations with greater ease. He can entertain alternative views of himself. ("Sometimes I do well in arithmetic, but I have trouble with word problems." "I can express myself clearly, but sometimes I offend people.") Whereas people in an earlier stage tend to resolve doubt by reference to formulas and easy solutions, this person is able to remain in doubt longer and to consider more alternatives. His awareness of others' intentions, however, can result in an "other-directedness" that renders him overly dependent on the approval of others.

INTERDEPENDENCE. In the most mature stage of conceptual development, a person possesses the most complex and flexible system of concepts, which enables him to adapt most easily to difficult and stressful situations. The interdependent person does not see conflicts of interest as necessary or long-lasting; he is less emotional about interpersonal difficulty; and he can understand the role of other persons and approach situations in a way satisfactory to both himself and others. When faced with a difficult problem, he tends to be able to suspend judgment while seeking information that will make a decision more rational. When he is criticized or confused or when he is confronted by a conflicting belief, his reaction is to find more information and to examine his beliefs to see if they need revision. Faced

---

[13] See Harvey, Hunt, and Schroder, *Conceptual Systems and Personality Organization* for a more complete description of these stages of conceptual development.

with a job, he tends to be task-oriented, although aware of others and their needs.

In short, the stage of interdependence is the desirable one, both from a point of view of personal adjustment and an ability to live a full life and from the point of view of society. A democratic society fairly demands interdependent citizens. In a totalitarian country they would be considered most troublesome.

What Conditions Influence Conceptual Development?

Harvey, Hunt, and Schroder's theory of development is by no means entirely tested. They present impressive evidence, however, that various training conditions or environments in which a child is raised or schooled powerfully influence conceptual development. Their thesis is that the way a child is treated at school and at home either helps him develop conceptually or tends to arrest his development at an immature stage. We shall next consider what they call "training environments," or the conditions under which schooling takes place at home and in formal settings. They describe training environments in terms of a unilateral-interdependent dimension.

UNILATERAL TRAINING. This kind of training is characterized, first of all, by the imposition of external rules and criteria of judgment. It may take the form of rules which are imposed and backed up by threat. ("I will tell you the right way to get the answer. Your grade will depend on your using the right way as well as on the correctness of the answer.") Or it may take the form of criteria which imply that authority does not err— suggesting that criteria of rightness are found outside the immediate situation. ("The book is right. It was written by an authority and has to be right.")

Under unilateral conditions, knowledge is seen as rigid and definite. ("There are three causes of the American Revolution. They explain why we had to go to war against the British.") The student is rewarded chiefly when he arrives at answers that have been selected beforehand. ("Will you stand and recite the three causes of the American Revolution.") The object of training is relatively fixed and definite. ("Your job for the year is to read all the passages in this book so that you'll be ready for next year's book.")

Also, under unilateral conditions, the child is valued for his achievement rather than for his efforts to search out ideas and information. ("You can't do any more reading until you've learned the week's spelling words. You seem to learn everything except what I want you to learn. Mary is a good girl. She does what I ask and then does something quiet.")

Harvey, Hunt, and Schroder make the assumption that unilateral training tends to arrest children at the simple stage of conceptual development. It tends to promote dependence on authority, stereotyping, rigid interpersonal relations, and a dislike for the doubt and confusion that pervades any really thoughtful attempt to find answers.

INTERDEPENDENT TRAINING. This kind of training is characterized by an attempt to help the child understand himself and his relations with others, as well as to help him to inquire into his world through experiment. Search, rather than rote learning, is rewarded. ("You've done a good job of looking for information, but the answer still doesn't satisfy me. Let's write to the museum and see if they can help us there.") The emphasis is on hypothetical constructs. ("Do you think water put out the candle? I wonder how we could conduct the experiment to see if you are correct.")

Perhaps most important, the learner is valued for himself. His achievement and his personal worth are not equated. ("Well, you seem to have missed a lot of the questions this week. Can we work out a new way of studying? Charley has some trouble too. I wonder if you can work together.")

It should be evident that interdependent training is designed to help advance conceptual development—to teach people to hold their knowledge and standards as tentative and emerging, to make them responsible for decisions, and to help them relate to others in cooperative inquiry. The organism is thus encouraged to form freer and more vigorous relationships with others, to tolerate uncertainty about knowledge and to seek and weigh evidence, and to treat others and himself with dignity. Failure, consequently, is treated as a source of information. ("Well, this time all the plants died again. Where shall we look for the cause?") The child has to share in the development of standards of performance. ("What do you think of your progress? Are there places where we can improve this job?")

The interdependent training environment is one of leisure and relaxation for children that requires utmost patience. It takes time for students to arrive at realistic standards, and they will make many mistakes along the way. The position presented here, however, is that unilateral conditions tend to retard the conceptual development of children, while interdependent conditions advance conceptual development.

A number of interesting experiments relate to the theory just presented. The famous studies by Kurt Lewin, Ronald Lippitt, and Ralph White more than a quarter of a century ago stressed "authoritarian" and "democratic" social climates. It was found that in these two social climates the interpersonal relations of children were quite different; children were more cooperative and treated one another with greater dignity after exposure to democratic conditions.[14]

Harold Anderson and Helen Brewer studied young children who were exposed to "dominative" or "integrative" behavior by their teachers. Even five-year-olds who were being dominated by their teachers tended to dominate, or attempt to dominate, their peers, while children who were being treated with greater consideration and respect tended to be more integrative and respectful with their classmates.[15]

We need to examine carefully the theses that training environments are infectious, that rigid environments produce rigid people, and that interdependent conditions produce people who will have open minds and flexible conceptual systems. It seems very likely that the predisposition to be open- or closed-minded is established in the very early years of life. Furthermore, the influence of the school may be dependent not only on the amount that the child learns but also on the *way* he learns and the way he is treated by other people while he is learning.

Democracy tries to keep issues open and solutions tentative. The person who wants authoritarian control and simple solutions to problems is the enemy of democracy. Hence the question of conceptual style and of the conditions that create open minds is of critical importance.

Implications for Teaching

What does the foregoing have to say for our strategy of social education? What kind of social environment should be planned and what techniques of instruction have to be learned in order to carry out the plans? If we accept open-mindedness as one of our educational goals, then we have to consider the conditions that bring it about. What, in other words, makes up the kind of "training environment" that helps children grow toward openness? What kind of environment is appropriate for different kinds of children, and how can we tell how to modify conditions to suit the needs of individuals? These conditions will be considered in terms of several categories of teacher activities.

---

[14] Kurt Lewin, Ronald Lippitt, and Ralph O. White, "Patterns of Aggressive Behavior in Experimentally Created Social Climates," *Journal of Social Psychology.* X (1939), 271–99.

[15] Harold M. Anderson and Helen M. Brewer, "Domination and Social Integration in the Behavior of Kindergarten Children and Teachers," *Genetic Psychology Monographs,* XXI (1939), 287–385.

THE TEACHER REWARDS AND PUNISHES. In myriad ways, from smiling encouragingly to admonishing with words, every teacher encourages certain kinds of child behavior and discourages others. We can distinguish several kinds of behavior by which teachers reward and punish.

Search behavior. The teacher can plan classroom activities so that it is easy for the children to make inquiries into the environment. The teacher can go out of his way to encourage attempts to search out answers and pursue interesting questions. An interdependent environment is necessarily characterized by search behavior; it is improved by constant practice and continually rewarded. In order to build an interdependent climate, the teacher has to reward search continually in ways that lead the child to understand and explain through cooperative investigation.

Attainment of information. In every good classroom many facts and ideas are learned, and the teacher needs to reward this increase in knowledge constantly. A problem arises, however, in that most of us have greater facility in rewarding the attainment of knowledge than we do in rewarding search or problem-solving activity. This is especially true when the search behavior does not uncover anything particularly important. Most of us, for example, have seen more tests that determine whether knowledge has been acquired than tests that find out whether we are learning to be better inquirers. Nonetheless, knowledge is important, and its attainment should be praised in balanced measure.

Following directions and conforming to rules. Every classroom needs organization, and an interdependent environment implies, most of all, that each individual is learning to restrain his own behavior and to develop with others the regulation of group activity. In a relatively unilateral environment the rules become the thing and the teacher spends much time rewarding those who conform and punishing those who do not. Hence the rules take on much significance. In a relatively interdependent environment the search for rules of behavior is as important as learning to live within rules. Failure to conform becomes not simply an object of censure but something to be looked into and studied. The good teacher needs to learn not only to reward conformity but also to encourage inquiry into the nature of rules and to stimulate the cooperative activity necessary to produce rules.

THE TEACHER HANDLES INFORMATION. In the course of a unit of study the teacher handles thousands of pieces of information and helps children to learn hundreds of concepts which organize the forest of ideas making up content. How the teacher handles this information is critically important.

The teacher helps the children find information. He helps them to locate reference books and develop the skills for using them. He helps them locate people in the community who are good sources and teaches them how to interview artfully. He helps them identify worthwhile questions to guide search, and he helps them organize the search itself. In an interdependent environment this is a major function of the teacher. He is guide, critic, and companion in search.

The teacher helps the children evaluate information. He helps them learn to test hypotheses, to assess the authenticity and reliability of information, and to look at things from many points of view. He helps them evaluate the quality of their thinking, to decide whether conclusions are warranted and whether ideas need revision. One of the teacher's critical functions in an interdependent atmosphere is to help the children evaluate information and reformulate problems on the basis of that evaluation. Interdependence makes all ideas fair game—and demands that supporting facts be continually examined, that logic be scrutinized, and that better solutions always be sought. If the classroom is pervaded by a spirit of curiosity and inquiry, then the atmosphere for open-mindedness and flexibility has been established.

The teacher asks questions. In unilateral environments the questions all seem to have but one answer (What year did the Mayflower land?). The interdependent environment is characterized by questions that require conclusions, reasons, and personal opinions (From the evidence we have, what might be the reasons that the Puritans came to this country?). Where the teacher asks questions that require only simple, factual answers, the inquiry in the classroom is subtly deadened. Where the questions require search, inquiry and interest are heightened.

The teacher gives information. While it requires consummate skill to lecture effectively to children of elementary age, the teacher nonetheless is the child's most valuable source of information. Carefully planned presentations by the teacher constitute one of his important functions. Under unilateral conditions, however, we tend to find that the information is presented as if law were being made. It is unequivocal, correct, and not to be challenged. In an interdependent environment the presentation of information is interspersed with opportunities to weigh the information and see what it adds up to. Some laymen have the idea that the elementary school years are simply the ones when the "basic facts" are poured into the child in preparation for the years ahead when real thinking begins. The tragedy is that if thinking does not begin in the early years, all we will have in the later years is a closed mind.

The teacher makes conclusions and generalizations. In unilateral environments this is one of the teacher's main functions. Many beginning teachers have seen so much of this activity during their training that it takes them a long time to learn to resist doing intellectual work for their

children. To be sure, there are times when the teacher must offer generalizations—carefully buttressed by facts. But nearly always, in the interdependent climate, the child has the burden of making conclusions and
defending them. When the teacher states them, he does so in such a way
that challenge is encouraged and the reasoning he used is visible to the
learner.

THE TEACHER ORGANIZES THE CHILDREN. Every classroom must be
organized so that work may proceed efficiently. But the methods used by
the teacher to decide on and effect organization are crucial to the child's
social development.

The teacher determines procedures. Unquestionably the teacher is
the appointed leader; and, especially with extremely young children, some
procedures have to be thought out beforehand. However, as the child
becomes able (and every school-age child is somewhat able), he should
take part in determining how his work is to be organized. *If he cannot
share in this decision process, a unilateral climate tends to prevail.* If the
teacher determines nearly all the questions to be explored, all the means
used to collect and analyze information, and all the ways in which committees are organized, then the child will not be encouraged to look to
himself for leadership and responsibility. He will not learn interdependence
and self-reliance.

The teacher helps the child determine procedures. In the interdependent environment the teacher does not leave the children completely
to their own devices, but he does counsel them continually to develop
reasoned plans in an air of mutual agreement. The child is involved in the
debate about ends and means and shares in the allotment of authority.

DETERMINING STANDARDS. In every activity of life, human beings
require some means of determining the adequacy of their performance.
In school, the teacher and his students must be able to answer these questions: Are we learning enough? Is our inquiry getting more effective? Are
we getting along better? The teacher must see that standards are evident
so that growth can be judged. Here again we will suggest two types of
pedagogical behavior.

The teacher determines standards. When the teacher imposes all
the standards and assumes all responsibility for evaluation, we have one
of the conditions for unilaterality. The child must learn, however, that rules
do not come ready-made. If he is to develop flexibility, he must understand
that rules are emergent, temporary standards demanding constant revision
and reapplication to new situations. At times the teacher may need to
impose standards. But whenever the child *can* participate in making and

enforcing standards and does not, then we have the conditions of uni-laterality.

The teacher helps the children determine standards. As the children grow toward maturity, they can assume increasing responsibility for estab-lishing standards and the means of living up to them. The interdependent climate depends on the children's ability to join in the search for means of judging progress. The open mind knows what rules and standards are and knows how to take part in their formulation. He knows because he has had practice from early childhood. The closed mind thinks he can derive stand-ards merely from authoritative sources, because in his early years he did not have to share in making guidelines for progress.

Making a Training Environment

All the varieties of teaching behavior described above are present in every normal classroom. How these behaviors are proportioned, however, determines the differences in the training environment of the child. The following diagram summarizes the kinds of behavior that a teacher can develop in order to create the kind of training environment he believes is appropriate.

Interdependent Environment		Unilateral Environment
Teacher helps children determine	Standards	Teacher determines
Teacher helps children determine	Procedures	Teacher determines
Directed at search	Rewards	Directed at following rules
Teacher helps children find and evaluate	Information	Teacher gives conclusions

ONE TREATMENT FOR ALL? Remembering that (theoretically at least) unilateral conditions are more likely to arrest conceptual development and that interdependent conditions are more likely to advance social develop-ment, we should nonetheless consider whether any one set of conditions is "good for all at all times." It seems reasonable to suppose that different environments are good for people in different stages of development.

For example, extremely rigid children, plunged into an open and interdependent environment, might, instead of assuming more responsibility, simply be frightened and withdraw into ritualistic behavior. A considerably modulated or muted interdependent environment might be best for them. Among the culturally deprived or under other conditions where socialization is erratic and partial, a moderately interdependent environment is probably advisable, at least until the children have internalized sufficient values to permit them to operate effectively in productive harmony. Thus we may suggest the following principles for the application of training conditions:

For very young children	Partial interdependence
For very rigid children	Partial interdependence
For certain culturally deprived children	Partial interdependence
For rapidly developing children	Full interdependence

If the teacher applies these principles, the very young child should be able to live under conditions permitting him first to internalize a few norms and rules and then later to develop norms and rules in cooperation with others. By providing him early with some rules to follow, we give him some anchors to behavior. But by gradually helping him to develop some standards, develop some procedures, and evaluate information and conclusions, we encourage his growing interdependence. (We might add only that the rigid child would probably also need to engage in a great deal of guided group activity in order to have peerage models for his own behavior.) Finally, when the child begins developing openness at a rapid rate, he should be placed in an atmosphere of complete interdependence and be given full responsibility for evaluating ideas, information, procedures, and standards. So doing, we help to push him toward independence and give him the opportunity for those interpersonal activities he needs in order to develop mutual dependence and trust.

Even when children of different levels of development are found in the same classroom (and this is most often the case), the teacher can find ways of varying his guidance methods. He can get the more open-minded children to participate in inquiry-centered groups; he can get the more rigid children engaged in structured problem-solving activities; and he can get the immature and deprived children to join in socializing games. All of these activities are possible within the same classroom, and many of them, particularly structured but socializing games, are appropriate for all even though aimed at a few. Nearly every unit activity provides many roles fulfilling the conditions dealt with in this chapter.

Summary

Open-mindedness and a flexible belief system are desirable goals of social education, and it appears that the *social climate* of the school and classroom is a potent element in promoting the child's social development. Properly conducted, a class can develop an inquiring person capable of both independence and an ability to evolve meaningful relationships with other people.

Therefore the teaching strategy has to provide for the development of a suitable social climate just as it has to guide inquiry into the subject disciplines. In fact, it is probably impossible to teach the methods and ideas of the social sciences *except* in an atmosphere of interdependence. Unilateral conditions are anathema to scientific procedures.

INQUIRIES

1. Read Edward L. Walker and Roger W. Heyns, *An Anatomy for Conformity*. Identify the conditions that Walker and Heyns believe lead to conformity or interdependence. Compare their analysis with the one in this chapter.

2. Read and criticize Chapter 9 of Stuart Chase, *The Proper Study of Mankind*. He provides a delightfully written overview of some provocative studies of group behavior.

3. Read David Riesman, *The Lonely Crowd*. Compare the effects of other-directedness with the effects of unilateral and inter-dependent environments as described here.

4. It was suggested, in the chapter summary, that unilateral conditions and the practice of social science are incompatible. Why is this so? Or do you think it would be possible to teach the disciplines in unilateral conditions?

5. Is there a conflict between the maintenance of open-minded-ness and the development of strong patriotic sentiments?

6. What are some of the difficulties involved in having young children share in the determination of standards? How can these difficulties be overcome?

7. In this chapter it was suggested that not every individual will thrive under the same conditions. Inquire more fully into means for modifying the training environment to accord with the development of particular children.

References and Readings

ADORNO, T. W., and others. *The Authoritarian Personality*. New York: Harper, 1950.

ALLPORT, GORDON W. *The Nature of Prejudice*. Reading, Mass.: Addison-Wesley, 1954.

ANDERSON, HAROLD M., and BREWER, HELEN M. "Domination and Social Integration in the Behavior of Kindergarten Children and Teachers," *Genetic Psychology Monographs*, XXI (1939), 287-385.

BROWN, INA CORINNE. *Understanding Other Cultures*. Englewood Cliffs, N.J.: Prentice-Hall, 1963.

BRUNER, JEROME S.; GOODNOW, JACQUELINE; and AUSTIN, GEORGE A. *A Study of Thinking*. New York: Wiley, 1956.

CHASE, STUART. *The Proper Study of Mankind*. New York: Harper, 1956.

FESTINGER, LEON. *A Theory of Cognitive Dissonance*. Evanston, Ill.: Row, Peterson, 1957.

HARVEY, O. J.; HUNT, DAVID E.; and SCHRODER, HAROLD M. *Conceptual Systems and Personality Organization*. New York: Wiley, 1961.

JOYCE, BRUCE R.; SIEBER, JOAN; and LAMB, HOWARD. "Conceptual Systems and Information Processing: A Study of Teachers." Unpublished manuscript.

LEWIN, KURT; LIPPITT, RONALD; and WHITE, RALPH O. "Patterns of Aggressive Behavior in Experimentally Created Social Climates," *Journal of Social Psychology*, X (1939), 271-99.

NEUGARTEN, BERNICE. "Social Class and Friendship Among School Children," *American Journal of Sociology*, LI (1946), 305-13.

RIESMAN, DAVID. *The Lonely Crowd*. Garden City, N.Y.: Doubleday, 1953.

ROKEACH, MILTON. *The Open and Closed Mind*. New York: Basic Books, 1960.

WALKER, EDWARD L., and HEYNS, ROGER W. *An Anatomy for Conformity*. Englewood Cliffs, N.J.: Prentice-Hall, 1962.

WARNER, W. LLOYD. *American Life: Dream and Reality*. Chicago: Univ. of Chicago Press, 1953.

Chapter 7

THE CAPACITY TO LEARN

In any discourse on the strategies of teaching there must be some exploration of theories that explain learning. What conditions promote learning and help learning to persist? What do we know of the child's ability to think? Are there optimal ages for particular kinds of learning—learning concrete facts, for instance, as distinct from learning generalizations? We must have some guidelines for helping the child to grow intellectually. We must not try to impose upon him learning for which he is not ready or, equally bad, delay important ideas past the time when he can best absorb them. Clear evidence and clear answers in these matters are currently very limited. There exists only fragmentary evidence about many of the important issues in social education, such as the development of social values, ideas, and skills. However, some of the research that *is* available is critically important, and some of the existing theories about the development of the social, intellectual animal have great implications for teaching strategies.

The Ability to Generalize

The nature of intelligence has long been the subject of serious controversy. Philosophers, psychologists, teachers, and laymen have all debated the degree to which learning ability is fixed by heredity or influenced by environment. A major issue has been whether an early measurement of intellectual ability (such as an intelligence test) predicts performance on later tests. To some extent, examiners have found that early measures do predict later ones, but increasingly the development of intelligence is being viewed as an outcome of the dynamic interaction of the individual and his environment; the mental operations that an individual can perform are believed to be closely related to the number and quality of the experiences he has undergone. Rich experience early in life can considerably influence later development, and certain types of experience even late in life can also influence intellectual capacity.[1]

The intelligence quotients of many children of lower-class parents tend to fall during the school years, while the intelligence quotients of upper-middle-class children have been observed to rise somewhat. Apparently what we regard as intellectual capacity is affected by experience, at least through the years of adolescence. The present view is that experience has its greatest effect on intellectual capacity during the first four or five years of life, its next-greatest effect during the next four or five years, and its least effect thereafter.

The noted Swiss psychologist Jean Piaget has contended that critical to intellectual growth is the development of intellectual structures or organizing schemata, which may be likened to the systems of concepts discussed in our earlier chapters. Piaget describes these schemata in terms of advancing stages of sophistication; at certain ages the child's ability to organize concepts rises to new levels, and he develops more advanced types of thinking. For example, Piaget contends that up to the approximate age of eight the child reasons only particular cases. He cannot carry on a generalized argument. He has trouble reasoning from the point of view of another person. And he feels no need for the logical examination of ideas.

Until about the age of eleven he is able to reason generally, but only in terms of concrete cases. That is, he can see that the population growth of two countries was related to the spread of railroads, but he cannot handle the idea as an abstract proposition (In grasslands where European culture was imported, population growth tended to follow the spread of railroads).

About the age of eleven, according to Piaget, the child begins to be able to assume the viewpoint of others and to reason from another's beliefs. It is at eleven or twelve years that his schemata have become sufficiently developed to enable him to carry on formal abstract reasoning and to engage in real deductive activity. At about the age of twelve he is able to fully explain causal relationships.[2]

For the benefit of teachers, the British educator E. A. Peel has described and interpreted Piaget's stages of concrete thinking.[3] Peel has especially examined how the stage of "concrete thinking" might have implications for school instruction. In the stage of concrete thinking, a child

---

[1] See J. McVey Hunt, *Intelligence and Experience* (New York: Ronald Press, 1961), and Benjamin S. Bloom, *Stability and Change in Human Characteristics* (New York: Wiley, 1964).

[2] See Jean Piaget, *Judgment and Reasoning in the Child* (New York: Humanities Press, 1947) and *Origins of Intelligence in Children*, trans. Margaret Cook (Washington: American Council on Education, 1956).

[3] E. A. Peel, *The Pupil's Thinking* (London: Oldbourne, 1961).

in social studies should be capable of discerning how the roles of a mother in Chicago compare with the roles of a mother in Samoa. However, he might have difficulty deriving generalizations from these specific examples. He may be incapable of formulating the general idea that maternal roles in primitive societies are in certain ways similar and in certain ways dissimilar to maternal roles in highly complex, technologically developed societies. In other words, the child can "get the point" of the specific examples, but he cannot fully develop the general idea that the examples represent.

concrete

Piaget's work has been attacked on the ground that the age limits for his stages are incorrect, for psychologists in countries other than Switzerland have reached somewhat different conclusions. Peel contends that the given ages are approximate and that if one recognizes that individuals reach various stages at different ages, Piaget's work has been substantially confirmed.

> We may conclude that Piaget's claims have been substantially confirmed when mental ages are substituted for chronological ages, always bearing in mind that individuals may tend to use concrete thinking even when they are capable of formal thought.[4]

If Piaget is correct in saying that the pre-seven-year-old (approximately) is unable to see abstract relations and that the pre-twelve-year-old (again approximately), though able to determine relations, is still incapable of abstract expressions of relations, then the job of the elementary school needs to be examined carefully. For example, elementary instruction could then place emphasis on helping children to find relations in concrete data (How many of the colonies allowed religious freedom? Which didn't? Was there more religious strife in one kind or in the other?). Correspondingly, it might be fruitless to try to develop general propositions (On the whole, for the first hundred years, the United States successfully followed George Washington's advice to avoid foreign entanglements); conceivably only the most advanced elementary children would be capable of such abstract reasoning. Everyone knows what happens when children learn verbal expressions that they do not understand. Besides the waste involved, boredom and a sense of futility quickly set in.

The author and his wife recently completed a research study dealing with children's causal thinking in natural science. Some of the results illustrate the extent to which children will use words meaninglessly if their concepts are vague and if they have mechanically learned abstract rules

---

[4] *Ibid.*, p. 178.

and principles. In the study some sixth-grade children observed a physics experiment. The teacher held before them a glass brimful of water. Over the top of the glass he slipped a piece of paper and then inverted the glass and removed his hand. The paper adhered to the glass, and the water did not spill. The following are some of the verbal "explanations" given by the children:

> "The suction of the water is holding the paper on."
>
> "No air is escaping."
>
> "The air inside the jar held the paper so it would not fall."
>
> "There is a vaproon in the jar and when you turn it over the water doesn't come out."
>
> "Centrifical force stops the water and the card from coming out."
>
> "It is staying there by water precher."
>
> "The suchon of the air outside of the jar is trying to get in the jar."
>
> "Because there is no oxygen on it and so the paper sticks."
>
> "The precher of the jar."
>
> "All the oxygen goes to the bottom of the jar so the paper stays on top of the jar."[5]

It is apparent that young children can lapse into senseless verbalisms when the words they learn are not completely understood. The quotations above reveal a fairly good "scientific" vocabulary—but it is a vocabulary unbacked by knowledge to make it meaningful.

According to numerous status studies, it is similarly true that children possess great *quantities* of surface information about social issues and about topics developed in the social studies, and that they are awake to the transient vocabulary of newspaper headlines. But, significantly, the studies also show that their information is of extremely mixed accuracy. They know the words, the verbalisms, but they do not know consistently the real meaning of the words. (The accuracy or inaccuracy of understanding varies, however, from child to child, and differences between children of the same age or grade level are often greater than the differences between children of different grade levels.)

Obviously all these factors point to the need for serious research. We need to find out the limits of a child's formal reasoning power, especially in terms of school learning. Only then can we determine what kinds of experience and education are appropriate for him.

---

[5] Bruce R. and Elizabeth H. Joyce, "Children Explain Science Phenomena: A Study of Verbalisms" (unpublished manuscript).

Improving Children's Thinking

Children are not the only people who make errors in formal thinking. The British psychologist Victoria Hazlitt, with convincing evidence, has argued that the differences between adult thinking and child thinking are the result of experience rather than capacity.[6] M. E. Oakes, too, has conducted research showing that the same kinds of errors Piaget found in the thinking of children can also be found in the thinking of adults.[7] Edna Heidbreder found that individuals do vary widely in their ability to approach concepts, but she also found that the processes or methods used to form concepts were similar in adults and children. Her work has some direct implications for social studies instruction, for when she asked children to form concepts from several kinds of clues, she discovered that concepts based on "number" clues are the last to be formed.[8] The implication is that concepts based on number are less obvious than concepts based on other kinds of clues. Many social studies concepts are based on number ideas. Maps, in fact, are actually mathematical representations of reality, as are globes. The ideas of scale, latitude, and longitude, as we shall see, come hard to most children. Charts and graphs also involve mathematical ideas; but they, along with tables, are essential sources of certain kinds of learning.

The social studies deal constantly with causation, whether seeking reasons for social legislation, explanations of business failures, the relation between climate and crops, or reasons why this nation has high production and that one low. Thus it is essential that the teacher carefully examine evidence not only about a child's ability to think but also about the means of accelerating and improving his thinking. The growing evidence is that training *can* improve thinking ability. Says Peel:

> Not many experimental inquiries have been carried out on this topic, but they tend to show that added experience, in the preoperational stage of manipulating, combining, dividing up, and matching up materials and objects leads to an acceleration of the onset of the concrete stage of thinking. . . . At the later stage of the transition from concrete to formal thought, added experience of the pupil in carrying

---

[6] Victoria Hazlitt, "Children's Thinking," *British Journal of Psychology,* XX (April 1930), 354–61.

[7] M. E. Oakes, *Children's Explanations of Natural Phenomena* (New York: Teachers College, 1947).

[8] Edna Heidbreder, "The Attainment of Concepts, Part III: The Process," *Journal of Psychology,* XXIV (1947), 93–138.

out experiments combined with comments, suggestions, and criticisms by the experimenter or teacher can bring about the change to formal judgments.[9]

R. H. Ojemann carried on an experiment which demonstrated that social studies teachers who emphasized causal thinking improved the causal thinking of their children.[10] Ethel Maw taught teachers to use twenty lessons so framed that they produced definite effects on children's scores in problem-solving tests.[11] J. I. Lacey and K. M. Dallenbach have concluded that proper training of the child can hasten the appearance of the successive stages of causal thinking.[12] More recently, J. Richard Suchman developed some techniques for teaching children methods of inquiry. He assumed that exploration, manipulation, and the quest for mastery are intrinsically motivating, and he joined to this assumption the belief that children can be taught more effective ways of thinking by being led to analyze problems. He was able to train teachers to handle what he calls "inquiry training," and his results indicate that children do develop more efficient and analytical problem-solving techniques as a consequence of the training.[13]

Hilda Taba and Freeman Elzey are presently engaged in an interesting research program that may help us learn how to shape teaching strategies for developing thought processes. They are exploring means by which certain defined formulas or "models" of thinking, such as concept formation, can be used as "maps" for lessons. They have suggested that in order to teach a given mental process, we should shape the lesson so that the child forms concepts in an efficient manner. Thus we get him to "practice" the mental process we want him to develop.[14]

It seems fairly plain that a teaching strategy emphasizing the development of more effective thinking can be successfully applied to children. Although many elementary school children possess only limited thinking ability and do not naturally use generalizations effectively, what they can do is considerable and is open to improvement.

---

[9] Peel, p. 181.

[10] R. H. Ojemann and others, "The Effects of a 'Causal' Teacher-Training Program and Certain Curricular Changes on Grade-School Children," *Journal of Experimental Education*, XXIV (December 1955), 95–114.

[11] Ethel Maw, "An Experiment in Teaching Critical Thinking in the Intermediate Grades" (Ph.D. thesis, Univ. of Pennsylvania, 1959).

[12] J. I. Lacey and K. M. Dallenbach, "Acquisition by Children of the Cause-Effect Relationship," *American Journal of Psychology*, LII (1939), 103–10.

[13] J. Richard Suchman, "Inquiry Training in the Elementary School," *Science Teacher*, XXVII (November 1960), 42–47.

[14] Hilda Taba and Freeman F. Elzey, "Teaching Strategies and Thought Processes," *Teachers College Record*, LXV (March 1964), 524–34.

SPACE AND TIME. Children seem to find the two mental perceptions of time and space particularly hard to grasp. Concern over this difficulty has rationalized much of the topical design of present-day curricula.

Conceptions of space and time are essential to the study of geography and history, respectively, but a number of research studies have shown that children are slow to understand these ideas in a form recognizable by geographers and historians. As John Michaelis has stated:

> Although many time concepts are known by children in the intermediate grades, chronology and historical time cannot be grasped by most children until they are in junior or senior high school. Similarly, space concepts of sphericity of the earth, such as latitude and longitude, are not really learned by most children until they are in the upper grades or in junior high school.[15]

Michaelis also points out how the difficulty of space-time concepts influences the teaching of the faraway and the long ago.

> As children study life in the expanded community or a simple primitive culture, the major emphasis placed by the teacher is not on how long ago, how far away, or on the number of square miles. From the child's point of view, it is more a matter of comparing likenesses and differences in ways of living of others as compared with ways of living in his home and immediate community.[16]

Clarifying Children's Concepts

The evidence that young children have limited ability to generalize or think abstractly and conceptually and that they tend to use verbalized information inaccurately has had a fundamental effect on the design of curricula. The evidence has generally been interpreted to mean that the curriculum of the elementary school should emphasize the here and now and, especially in the primary grades, should center on the home and the family and on holidays and historical figures. In other words, the principle has been that the child can study only those things related to his immediate experience and not requiring much understanding of spatial, temporal, or ideational relationships.

---

[15] John U. Michaelis, *Social Studies for Children in a Democracy* (Englewood Cliffs, N.J.: Prentice-Hall, 1956), p. 74.
[16] *Ibid.*, p. 69.

The evidence does suggest that the younger child needs to acquire a great deal of firsthand experience on which to build his ideas. But can it be that this evidence has been overinterpreted to mean that he cannot effectively study *anything* lying outside his immediate life environment? As early as 1932, Joy M. Lacey, after researching the problem, concluded not only that many children's concepts were confused and inaccurate but also that primary-grade curricula were so thin in content that they gave the child no chance to clarify his ideas.[17] Much later, in the 1950s, J. D. McAulay's interviews with primary-grade children led him to much the same conclusion. He found that the home-and-neighborhood-centered study of the primary grades emphasized concepts which the children had acquired prior to school or prior to the grade in which concepts were first emphasized. Consequently the curriculum did not extend the children's understandings.[18]

Ralph Preston has argued that the limits of children's thinking should not entirely restrict the range of content; rather the evidence indicates the necessity for treating fewer topics, but these in depth, so that the child can acquire sufficient firsthand experience on which to build difficult ideas and have adequate time to clarify his concepts.

> While there are obvious limits to the school child's critical understanding, there is impressive evidence that children are quite capable of engaging in certain mature types of understanding. The full development of these capabilities and processes calls for the concentrated and unhurried application upon carefully selected bodies of content. A major condition is then present under which the child can learn to "think deep."[19]

Arthur Jersild's observations point in the same direction—that the wise way to handle children so that they will acquire the experience and understanding necessary to build clear ideas is to have them engage in depth studies of a few topics rather than in a superficial study of a great many things. He calls the process the "seasoning" of ideas:

> In many areas it appears that in order to grasp certain meanings it is necessary for the child to have an accumulation of impressions and experiences distributed over a limited period of time. It has been

---

[17] Joy M. Lacey, *Social Studies Concepts of Children in the First Three Grades* (New York: Teachers College, 1932).

[18] J. D. McAulay, "Social Studies in the Primary Grades," *Social Education*, XVIII (December 1954), 357–58.

[19] Ralph C. Preston, "Teaching for Depth," *Childhood Education*, XXXVI (January 1960), 213.

found that impressions concentrated within a short period of time, even when quite dramatic and charged with emotion, are not likely to produce the same grasp of the subject as a child will obtain through a gradual accumulation of impressions and information over a longer period of time.[20]

A recent study by Melvin Arnoff demonstrated the feasibility of teaching concepts of government to children in grades 2 to 4. He reported that second-graders appeared to learn as rapidly as the older children. Concluding that traditional ideas of grade placement are outmoded, he stated:

> No longer tied to previous concepts of grade placement, the schools must bear the responsibility for developing social studies curricula which will prepare children to enter the world of their adult lives equipped to comprehend and harness the complex personal and global social forces which are no less important than the physical and chemical forces of our universe.[21]

Assumptions About Instruction

Only a few issues have been treated in this review of the literature on the intellectual development of the child, but they have been selected because they have particular implications for the revision of social studies instruction.[22] Some of these implications may be summarized in the form of assumptions to be considered when constructing the teaching strategy.

Assumption 1. The child's intellectual development depends on his experience. To introduce him to a new idea, we need to give him experiences to which that idea is relevant. It is easier to teach the child about things which he has already experienced, but that is not enough. The school must also lead him to new areas of reality.

Assumption 2. Proper instruction can improve the child's thinking ability. The elementary school child has difficulty reasoning from general propositions, but he can reason effectively when the hard facts are before him, and his ability to handle abstract ideas and to use more effective concepts in his inquiries can be enhanced considerably. Instruction has to

---

[20] Arthur T. Jersild, *Child Psychology*, 4th ed. (Englewood Cliffs, N.J.: Prentice-Hall, 1956), p. 459.

[21] Melvin Arnoff, "Adding Depth to Elementary School Social Studies," *Social Education*, XXVIII (October 1964), 336.

[22] For a more detailed treatment of this subject of child development, consult the books and journal articles listed at the end of this chapter.

be planned with this in mind, however.

Assumption 3. Depth studies—or studying a few topics thoroughly—can ensure that the children have enough time to acquire new experiences and to "season" new ideas and concepts. Time must be allowed for the development of thinking ability.

Assumption 4. Ideas of chronology and geographical space apparently come hard to children whose mental age is less than eleven or twelve. Until contrary evidence appears, the study of other times and places perhaps should not emphasize space and time concepts; apparently efforts have been wasted in attempting to teach these concepts for which the children need greater experience or maturity. However, depth studies can give children the vicarious experience of other times and other places. There is no question that children can learn much about distant eras and peoples even without the chronological or spatial perspectives of the professional scholar. For example, first-graders in Texas, trading information about the family and the home with first-graders in Japan, can learn a great deal about Japanese life without having the geographer's ideas about where Japan is.

Assumption 5. The development of concepts about society is accompanied by the development of a conceptual style, an open or a closed mind. Consequently the social climate of the school and the ways in which the child is helped to inquire into the world around him are as critical to his development as the care with which content is presented. The closed mind results when the child is handled unilaterally and rigidly. The open mind develops when the child is rewarded for searching out ideas and checking his opinions and facts in an interdependent atmosphere.

Social Attitudes

Thinking and feeling are inextricably bound together. Therefore our discussion of children's thinking is not complete without a consideration of the factors that affect the development of social attitudes and values.

In Chapter 6 we found that the child, soon after birth, begins to take on the values and attitudes of his social group and that his very personality becomes shaped in the process. Here, to illustrate how social attitudes develop, affect learning, and change, we might turn to a discussion of racial and ethnic attitudes.

People having racial or ethnic attitudes may be said to have a perception of "social distance"—that is, a desire to reduce contact with a racial or ethnic group or a desire to increase such contact.

Most such attitudes appear to develop between the ages of six and sixteen as an act of conformity to the social group of which one is a member.[23] In other words, if one's social groups, including the family, wish a high degree of social distance between their members and the members of another racial or ethnic group, then one is likely to take on that desire. Often, when a great deal of social distance is wanted, this desire is accompanied by a fear of the group in question and a feeling that its members are dangerous or have other undesirable characteristics.[24]

Even very young children are aware of prejudice and are involved in it. Helen Trager and Marian Radke found in Philadelphia that kindergarten and first-grade children coming from homes prejudiced against a minority group already showed this prejudice in word and action.[25] In the Philadelphia studies it was noticed that friendly contacts in the classroom did not prevent the growth of prejudices. Prejudices were seemingly absorbed from the home and neighborhood even while the children were having friendly school experiences with the group in question. Trager and Radke have contended that the teaching of general democratic principles does not reduce prejudice either.[26] Hyman Meltzer has reported the same general finding—that there seems to be little relation between the course of study and the rise of prejudice.[27]

Reviewing the research into attempts to alter racial and ethnic attitudes, Arnold Rose concluded that only one kind of experience appeared to affect such attitudes: when the child is having friendly contact with members of the group toward which he holds a prejudice, he must be caused to *evaluate* his attitudes.[28] This evaluation, made in an objective manner, will help him free himself of unwitting prejudice.[29]

---

[23] Gordon W. Allport and Bernard M. Kramer, "Some Roots of Prejudice," *Journal of Psychology*, XXII (July 1946), 9–40.

[24] Bernard M. Kramer, "Dimensions of Prejudice," *Journal of Psychology*, XXVII (April 1949), 389–451.

[25] Helen G. Trager and Marian Radke, "Early Childhood Airs Its Views," *Educational Leadership*, V (1947), 16–24.

[26] Marian Radke, Helen G. Trager, and Hadassah Davis, "Social Perceptions and Attitudes of Children," *Genetic Psychology Monographs*, XL (1949).

[27] Hyman Meltzer, "The Development of Children's Nationality Preferences, Concepts, and Attitudes," *Journal of Psychology*, XI (1941), 343–58.

[28] Arnold Rose, *Studies in the Reduction of Prejudice* (Chicago: American Council on Race Relations, 1948).

[29] Robin M. Williams, Jr., *The Reduction of Intergroup Tensions* (New York: Social Science Research Council, 1947), surveys the research bearing on the issues and problems involved in ethnic, racial, and religious attitudes. Though published in 1947, the survey is still instructive in dealing with issues of concern to educators, and every teacher should know the book and its implications for the classroom.

All this evidence seems clearly to indicate the following:

Social attitudes are absorbed from social groups beginning in very early childhood.

Attitudes to some extent arise independently of contact with the objects of the attitudes.

Favorable experience with the object of a negative attitude is not likely to change the attitude.

General teaching about attitudes is not likely to affect attitude formation.

Teaching that provides experience with the object of the attitude and combines this experience with an evaluation of the attitude will have some chance of helping individuals free themselves from their prejudices.

Summary

A child of elementary school age seems to have limited ability to use general propositions, although the evidence is mixed. More definite is the difficulty he has in using concepts relating to time and geographical space.

Pressed to cover a great deal of content superficially, the young child tends to verbalize: that is, he learns the words for things without really understanding them. However, where he has sufficient evidence and experience, he thinks quite capably; this leads us to the conclusion that instruction should be organized around depth studies that provide him with considerable experience about a relatively few things and give his ideas time to season, or develop.

The organizing concepts of the subject disciplines have to be developed out of a rich foundation of experience. Probably "observed concepts" (see Chapter 4) are most appropriate for younger children, for observed concepts are made by classifying firsthand experience. Probably, too, children should become accustomed to illustrating their concepts with concrete examples. When a child uses the word *colony*, he should be prepared to mention examples of colonies.

Since there is some question about the ability of younger children to use abstract propositions effectively, the introduction of organizing concepts should be closely tied to the most concrete examples possible.

Hence, when introducing the concept "authoritarian" (from political science), one should probably begin with examples of authority within the child's experience. Then, when the concept is well established, one might turn to the local government and catalog the sources of the mayor's authority and the limitations on it. One could then proceed to examine the government in, say, pre-Castro Cuba, an example of authoritarian but noncommunistic government clearly illustrating the distinction between authoritarianism and communism. The study of the Cuban nation, contrasted with the local government and the previous examination of authority, ensures that the children will be well supplied with clear examples of the concept.

Then the children might be led to set up a mock authoritarian government in the classroom, drawing from what they have learned and contrasting authoritarian government with their usual democratic organization.

The teaching strategy for organizing concepts, then, might be summarized as follows:

1. Observed concepts are more suitable for younger children.
2. All concepts must be developed out of a base of experience.
3. As they develop concepts, the children should learn to illustrate them clearly.
4. New ideas should be put to work immediately, so that they can be clarified and reinforced and their usefulness demonstrated. Thus the mock government suggested above helps the children to find what they know and don't know and causes them to use the new idea in an active situation.

Where important ideas are related to attitudes that the children pick up from their social milieu, it should be remembered that ideas change slowly and only after intense experience accompanied by self-examination. The facts alone will not do the job.

5. To learn more effective thinking processes, the child must have a great deal of practice in thinking. If we wish to promote the ability to form and use generalizations, then the children need to have much guided practice in forming and using ideas.

INQUIRIES

1. Compare *Elmtown's Youth*, August Hollingshead's study of the influence of social class origins on adolescent social behavior, with the description given here of the influence of social milieu on attitude development.

2. On page 8 of *Children's Thinking*, examine David Russell's conclusions about the development of children's social ideas. What are the implications for the teaching of social science in elementary schools?

3. In *The Child's World: His Social Perception*, read Frank and Elizabeth Estvan's account of the difference in social perception between rural and urban children. What are the implications for the social studies?

4. It may be that attention to the concepts of the disciplines will increase children's ability to handle abstract propositions. Or it may be that the more abstract concepts of the social sciences in any form will be out of the reach of young children. Examine this issue carefully.

5. The position taken in this volume is that historical eras can be approached by children so long as historical concepts of time are not emphasized. Is this possible? Should history be taught at all in the elementary school?

References and Readings

ALLPORT, GORDON W., and KRAMER, BERNARD M. "Some Roots of Prejudice," *Journal of Psychology*, XXII (July 1946), 9–40.

ARNOFF, MELVIN. "Adding Depth to Elementary School Social Studies," *Social Education*, XXVIII (October 1964), 335–36.

BLOOM, BENJAMIN S. *Stability and Change in Human Characteristics*. New York: Wiley, 1964.

ESTVAN, FRANK J. and ELIZABETH W. *The Child's World: His Social Perception*. New York: Putnam, 1959.

HAZLITT, VICTORIA. "Children's Thinking," *British Journal of Psychology*, XX (April 1930), 354–61.

HEIDBREDER, EDNA. "The Attainment of Concepts, Part III: The Process," *Journal of Psychology*, XXIV (1947), 93–138.

HOLLINGSHEAD, AUGUST DEB. *Elmtown's Youth*. New York: Wiley, 1949.

HUNT, J. McVEY. *Intelligence and Experience*. New York: Ronald Press, 1961.

JERSILD, ARTHUR T. *Child Psychology*. 5th ed. Englewood Cliffs, N.J.: Prentice-Hall, 1960.

JOYCE, BRUCE R. and ELIZABETH H. "Children Explain Science Phenomena: A Study of Verbalisms" (unpublished manuscript).

KRAMER, BERNARD M. "Dimensions of Prejudice," *Journal of Psychology*, XXVII (April 1949), 389–451.

LACEY, J. I., and DALLENBACH, K. M. "Acquisition by Children of the Cause-Effect Relationship," *American Journal of Psychology*, LII (1939), 103–10.

LACEY, JOY M. *Social Studies Concepts of Children in the First Three Grades.* New York: Teachers College, 1932.

McAULAY, J. D. "Social Studies in the Primary Grades," *Social Education*, XVIII (December 1954), 357–58.

MAW, ETHEL, "An Experiment in Teaching Critical Thinking in the Intermediate Grades." Unpublished Ph.D. thesis, Univ. of Pennsylvania, 1959.

MELTZER, HYMAN. "The Development of Children's Nationality Preferences, Concepts, and Attitudes," *Journal of Psychology*, XI (1941), 343–58.

MICHAELIS, JOHN U. *Social Studies for Children in a Democracy.* Englewood Cliffs, N.J.: Prentice-Hall, 1956.

OAKES, M. E. *Children's Explanations of Natural Phenomena.* New York: Teachers College, 1947.

OJEMANN, R. H., and others. "The Effects of a 'Causal' Teacher-Training Program and Certain Curricular Changes on Grade-School Children," *Journal of Experimental Education*, XXIV (December 1955), 95–114.

PEEL, E. A. *The Pupil's Thinking.* London: Oldbourne, 1961.

PRESTON, RALPH C. "Teaching for Depth," *Childhood Education*, XXXVI (January 1960), 211–13.

RADKE, MARIAN; TRAGER, HELEN G.; and DAVIS, HADASSAH. "Social Perceptions and Attitudes of Children," *Genetic Psychology Monographs*, XL (1949).

ROSE, ARNOLD. *Studies in the Reduction of Prejudice.* Chicago: American Council on Race Relations, 1948.

RUSSELL, DAVID H. *Children's Thinking.* Boston: Ginn, 1956.

SUCHMAN, J. RICHARD, "Inquiry Training in the Elementary School," *Science Teacher*, XXVII (November 1960), 42–47.

TABA, HILDA, and ELZEY, FREEMAN F. "Teaching Strategies and Thought Processes," *Teachers College Record*, LXV (March 1964), 524–34.

TRAGER, HELEN G., and RADKE, MARIAN. "Early Childhood Airs Its Views," *Educational Leadership*, V (October 1947), 16–24.

WILLIAMS, ROBIN M., JR. *The Reduction of Intergroup Tensions.* New York: Social Science Research Council, 1947.

STRATEGIES
FOR TEACHING
THE SOCIAL SCIENCES

Chapter 8

PUTTING IDEAS TO WORK: STRATEGIES FOR PLANNING LESSONS

In the guidance of the day-to-day activities of his pupils lies the teacher's greatest influence. There are many kinds of lessons that he may conduct. Some lessons result from pupil interest and natural inquiry. Some the teacher cunningly contrives for weeks ahead so that the children are unwittingly drawn into pursuit of one of the teacher's own interests. Some lessons are built around the acquisition of rote skills, and some are attempts to shape attitudes. In some lessons the chief tool of instruction is the word of the teacher; in some it is the social climate he has created with the children. Our present concern is the strategy used to select and contrive these lessons.

The Selection of Objectives

Nearly all the important objectives of the social studies take a long time to achieve. Good citizens are a long time in the making. For this reason the teacher needs to carry in his mind the long-term objectives that will be accomplished only by the cumulative impact of years of teaching. He also needs to keep the few basic objectives in mind so that when the children spontaneously generate interesting inquiries and when current affairs offer unexpected opportunities for teaching, he can capitalize on these unforeseeable events.

In general, all social studies lessons should serve the three objectives defined at the beginning of this volume:

Humanistic education—to help the child comprehend his life and find meaning in it.

119

Citizenship education—to enable the child to comprehend his society and participate creatively in it.

Intellectual education—to help the child learn and use the organizing concepts of the social sciences.

Although these goals are too broad and inclusive to be themselves the objectives of particular lessons, they can serve as a guide and screen. If each lesson and unit activity in the elementary school serves these three ends in some way, then the cumulative impact of the curriculum can be great. Activities not likely to contribute to the realization of these objectives can be screened out. Nevertheless, more specific objectives need to be defined for each lesson.

As a specific strategy, each lesson needs to concentrate on behaviors and ideas that can reasonably be learned during the period of the lesson. Some lessons will be built around the acquisition of specific facts, such as the names of the legislative and judicial officers of the local community. Some will be built around an ability to evaluate information, such as the differing evidence and viewpoints of two editorials discussing the same issue. Some will be directed toward learning a general idea, such as the relations between different businesses in the community. Some will be deliberately designed to promote the use of an organizing concept of one of the social sciences, such as the economic distribution of labor in the family or in the local fire department.

Most important, the specific goal of each planned lesson should be clearly identified and screened to ensure that it reinforces the general objectives of the program. Even spontaneous lessons, capitalizing on an unusual event or a child's spur-of-the-moment idea, need to be quickly shaped by the teacher so that he can identify its purpose and hence be in a position to guide it.

At first many beginning teachers have some difficulty seeing how attitudes relate to instructional goals and how lessons can be built around attitudes. But some lessons can center on an *awareness of attitudes;* first-graders, for example, can learn about the attitudes that Japanese children have toward their parents or toward religion. Or some lessons can be built around an *awareness of the causes of attitude;* fourth-graders, for instance, can see the changes in ways of life among the Pueblo Indians as a result of their contact with Northern European culture. Still other lessons can attempt to help children learn to project themselves into the shoes of other peoples. For this purpose we might have Northern children study racial strife in St. Augustine, Florida, for example, and try to express the opinions of all sides.

One teacher has developed a particularly effective approach to lessons designed to increase a child's ability to assume the viewpoint of another.[1] In one of the lessons the children are asked to take the role of revolutionary leaders who have just taken over the government of a small island country. (Earlier the children are presented with a good deal of information about the country, the size of its army, the issues which brought about the revolution, and so on.) Now in power, this "revolutionary group" discusses what to do with the leaders of the regime just overthrown—shall they eliminate them, as Castro did, and so forth. Throughout the debate the teacher absents himself, but the conversations are tape-recorded.

After the debate the children listen to the tape recording and analyze their several contributions to it. They are asked questions to help them identify the feelings they had. The teacher who developed this technique has found that some children admit that they can begin to see how nervous a revolutionary force would be and how its fear of the old regime could incite the execution of the old leaders. Others express the revulsion they felt at the suggestion of an execution and the emotion they felt in trying to get the group to take a humane course. Interestingly, on one occasion, the discussion paid unexpected dividends when one "leader" admitted that he had called on one member for advice because he knew this person would agree with him. Thus opened another line of understanding.

Selecting Content

As we pointed out in Chapter 5, there is so much possible content for the social studies that sorting out the possibilities is a major task. Every time the teacher plans a lesson or helps the children to plan an inquiry, he decides to expose them to some content and to deny them the opportunity to study other content. In Chapter 5 the discussion of the strategy for selecting content centered on the analysis of human groups. That discussion needs to be extended to the planning of specific lessons.

There are four general sources from which content may be selected:

1. *The social life of the students themselves* as they interact in and out of school. In other words, the class members themselves are a subject for study.

2. *The society in which the class members live* (from the level

---

[1] To George I. Brown of the University of California at Santa Barbara and Robert Sinclair of the Center for the Study of Instruction, National Education Association, are owed my gratitude for giving me the opportunity to observe lessons like these at a Harvard University summer session in 1963.

of the local community to the national level). The several levels of society are studied in terms of their effect on the child and his effect on them.

3. *Contemporary cultures other than the students' own.* The interaction between world culture groups may be particularly emphasized. The child needs to be exposed to world cultures; and, subject to the limitations discussed in Chapter 7, he should be able to cope with such content.

4. *The history of human society.* In the past, the history of other culture groups has been neglected, as have certain ages in Western history—the Renaissance and the Middle Ages.

The following outline lists some major subtopics within each of these four content areas.

CONTENT SOURCES

The Social Life of the Student
    His family life
    Democracy in his class group
    The media of communication as they affect him
The Student's Contemporary Society
    His community—its social, economic, and political aspects, its
        history and geography
    His state and nation—their social, economic, and political as-
        pects, their history and geography
    The ways in which contemporary society affects his behavior
Other Cultures
    Primitive cultures in today's world
    Highly developed cultures
    Underdeveloped cultures
The History of Human Society
    Pivotal periods in Western civilization
    Pivotal periods in the history of the United States
    Pivotal periods in the development of Eastern culture
    Cultural diffusion through time

Because each of these subtopics is still too large to be the subject of single lessons or even extensive depth units, they each in turn need to be divided and redivided until they can fit shorter units of study. However, they illustrate the wide range of content around which lessons can be built, and the better social studies program probably is balanced among the four areas. (The development of a balanced curriculum will be discussed in the next chapter.)

In developing a lesson, the teacher must decide on the topical aspects to be emphasized. Will a community or cultural group be studied from the standpoint of economics, political science, history, or some other discipline or combination of disciplines? What organizing concepts will be used and, consequently, better learned? Consider a teacher who has decided that a lesson will deal with "Travel in the City." He might emphasize the social aspects of modern transit, such as the widening horizons that it opens up for people or the demands it makes on social attitudes in order to make the city pleasant and safe. In such a study the major questions will derive from sociology. On the other hand, an economic emphasis might be preferred, in which case the lesson might focus on questions of a different kind: What is being produced by transit workers? Who are the consumers? What kind of system determines prices?

Several elements of a strategy for planning lessons have now been identified:

1. Lessons need to be planned so that they are harmonious with the basic goals of the social studies—humanistic, civic, and intellectual education.

2. Each lesson must concentrate on ideas and behaviors that can reasonably be learned within the span of the lesson. The objective might be to have the students learn a small cluster of facts or analyze information, using one of the organizing concepts of the social sciences. Or it might be to stimulate an awareness of attitudes or to increase the children's ability to understand empathetically the views and opinions of other people.

3. Content needs to be selected. Four sources provide content: the social life of the child, life in his society, life in other societies, and life in past times.

4. The aspects of content that are to be emphasized must be identified. Human groups can be studied from the viewpoint of anthropology, sociology, economics, political science, geography, or history. The choice of the discipline determines, in turn, the choice of the concepts to be emphasized.

Planning for the Development of Open Minds

In Chapter 6 we described the conditions likely to produce open or rigid belief systems. How is this information useful in planning lessons?

The planning of *every* lesson needs to consider the learner's growth toward interdependence. The learner must have as much opportunity as possible to share in the development of plans and standards. He must be encouraged to examine his ideas and revise them when necessary. He must be urged to find more ways of cooperating fully with his fellow students. In short, the social climate of each lesson should be planned with the same care used to select content. Each lesson should constitute a cooperative inquiry by both teacher and student, who together share in—and, if need be, analyze—every stage and phase from start to finish.

This does not mean that the student shares in the *planning* of every phase of every lesson. A lesson to teach him to analyze character motives in a novel might well be planned by the teacher entirely beforehand. But the *progress* of the lesson—the discussion, the testing of ideas, the analysis of the lesson itself—would be mutual and open. The conduct of the lesson would encourage the free flow of ideas, the testing of ideas one against another, and the logical defense of one's opinions and ideas.

Planning for Thinking

In Chapter 7 we offered evidence that a child's reasoning can be improved by instruction that emphasizes problem solving and inquiries into causation. Hence it seems that causal thinking should be emphasized in the planning of lessons. The child must be brought to examine his reasoning and to try consciously to improve it. Knowledge needs to be regarded as tentative and changing; thus the child must examine each idea to see whether it fits the facts and whether it stands up to a comparison with other ideas.

We should recognize that children need to acquire firsthand experiences from which they can draw generalizations. At the same time we must keep in mind that children are capable of learning verbal rules without understanding them. Lessons must be planned so that general ideas are carefully illustrated; each child must be led to defend his verbal statements by giving examples of what they mean. On the other hand, if the lesson can be designed so that the child, instead of proving ideas deductively, produces ideas *inductively*, so much the better. A child's thinking improves much more if he first encounters data and *then* builds up ideas based on the data. Cooperative inquiries are of this inductive kind: the entire class or a few individuals pursue an important question; they collect information pertaining to the question; then they analyze the information and come up with a tentative conclusion. With inductive lessons the teacher has no doubt about whether the children can defend their ideas, for the ideas have arisen out of the data. When he teaches deductively (and for some purposes he must) and presents an idea (followed by illustrations), he finds that some children will learn the abstract words defining the idea but will have no real conception of the idea itself. Consequently many educators recommend that lessons proceed according to the following steps:

1. Identify questions to be answered or problems to be solved.
2. Organize the search for solutions or pertinent information.
3. Make hypotheses about possible answers to the question, about possible solutions to the problem, or about ideas that might tie the data together.
4. Test each hypothesis against other hypotheses or against more data.
5. Revise the hypotheses and plan further inquiry.

By no means is this the only lesson procedure that can encourage good thinking. Since, however, such a line of inquiry proceeds much like the investigations of the social scientist, it lends itself well to the teaching of the organizing concepts of the social sciences. Its aspects of cooperative inquiry also make it amenable to the development of an interdependent social climate.

Planning for Attitudes

Wherever there are people, there are attitudes; and in view of the evidence given in Chapter 7, apparently five- and six-year-olds are no exception. Attitudes in the learning process are important. Children, even five-year-olds, not only learn subject matter but simultaneously acquire attitudes. Even while solving problems together, children may develop a distaste or liking for inquiry and may indeed take desirable or undesirable attitudes toward their fellows. Therefore a planning strategy has to relate to attitude development.

The planning strategy for developing desirable attitudes should avoid brainwashing, cajoling, and extreme social pressure and instead rely on more gently persuasive guidance and appeals to the mind. The school will find within it children who are very loving and children who are antisocial. It will house some who will end up on the right political wing and some who eventually will flirt with the left. While they are in school, some children will form racial prejudices, while others will become humanitarians.

The school must care deeply about all this. But it has to welcome children representing every political belief and every social norm. And it has to restrict itself to rational means of examining these values.

The teacher has the right and the obligation to see that the attitudes of the children become subjects of examination when he thinks this is appropriate. He has the right to insist on cooperative inquiry and the free play of ideas in the classroom. From that point, however, the strategy of instruction should depend on examination of values, not their suppression.

When the children examine the values of an Eskimo community, they will end up examining their own position. When they study the conditions that make life in the community or the classroom more livable, they will be examining their values. And so they must in a democracy.

An Outline for Teaching Attitudes

That a teaching strategy for conveying attitudes as well as content can be successfully developed and applied has been proved by Barbara Powell, of Newark, Delaware. Her outline for the strategy appears in part below.[2] It deals with the liaison between the towns of Newark, Delaware, and La Garde-Freinet, France, which have proclaimed themselves "twin cities" and now exchange visitors and cultural products and even maintain a student exchange program for older children. The result has been that Newark abounds in experienced native informants on virtually every phase of life in La Garde-Freinet. With the help of film slides, visitors, artifacts, and whatever else can be obtained directly from the French town, the Newark children are especially advantaged in the study of another culture. (And they learn more about their own culture, for a foreign visitor often points out things that would otherwise be taken for granted by a native.)

Mrs. Powell's teaching strategy drew from several of the social sciences. By entwining the study of physical geography, economics, and government with questions designed to explore "what these people hold important," she was able to include the study of attitudes and values. Basically, the strategy of the lessons was comparison. The sequence of the lessons called for cooperative planning, followed by data collection, followed by data analysis.

---

[2] This outline is taken, with minor changes, from a paper submitted by Barbara Powell for a course taught by the author at the University of Delaware in the summer of 1960.

HANDS ACROSS THE SEA
*A study of the twin towns of Newark, Delaware,
and La Garde-Freinet, Var, France*

EXPLANATORY NOTE: In the summer of 1959, through the efforts of
a few people in Newark and of a former exchange student at the university, now a resident of La Garde-Freinet, "twinning" of these two
towns was completed under the sponsorship of the United Towns
Organization, an international agency with offices in Paris. In the fall
of 1050 the mayor of La Garde-Freinet visited Newark, bringing many
samples of products produced in his town, and was accorded a public
reception by the officials of Newark. Much interest has developed,
especially in the senior high school French classes. This outline is an
attempt to make the twin cities a suitable and profitable study for
the fourth grade.

I.   Themes
     A.   To develop understandings of a different culture
     B.   To promote awareness of the essential similarities of peoples
     C.   To encourage friendship through communication and through
          sharing with other peoples in the interest of world harmony

II. Objectives
     A.   Development of attitudes of tolerance for differences be-
          tween peoples
     B.   Introduction to the history of these communities
     C.   Knowledge of the physical and economic geography of the
          areas
     D.   Comparison between daily lives of people in these commu-
          nities
     E.   Appreciation of the culture of both populations
     F.   Acquisition of elementary map skills, including comprehen-
          sion of distances and altitudes
     G.   Introduction to working and planning in groups
     H.   Knowledge of some elementary French words and expressions

III. Introductory activity to set purposes
     A.   Teacher-collected display of products and artifacts, including
          cork objects, sachets, perfume, chestnut jam, mushrooms,
          honey flavored with lavender, dolls in Provençal costume,
          handwoven rugs, jars of olives
     B.   Questions to stimulate interest
          1.   Where do the children think these things came from?
          2.   How many children have been in a foreign country? What
               made it "foreign"?
          3.   Would they like to take a trip to this one?

4. If they were to take a trip to the town that produced these objects, what would they be interested in finding out?
5. What questions would a typical boy and girl from this French town be likely to ask them about Newark?

C. Purposes set by children, guided by teacher to cover planned content in a program flexible enough to incorporate other ideas and to eliminate those eliciting no interest

IV. Planning a trip to La Garde-Freinet
   A. Content
      1. Location on map—route to be taken—how far is it to Le Havre?
      2. Passports—what are they and how do we get them?
      3. Steamship—how much does ticket cost?—what is life like on a big ship?
      4. Train—from Le Havre to Marseilles—are French trains different?—what kind of terrain will our train take us over?
      5. Omnibus to La Garde-Freinet—roads, traffic, tourists
      6. What shall we wear? Will it be hot, cold, rainy, windy?
   B. Activities
      1. Tracing route to be taken on world map
      2. Collecting pictures of French steamship, train, bus, countryside, people
      3. Making passports, using some parent's as sample
      4. Reading travel folders
      5. Group research on climate; making maps of rainfall; gathering information on temperature and winds; using sand table for relief map of area
   C. Resources
      1. Travel circulars from French Line, New York; French Embassy, Washington, D.C.; Ministère des Travaux Publics, des Transports et du Tourisme, Paris IV
      2. Pictures from magazines such as *Holiday* and from Sunday travel sections of newspapers
      3. Information on passports, climate, relief map from *World Book* encyclopedia

V. Information we will take to La Garde-Freinet about Newark
   A. Content
      1. The land
         a) Physical location, area, population, altitude, physical features
         b) Climate—effect on land use, occupations
         c) Natural resources—soil, streams

    2. The people and their work
- *a)* What do we do for a living?
- *b)* Do we all speak the same language?
- *c)* What are our houses like? Our schools? Our industries?

    3. How our town is governed
- *a)* Mayor and council
- *b)* Police and fire protection
- *c)* How our state helps—roads, sewers
- *d)* How we support our town

    4. Our means of recreation
- *a)* Sports and games—baseball and Little League; dancing, scouting, bowling, football, etc.
- *b)* Radio and television, movies
- *c)* Music—instruments, singing, records
- *d)* Festivals—Christmas, Easter, Mardi Gras and Halloween, July 4

    5. A day in the life of an American nine-year-old
- *a)* House and family—parents, sisters and brothers
- *b)* Food—where it comes from, how it is prepared, typical meals
- *c)* Clothing—for school, for dress-up, for festivals
- *d)* School day—classroom, teacher, books, how one travels to school.

B. Activities
1. Preparing map of Delaware, locating Newark
2. Making relief map of papier-mâché showing canal, towns, etc.
3. Individual research in sources such as *World Book* or other encyclopedia to get overall picture of Delaware
4. Locating school, home, public buildings on town map
5. Drawing typical house in development, farm, large old home
6. Field trip around Newark locating places found on map
7. Visit from town official on subject of Newark's growth and problems, specifically such problems as traffic, new houses to replace those beyond repair, swimming pool
8. Collecting postcards and snapshots of Newark for scrapbook

VI. Information we will want to bring back from La Garde-Freinet
    A. Content
       1. The land
- *a)* Location of town, area, population, physical features
- *b)* Climate and its effect on land use, architecture, occupations

   c) Natural resources
  2. The people and how they live
   a) What are these people like? What do they hold to be important?
   b) How do they make their living?
   c) What industries do we find here?
   d) How do they travel?
   e) Their language
  3. Their government and services
   a) Brief history of town, department, province
   b) Present government of town, officials, law enforcement
   c) Schools and education in general
  4. Their pleasures
   a) Literature—legends, proverbs
   b) Music—songs, nursery rhymes, national anthem
   c) Sports and games—Tour de France (cycling), football, tennis, boules
   d) Fine arts—local arts and crafts; inspiration for Matisse, Cézanne, Van Gogh
   e) Festivals—14th July, Christmas, New Year, Easter, Mardi Gras
  5. A day in the life of a French nine-year-old
   a) His house and family
   b) Food—where it comes from, how it is prepared, typical meal
   c) His clothing—for school, holidays, festivals
   d) His means of recreation
   e) Typical school day
 B. Activities
  1. Preparing map showing location of town
  2. Making relief map showing river valley, Mediterranean, mountains
  3. Using sand table to create typical village, with special attention to accuracy in depicting type of house and architecture
  4. Interview and discussion with people who have recently been there (By the end of each summer, several Newark residents will have spent some time in this town.)
  5. Learning French songs, some already familiar, from records (Cooperation with music teacher for best results!)
  6. Collecting scrapbook material by entire class, including also stamps, coins
  7. Research by small groups on different aspects of French life; reports to class illustrated by scrapbook material

8. Flags—small group to work on producing French flag, La Garde flag, Delaware flag
9. Gathering of collection of artifacts from this region—reproductions of paintings done by artists here, local crafts, costumes (Teacher will have to arrange to borrow most of these from people who have toured the region. Class will help make labels explaining each item.)
10. Murals to be made by group of children depicting day in life of French child and Delaware child
11. Preparation of program for parents explaining work done and the exhibits, culminated by serving of refreshments prepared from French cookbook (All foods to be given their French name. Cooperation of parents essential here!)

Summary

In this chapter we have begun to apply our ideas about the social sciences and about children's thinking to the problems of planning for instruction. We have suggested a teaching strategy that unites the overall objectives of the social studies, the nature of the social sciences, and the development of thinking ability and social attitudes. In the next chapter we shall extend our strategy to the problems of curriculum planning.

INQUIRIES

1. During a current-events session, one of the fifth-grade children asks you how the United States and West Germany could become allies so quickly after they had fought such a bloody war. Describe your strategy for planning a lesson dealing with his question.

2. Your first-grade class is studying Japan. Some of the children think that the Japanese houses and clothes are very funny indeed. What is your teaching strategy for helping them examine this attitude?

3. Your second-graders are studying the local bakery. One of its managers shows the children a new machine that will do the work of three employees. Returning to school, the children ask

you what will become of the three employees who are replaced by the machine. What is your teaching strategy for a lesson dealing with the children's question?

4. How can the social climate be utilized in a planning strategy? Identify some situations in which the social climate would definitely be a useful instructional tool.

5. Select one of the social sciences and identify several of its important concepts. Build a teaching strategy for helping children learn those concepts.

References and Readings

ASHTON-WARNER, SYLVIA. *Teacher*. New York: Simon & Schuster, 1963.

AUSUBEL, DAVID. "A Teaching Strategy for Culturally Deprived Pupils," *School Review*, LXXI (1963), 454–63.

DUFFEY, ROBERT V. "A Study of the Reported Practices of 538 Temple University Graduates and Students in Their Teaching of Social Studies in the Elementary School." Unpublished Ed.D. thesis, Temple Univ., 1954.

JOYCE, BRUCE R. and ELIZABETH H. "Searching for Strategies for Social Education." Unpublished manuscript.

KENWORTHY, LEONARD S. *Introducing Children to the World*. New York: Harper, 1956.

MICHAELIS, JOHN U. *Social Studies for Children in a Democracy*. Englewood Cliffs, N.J.: Prentice-Hall, 1963.

PRESTON, RALPH C. *Teaching Social Studies in the Elementary School*. New York: Rinehart, 1958.

RAGAN, WILLIAM B., and MCAULAY, JOHN D. *Social Studies for Today's Children*. New York. Appleton-Century-Crofts, 1964.

Chapter **9**

PUTTING IDEAS TO WORK: STRATEGIES FOR PLANNING CURRICULA

One of the most difficult professional tasks is to develop a curriculum that, from year to year, will have a cumulative effect on the child's intellectual and social growth. Each year's fund of knowledge and understanding should build on and amplify what went before. What makes the development of such an instructional plan so hard, however, is the delicate choices that must be made: on the one hand the planner must avoid an unnecessary duplication of effort from one grade to the next; but on the other hand he must allow himself a certain flexibility of action in order to encourage free cooperative inquiry and exploit current topics of interest that are not easily anticipated far in advance. The curriculum plan must be neither rigid nor directionless.

If the curriculum is underplanned, life in school can become a formless mass. If it is overorganized, the spontaneous flow of ideas that is the lifeblood of education becomes inhibited. If it is not balanced, then instruction loses both variety and perspective. Balance, it may also be said, requires a proper distribution of social science study; for example, because many middle-grade social studies curricula are overbalanced toward economic geography, many students today are learning too little about the ideas and approaches of the other social sciences.

The Project on the Instructional Program of the Public Schools, sponsored by the National Education Association, has provided a clear set of criteria that can be used by school faculties and other educators to improve curricular planning.[1] In the pages following, we shall discuss these criteria one by one.

---

[1] National Education Association, Project on the Instructional Program of the Public Schools, *Schools for the Sixties* (New York: McGraw-Hill, 1963). The Project on Instruction (as this project is popularly called for purposes of

Criterion 1: A Statement of Objectives

The first criterion formulated by the Project on Instruction asserts that *a clear statement of objectives should guide the determination of learnings to be sought in the classroom.* That each teacher should plan his lessons and units in definite relation to the overall objectives of the curriculum has already been stressed in Chapter 8. Unless this relation is firmly established, the school's year-by-year effect on the child is not likely to be cumulative. Because nearly all important social learnings take a long time to develop, the faculty needs to decide on the critical learnings to be emphasized as the essential long-term goals of the school. In Chapter 1 we stated three critical areas that are believed to be the primary goals of the social studies. Each school faculty needs to have a similar statement, phrased so that each teacher can use it for planning class activities.

Unfortunately, school systems commonly lack a comprehensive and reasonably consistent set of objectives to guide them in making other curriculum decisions. More often than not, schools possess a rather vague statement of philosophy and of goals for each subject taught.[2]

Schools need to remedy this vagueness. A purposive statement should be clear enough so that the teacher can use it to plan lessons, broad enough so that it describes the kind of citizen and person the school hopes to foster, and selective enough so that the few objectives included can be remembered easily without constant reference to the printed page.

Criterion 2: Sequential Instruction

The second criterion of the Project on Instruction states that *the curriculum should be organized so that one experience builds on another*

---

abbreviation) originally consisted of a national committee which, under the direction of Ole Sand, identified critical decision areas for schools and the criteria for making the decisions. The project reports appeared in seven volumes, of which *Schools for the Sixties* published by McGraw-Hill was one. The others, published by the National Education Association, are *Education in a Changing Society* (1963), *Deciding What to Teach* (1963), *Planning and Organizing for Teaching* (1963), *The Scholars Look at the Schools: A Report of the Disciplines Seminar* (1962), *The Principals Look at the Schools: A Status Study of Selected Instructional Practices* (1962), and *Current Curriculum Studies in Academic Subjects* (1962).

[2] National Education Association, Project on the Instructional Program of the Public Schools, *Planning and Organizing for Teaching* (Washington: National Education Assn., 1963), p. 25.

with cumulative effect on the behavior of the child. The plan defining the sequence of topics and ideas to be studied through the grades should indicate those learnings to be emphasized in the early grades and those more appropriate for the later grades. But in determining the proper sequence, the curriculum planner must consider not only his subject matter (how the social sciences are each logically organized) but also the intellectual capacity of the child at successive ages.

In each curricular area, the vertical organization of subject matter should take account of (*a*) the logical structure of the subject, (*b*) the difficulty of material as related to the student's intellectual maturity, and (*c*) the relation of the field to other fields (that is, the relation of social sciences to language arts, arithmetic, natural science, and other disciplines).[3] Let us consider the first two desiderata—the structure of the social sciences and the capacity of the child. (Criterion 4, discussed later, deals with the integration of the various curricular areas.)

PATTERNING THE CURRICULUM ON THE SOCIAL SCIENCES. The curriculum should be designed so that the organizing concepts of the various social sciences are gradually developed by the child in his study of human interaction. Studying the family in the first grade, for example, the child can begin to learn the ideas and questions the sociologist uses in analyzing roles. He can also begin to learn how the economist analyzes production in terms of division of labor. As the child studies his community a year or two later, he can extend the concept of role to apply to municipal government and community decision-making and broaden the concept of division of labor to apply to factories and shops.

Comparative studies of human groups are also important through the grades. The logical structure of anthropology implies that *to establish the concepts used by the anthropologist, curricular plans must provide for the pairing of culture groups.* For example, American and Japanese families might be paired for study in the first grade, the Mexican and the French governments for study in an upper grade, and so on. In similar fashion, the geographer emphasizes the interaction of culture and natural environment. In order to "see" a culture, one must perceive how two cultures react to the same kind of environment. Hence the structure of geography also requires comparative study: the Sahara and the American desert might be compared, or the Congo and the Amazon basins.

The body of organizing concepts of each discipline provides a kind

---

[3] National Education Association, Project on the Instructional Program of the Public Schools, *Deciding What to Teach* (Washington: National Education Assn., 1963), p. 44.

of intellectual map which the curriculum planner can use to make sure that each social science is adequately introduced and explored. In economics, for example, emphasis on production one year might be followed by emphasis on exchange the next, followed by emphasis on distribution, followed another year by an analysis of all three concepts together. In sociology, an emphasis on norms might be followed by an emphasis on sanctions, then roles, values, and institutions; then in an upper grade all these concepts could be seen operating together. A fourth-grade study of values and roles in a primitive society might be followed by a fifth-grade study of institutions in a nineteenth century frontier community, followed by a sixth-grade analysis applying all these concepts to a study of the classroom group itself. (It should be noted that although the social studies curriculum needs to embrace the organizing concepts of every social science, the child should not be challenged with concepts from all of the sciences simultaneously until he has learned them individually.)

THE STUDENT'S CAPACITY. The sequential organization of most present-day curricula is based on the child's intellectual capacity. Since young children learn most easily about things they have already experienced, the curriculum often starts with the study of things near at hand and proceeds to the study of things more removed in time and space. This is often called the "expanding horizons" or "expanding worlds" approach to social studies. Thus the topics "Home," "Family," and "Neighborhood" are often studied in the first grade, while topics more expansive—"Our City," "Our State," "Our Nation," "Our Hemisphere"—are studied in successive grades, and finally world geography is taken up in the sixth.

In order to develop understanding, the younger child does need more "concrete" experiences than the older child. Compared with the older child, the younger is disadvantaged in several ways. He has had less experience. In simple terms, he has seen less of life, thought less, heard less. Hence more time is needed to allow him to build experiences relative to any idea we want him to learn or inquire into. Moreover, he has less ability to deal with abstract ideas. He "gets the point" of something that is well illustrated, but he builds abstractions (especially verbal expressions of abstractions) only slowly. The child also has less ability to provide illustrations out of his own experience. Told something about rivers, an older person thinks of rivers he knows and "tries on" the idea. The child is less likely to apply ideas to experiences that are not immediately current. More often, we have to remind him of a river he knows or give him experiences with another one. Finally, the young child is more egocentric and impulsive. He can't reason as effectively from the point of view of another, and his attention wanders more frequently.

All these limitations, however, do not mean that we are necessarily restricted to an "expanding horizons" approach. In the first place, vicarious experiences of the far away or long ago can be created for the young child in terms of everyday experiences. In other words, when the child reads about something in another land or time, his teacher can offer analogies drawn from present, local conditions so that the child can associate the new idea with his present experience.

Secondly, the child can be given many facts to illustrate each new idea or concept. Ideas such as "Whig," "Tory," and "Thanksgiving" need multiple illustrations or they will be fuzzy and incomplete in the child's mind.

Finally, oversimplification, which is a temptation to the elementary school teacher, is to be avoided. It is better to emphasize a few honest but complex ideas than a host of distorted simple ones. The young child can learn realistic ideas. Because social life is complex, ideas about social life are complicated. Instead of accommodating the child's limitations by oversimplifying events (such as wars, civil rights demonstrations, and the like), the teacher would be far better off taking up fewer topics and exploring them deeply and honestly.

Criterion 3: Continuity of Instruction

The third criterion posed by the Project on Instruction asserts that *the curriculum should be planned so that there are identified a relatively few organizing centers around which activities can be built.* These centers provide continuity. They are the important ideas, values, issues, and skills which are introduced to the child soon after his arrival in school and which are repeated in more mature form again and again all through the school years.

To help students achieve an increasingly mature organization of knowledge, the school program should provide for continuity and increasing breadth and depth of content from one school year to the next. The principles and generalizations selected for development should be sufficiently limited in number that the learners have many opportunities to reinforce understandings and apply them. The simpler principles to be developed with young children should be so formulated as to provide a basis for, be in harmony with, and lead naturally into the more highly differentiated and elaborated structures that can be developed by senior high school students. Learners, whatever their age, should be helped to relate facts and knowledge to concepts or organizing principles so that they continually expand their conceptual frames of reference for each field of study.[4]

The organizing concepts of the social sciences, continually and more maturely applied to the analysis of human behavior, can provide the organizing centers of instruction in the social studies. Just as the human group can be the focus of content, whatever the topic, so organizing concepts can be applied to the analysis of the human group, whatever the topic. In the early primary grades the child can learn immature but accurate forms of the questions that social scientists ask. Gradually he can sharpen his questions until by the end of the elementary school he is able to form inferred and ideal-type concepts from all the disciplines.

Many social scientists have felt that it is not possible to develop a unified approach to all social sciences and that the disciplines should be approached separately. Lawrence Senesh's economics project, described in Chapter 4, represents an attempt to develop an approach to the social studies using the structure of a single discipline—economics. The advantage of this kind of organization should be plain: it is easier to sort out important ideas and see that they are well developed. However, the disadvantages should be equally obvious. The frame of reference of each discipline is relatively narrow. It is important that the child learn to apply to his analysis of human interaction not only the ideas of economics but the ideas of political science, anthropology, and the other social sciences as well.

In Chapter 5 we described a plan for focusing instruction on human groups and applying to the study of the human group the organizing concepts of the various social sciences, emphasizing one or two concepts at a time in the study of each topic and repeating year after year the emphasis on each concept until the concepts are fully developed.

Another, somewhat different integrative plan has been developed by Paul Hanna and his associates at Stanford University. Hanna has identified ten "areas of basic human activity" around which instruction can be built. Each area involves content from several of the social sciences, so that it "integrates" or "fuses" the disciplines. The following areas have been identified:[5]

---

[4] *Deciding What to Teach*, pp. 44–45.

[5] Paul R. Hanna and John R. Lee, "Generalizations from the Social Sciences," in *Social Studies in Elementary Schools*, 32d Yearbook of the National Council for the Social Studies (Washington: National Education Assn., 1962), p. 71.

Organizing and governing
Providing recreation
Protecting and conserving human and natural resources
Expressing religious impulses
Expressing and satisfying aesthetic impulses
Transporting people and goods
Producing, exchanging, distributing, and consuming food, clothing,
    shelter, and other consumer goods and services
Communicating ideas and feelings
Providing education
Creating tools, technics, and social arrangements

In a series of research studies, Hanna and his co-workers have provided a "map" of generalizations to be used to guide a curriculum built around these areas. In such an arrangement *continuity* can be built both by revisiting the basic areas yearly and by selecting certain key issues or generalizations and emphasizing them throughout the years. *Sequence* can be accomplished by arranging the generalizations in order of difficulty or in order of logical development.

Criterion 4: Integrating the Social Sciences with Other Disciplines

The fourth criterion of the Project on Instruction is that *the relation between the social studies and other curriculum areas should be designed so that they support one another.* Opportunities for reinforcing one curricular area with another arise from two conditions. First, the division of knowledge among academic disciplines is arbitrary, and considerable overlap exists between areas. Literature reveals the values of people, and thus the study of literature can be properly a social study. In maps, graphs, and models, social data are represented by means of mathematics. Geography and geology overlap greatly. Anthropologists use the methods of physicists to date artifacts and the methods of biologists to study human beings.

The second general reason that curricular areas can be integrated is pedagogical. Frequently an activity serving to achieve the objectives of one curriculum area can easily be used to achieve, simultaneously, the objectives of another curriculum area. For example, one reads and writes in the social studies. What could be more natural than to use social studies content as the vehicle for teaching reading and writing? Map making provides many opportunities for teaching scale and, for that matter, elementary geometry; in fact, some of the concepts of curved-line geometry are essential to an understanding of map projections and globes. A time line, so useful in history, is an application of a number line. The study of man's use of land or the distribution of plant life requires, naturally, some understanding of biology. Furthermore, knowledge that is not used in some context soon withers away. To study conservation of resources, the student applies knowledge learned in the natural sciences to his study of social science; thus the child gains a kind of understanding and fixation of knowledge that the natural sciences alone could not provide.

The well-planned curriculum provides for sufficient integration to allow the practical application of knowledge and uses the relationships between subject areas to reduce the number of separate topics that the student has to study.

At one time integration became a kind of object of instruction in itself, and the teacher was admonished to look for opportunities to fuse the curriculum areas. Units on topics such as "The Postman" became embellished with poems, songs, dramatic play, and art production. Although subject integration should intelligently integrate the child's intellectual life and make learning activities in one area promote learnings in other areas, it is not necessary to invent poems celebrating community helpers in order to integrate, for example, the study of economic life with the study of literature. Integration does not need to be forced; the opportunity is present naturally.

Criterion 5: A Proper Balance of Topics and of Social Sciences

The fifth and final criterion developed by the Project on Instruction for curriculum planners states that *the various subject areas must be studied in proper balance, with no subject area unduly predominating.* Time given to mathematics should not prevent the teaching of reading. Passion for poetry should not prevent attention to the social studies. No one social science should dominate social education to the point where the children do not learn others. In the past many curricula for the early grades have over-emphasized the study of the community to the neglect of wider areas. In the later grades the study of economic geography, government, and American history has swelled to the point of forcing out the other social sciences.

A careful balance should also be achieved among studies focusing on the class group, contemporary American society, world cultures, and historical periods. Although any one of these four areas could serve to introduce social science concepts, the child of the present century needs to understand not just one, but all of these areas. He simply has to know how to think effectively about his own social groups. He has to deal with his society. He has to know about other cultures—in fact, he will not understand his own until he does. And he has to have some idea of the movement of events through time.

Patterns in Present-Day Curricula

The pattern of social studies curricula does not vary from school to school as much as might be expected, considering the richness and variety of the social sciences. Both textbooks and curriculum guides have tended to utilize the "widening worlds" approach to curriculum organization. A faculty committee in South Bend, Indiana, for example, prepared a curriculum guide that included the following statement in the introduction:

> The social studies program in South Bend begins with the home, and gradually extends to the community, the state, the nation, the Western Hemisphere, and the Old World.[6]

This same curriculum guide goes on to describe a grade placement of topics somewhat in the order suggested by the above statement; "resource units" suggest activities and materials for child and teacher. These unit topics appear below:

Kindergarten
    Safety (Emphasis is on safety rules in school and home.)
    Preparation for Winter (Emphasis is on interdependence, especially in classroom behavior.)
    The Garden
    The Circus

Grade 1
    Family Life (Emphasis is on personal interdependence with others, health habits.)
    Daddies: What They Do and How It Affects Us

---

[6] *Living in This World of Ours* (South Bend, Ind.: Board of Education, 1956), p. 3.

The School Family
The Farm Family

Grade 2
The Grocery Store
We Work and Play Together
How We Get Letters
. Living Safely in the Community
Transportation

Grade 3
Homes
Clothes
Food (This unit and the two preceding provide for the study
of various periods in history, such as the Middle Ages, and
of other countries around the world. The objective is to
extend the child's acquaintance to places removed from
him, but in terms of life activities with which he is
familiar.)

Grade 4
Living in Indiana
Communities of Men and How They Live (Primarily the em-
phasis is on economic geography.)

Grade 5
Past and Present Population Movements in the United States
How People in the United States Make a Living

Grade 6
South Bend and Its Relation to the World (The unit includes
a study of local merchants and industries and of the pro-
curement of raw materials for them.)
Our Way of Life in the United States (Emphasis is on technology and on ideals, as expressed in historical documents
and present-day human actions.)

Numerous curriculum guides include a systematic history and geography of the United States and a systematic geography of the world in the
fifth and sixth grades. The South Bend curriculum committee preferred
to recommend an approach which stressed South Bend's relation to American history and to other nations; thus the local environment was the

comparative base for studying and interpreting other eras and places. The South Bend guide used a modified expanding-worlds approach, with emphasis on human relations and the local community.

EXPANDING HORIZONS: A TEXTBOOK APPROACH. In a modern social studies program, no textbook could conceivably be the sole, or even the major, source of working materials; nevertheless it is true that in many schools the organization of the textbooks adopted determines the organization of the curriculum. The curriculum is organized around the text. Ruth Ellsworth recently reported:

> Any survey of the organization of social studies curriculums in the elementary school must take into account the fact that for many school systems the organization is determined by the textbook chosen. Indeed, in curriculum guides one occasionally finds a statement that the guide has been prepared to help teachers in the use of textbooks adopted by the state or local school systems. However, most guides assume the use of a variety of books as well as other instructional materials.[7]

Consequently, it is illuminating to examine the patterns of organization used in textbook series. Most of them utilize the expanding-worlds approach, with emphasis on the community and local area in the early grades and on economic geography and American history in the upper grades.

The American Book Company Social Studies Series, published in 1961, illustrates these tendencies; the following is an abridgment of its tables of contents:

Book 1. *Our Home and Our School*
    At School
    Safe Work and Safe Play
    Family Work and Family Play
    Family Plans
    A Party at Home
    School Plans
    The School Pet Show

Book 2. *Our Neighborhood*
    Fire! Fire!

---

[7] Ruth Ellsworth, "Trends in Organization of the Social Studies," in *Social Studies in Elementary Schools*, p. 108.

How the Doctor Helps Us
People Who Help Us Get Food
A Long Bus Ride
The Work of the Post Office
The Men Who Work on Our Houses
The Playground Worker

Book 3. *Our Community*
Clothes for the People of Riverside
Food for the People of Riverside
The Buildings of Riverside
Getting to and from Riverside
How People in Riverside Get the News
The Schools of Riverside
How Riverside Protects Its Citizens
Enjoying Free Time in Riverside

Book 4. *Our State*
Our State
Farming
Grazing
Fruits
Forest Products
Fishing
Cities
Your State

Book 5. *Our Hemisphere*
Beginnings of Today's Americas
Growth of the English Colonies
Thirteen Colonies Become a Lasting Nation
The U.S. Grows Under Its Constitution
The Northeast
The South
The North Central Region
The Southwest
The Mountain West
The Pacific Region
Canada—Neighbor to the North
Neighbors to the South
Neighbors of Middle America
South American Neighbors

American Good Neighbors

Book 6. *Our World Neighbors*
   Learning About Our World
   The Dawn of Man's History
   Progress Made by Ancient Peoples
   The Middle Ages
   Western and Central Europe
   The Soviet Union and Eastern Europe
   Northern Mediterranean Lands
   The Near East and North Africa
   Asia's Southeastern Lands
   In the Far East
   South of the Equator
   Our World Neighbors

These topics exemplify the contents of most social studies books. The second-grade descriptions of community workers and the third-grade study of the city prepare the way for an emphasis on economic geography in the upper grades. In the fifth-grade book, U.S. history is intertwined with U.S. geography—namely, in the joint study of New England and the early English colonies. The same pattern is followed in the sixth book, in which a survey study of world history is followed by a study of nations now occupying the sites where the historical developments took place. This textbook series, like most others, dwells heavily on the products of factories and of the land. Beyond the early books the economic production of services is neglected; and intangible products, such as ideas and education, are virtually ignored throughout. The emphasis on economic geography is customary, as is the neglect of the concepts of the other social sciences.

It should be noted that when the expanding-horizons approach tries to survey the world completely by the end of the sixth grade, the tendency is to place the study of a great many places and eras in grades 5 and 6, with the result that all topics are dealt with quickly and superficially. The students, because they study nothing in depth, fail to gain the experiences on which to build generalizations. In many series, some nations are treated in only four or five pages, frequently with no more content than would be found in an encyclopedia article.

Not all publishing houses, of course, issue their social studies books in series. Some, like Fideler, prefer to publish individual books concentrating on single countries or single regions of the United States. Economic geography still dominates, but the coverage is intensive, since each volume runs to about 150 pages, even for the smaller nations.

A "BASIC LEARNINGS" APPROACH. The curriculum guide developed for the public schools of St. Paul, Minnesota, employs the expanding-horizons approach but, in an attempt at continuity, also pays attention to four "basic learnings in the social studies" which are to be stressed through the grades:

> People are interdependent and need to live in harmony.
> Man's environment influences his way of living.
> Living can be improved.
> People of the past influenced our way of living.[8]

The curriculum guide indicates that these basic learnings function in several ways:

> Basic learnings help tie all elements of the social studies program together, giving it unity, purpose, and direction.
> Basic learnings should be used by the teacher to plan the recurrence of concepts from different approaches, and on increasingly mature levels.
> Basic learnings can and should be approached from many directions and through many varied experiences.
> Basic learnings will be developed and applied by children as they meet them in meaningful situations important to them.[9]

The guide further suggests unit resources and advises the teacher that the curricular outline is not necessarily prescriptive. The teacher may select topics that seem appropriate to him and plan them cooperatively with the children.

> Planning the unit should involve pupil cooperation in every possible phase. In planning how the unit will develop, each class will help to chart its own path. On a problem-solving basis, the path of development will be determined by the interests and needs of the pupils as they express them in the cooperative planning stage.[10]

Significantly, the St. Paul guide merely suggests content topics that will contribute to the ends of the curriculum. The teacher is free to make the final decisions and to build the units with the children. Furthermore, the cooperative-planning approach implies that both the content units and the details to be learned will vary considerably from class to

---

[8] Elementary Social Studies Curriculum Committee, *Social Studies for Elementary School Children* (St. Paul: St. Paul Public Schools, 1959), p. 2.
[9] *Ibid.*, p. 3.
[10] *Ibid.*, p. 18.

class. The children's interests help to determine the shape of the instruction; indeed, the children assume part of the obligation for planning. In sum, the curriculum makers have deliberately tried to provide continuity in the social climate of the school. The ways the children act and interact are part of the content they study. The whole tenor or philosophy of the St. Paul curriculum guide is evident in its descriptions of the grades:[11]

Kindergarten and Grade 1
Everyday Life—at Home and in School
  The center of interest for the child is the home and family. School is the new, important change in his everyday living. Experience related to home and school will have the fullest meaning and produce the best results. Many of the activities initiated at the kindergarten level can be continued successfully on the first-grade level.

Grade 2
Living in Our Neighborhood
  In this grade, the experiences with neighborhood activities create new interests. The environment broadens from the familiar and personal events of home and school to the wider scope of life in the neighborhood. Interest in the people and in the services of the nearby community become very important.

Grade 3
Basic Needs of Our Community
  The child's interests and experiences at this grade level move to the larger community of a town or city. He becomes aware of the need for food, clothing, shelter, recreation, and companionship. He becomes particularly interested in how St. Paul endeavors to meet these needs for its people. The concept of interdependence becomes more meaningful.

Grade 4
Living in Our City and State
  Study of the exploration and colonization of the United States by various groups leads to an understanding of the background for the settlement of Minnesota. The child begins to see the city and state as organized units of society. He learns how Indians, explorers, fur traders, and pioneers contributed to the origin and growth of St. Paul and Minnesota. He becomes aware of the resources and opportunities of representative communities in the United States and compares St. Paul with them.

Grade 5
Living in Our Nation and the Americas
  From the background of their previous historical study of St. Paul

---

[11] *Ibid.,* pp. 5–6.

and Minnesota, children begin the historical and geographical study of the United States. They learn how geography influences the industries and ways of life in various communities. Intensive study is devoted to this relationship as it applies to Minnesota.

Children learn to appreciate the foresight, courage, and endurance of our forefathers and begin to understand the dynamic nature of our society. Modern life in various regions of the United States, Canada, Latin and South America is compared with that of Minnesota.

Grade 6
Living in Our World

The experiences provided in earlier grades serve as a foundation for understanding other cultures. Children learn that human activities in any land are directed toward the satisfaction of basic needs, and that customs differ only as people adjust their environment to their needs. They develop an understanding of interdependency of nations as they see how other peoples of the world have contributed to life in Minnesota and the United States. Some of the social processes and problems of modern societies are explored as they apply in our state, particularly education, churches, conservation of natural resources, and human resources. The government of Minnesota is studied as an outgrowth of Old World principles of democracy. Children begin to see the roles of the United States and other nations in world affairs.

This description of the grades reveals the balance of direction and freedom which the St. Paul guide provides the teacher. The guide identifies the important themes around which continuity can be built, but it leaves to the teacher the job of constructing with his children the activities to give those themes life and substance.

The Need for Curriculum Improvement

Gatherings of scholars are now busy preparing new materials for social studies—materials ranging from models of archaeological relics to books and films tracing ideas like "liberty." Some materials have even been designed for complete courses in one of the social sciences. Many of these newer curriculum materials are currently being tested and will soon be widely available to schools.

Textbook companies and the publishers of trade books are at work preparing new texts and other materials for social studies.

State, county, and local curriculum committees are meeting to write new curriculum guides and prepare resource units.

Apparently today's social studies teacher is about to be barraged with materials that he will have to analyze and integrate into his teaching strategy. How great is the teacher's responsibility for selecting materials and for developing curricular outlines? The Project on Instruction says:

> Local school faculties should have the freedom and the authority to make decisions about what to teach—and how to teach. Final instructional decisions should be made by the teacher, taking into consideration recommendations from appropriate local, state, and national groups representing the teaching profession, academic scholars, and the public.[12]

In order to exercise this authority, the teacher has to have a well-defined strategy to apply to the problems of decision making. He is going to have to select objectives, identify organizing themes, develop plans for sequence, select learning activities and organize them, and procure and (in many cases) create teaching materials.

In a country as diverse as America, many curricular plans should exist in each curriculum area, reflecting the spirit of inquiry and invention that needs to emanate from teachers. It is a matter of some discouragement that so many existing curricular patterns are cast in the same mold. While there are excellent rationalizations for this sameness, the expanding-worlds approach is not the only one that takes into account the psychological realities of childhood. In today's world, in fact, the first grade may not, in some communities, be a good time at all to study the family and the neighborhood. In many urban neighborhoods, for example, the children would discover that only a third of their number were acquainted with their fathers, and the topic "What Daddy Does" could be disturbing, to say the least.

Also, many primary-grade topics, such as "The Neighborhood," involve abstract ideas that can be fully developed only by the more mature child. If the family and the community are not studied in the upper grades as well as in the lower, there is little likelihood that these ideas will be satisfactorily developed. Indeed, very few curricula, even good ones, have been organized effectively around the central organizing concepts of the social sciences. Frequently generalizations have been identified, but the central concepts have received little attention. Finally, as we have noted before, the study of many regions, nations, and eras is often packed into the fifth and sixth grades, preventing depth studies and encouraging superficial coverage.

---

[12] *Deciding What to Teach*, p. 205.

Strategies for Curriculum Improvement

What are the questions that need to be answered when a curriculum is being planned? What are the tasks that must be performed?

1. Goals have to be identified.
2. Organizing centers on which continuity can be developed have to be identified.
3. Principles on which sequence can be ordered must be created and illustrated.
4. Instructional units or topics around which the teacher can plan instruction must be determined—in a manner that gives balance to the program.
5. Appropriate instructional materials have to be developed and organized.

IDENTIFYING OBJECTIVES. The first of the three goals of the social studies (as stated at the beginning of this book) is to "help the child comprehend his experience and find meaning in life." This goal was derived from an examination of the needs of the learner himself. What was emphasized was his relative helplessness in the face of the great booming society that stands ready to impose its values on him. He soon will learn the anxiety that is supposed to characterize the modern era and will find strange and incomprehensible those people of other cultures with whom, inevitably, he must deal. Reflecting on this state of affairs, one can reasonably give high priority to the child's search for personal meaning.

How one interprets this objective may vary, however. Some teachers may feel, for example, that to find personal meaning the child should be led to some kind of adjustment to the norms of his culture. Other teachers might emphasize the child's economic needs—his future need to earn a living and thus his need to begin to comprehend the economic world. Teachers in depressed urban areas might note the ego damage suffered by children as a result of their environment and might therefore stress the school's role in supplying to the child what a missing father cannot or in helping the child to cope with the feeling of worthlessness that comes from being on relief rolls. Still other teachers might concentrate on the child's interests and frame their curriculum to give these interests full play. Many facets of the child's personality might be considered, and conditions may be variously interpreted. But, however interpreted, the child's humanistic development *is* one of the primary goals of education.

The second objective of the social studies—education for citizenship and for effective participation in society—derives from a consideration of society itself. Quite simply, a really creative contribution to society depends on an understanding of how society works.

The forces that create totalitarian and fascist states are forces that would provide simple solutions to complex human problems. The totalitarian seeks to control human behavior—to make human beings more predictable and reduce the uncertainty that free speech and free communication produce. Democracy, on the other hand, representing the maximization of freedom, is a solution to political organization that demands a toleration of diversity and a complex adjustment of differences and demands that one learn to live with people who are not just like oneself; in many ways this is a harder solution to the problems of governing and being governed. There are moments when one weakens and wishes that there were more order. But democracy depends on abstinence from the final solution, from the total resolution of conflict that totalitarian systems attempt.

Reflecting on this condition of democracy, one can urge the development of a comprehending citizen, one who is oriented toward the production of creative change in his society and who comprehends freedom fully enough to tolerate the inevitable diversity and seeming confusion. The purely private man is useless to a democracy. So is the completely other-directed man who must depend totally on the norms and desires of the people around him. To produce the effective dedicated citizen requires that from his first day at school the child be involved in the loving and determined analysis of his society and of the ways he can help to improve it.

Reflecting on society, different people will emphasize different aspects and offer different interpretations of the needs of the citizen. Some may feel that the coming cybernetic revolution deserves special attention and that even the elementary school must train people to adjust to a computer civilization. Others may emphasize the civil-rights conflicts, and still others the citizen's need to attempt an understanding of the problems of the nuclear age and of the complex international involvements, East and West. Whatever his interpretation, however, the curriculum maker must examine the state of society and, in his interpretation, try to determine the behaviors that the social studies should develop in children.

The third objective of the social studies is to equip the child with the concepts and methods developed by the social scientists. The perplexing problem of intellectual content for the social studies has been that the ideas and facts which one *could* learn have become too massive for individual consumption. And most of what is presently known is fast becoming obsolete. It is now becoming apparent, however, that the most permanent part of the social sciences—and the most useful—are the modes of inquiry, the organizing concepts that can be applied to such a wide range of problems.

The strategy, then, for formulating objectives, is to study the child, his society, and the social sciences and to infer what objectives should guide the curriculum. This strategy is balanced. One does not forget the child, who after all is the *raison d'être* of the school. Neither does the school operate in a vacuum; the school and its children are inextricably tied to the culture of their society. Nor are the scholarly disciplines neglected. This strategy does not let any of these factors dominate the others. It does not allow considerations of social science content to dictate the curriculum without considering the nature of the child. Neither does it let the child's needs dictate all the decisions; it recognizes the roles of the society and the social sciences.

FINDING ORGANIZING CENTERS. The next task is to identify "organizing centers" around which instruction can be planned to ensure continuity through the grades.

These organizing centers are the complex, difficult-to-establish behaviors and ideas that need to be repeated and repeated with variety and amplification until their cumulative effect is felt.

There have been a variety of attempts, of course, to formulate means of continuity. For example, Paul Hanna's "areas of basic human activity," listed earlier, were meant to serve as organizing centers and *are* so used in the Scott, Foresman series, "The Basic Social Studies Program." (This series, however, has a sequential development that relies on the expanding-worlds principle.) In 1957 the National Council for the Social Studies designed fourteen themes which, because they are important for all citizens, might well serve as organizing centers for curricula in schools across the country.[13] For example, one theme, "the intelligent uses of the forces of nature," could be introduced in the primary grades as the children learn about the natural resources they themselves use; then in later grades it could be expanded into a consideration of the use of resources in state and national economies; and, finally, in senior high school the theme could be the subject of debates on the proper utilization of human resources, considered from the viewpoint of human freedom.

Important as these attempts are, let us remember that the pattern of the social sciences themselves can—as we have emphasized in earlier chapters—provide a continuity of study. Using the organizing concepts of the social sciences, the child can study human groups from one grade to

---

[13] National Council for the Social Studies, *A Guide to Content in the Social Studies* (Washington: National Educational Assn., 1957).

the next with increasing sophistication. If both concepts and groups are used as organizing centers, then the child progressively learns to analyze human groups in the fashion of the social scientist. If the child joins with others to study the human group in a spirit of cooperative inquiry, then an "interdependent atmosphere" becomes still another source of continuity, as the children increasingly learn to plan and conduct their own investigations.

Sometimes the focus could be confined to one of the social sciences, such as the study of political groups in the local community. At other times the emphasis might be on the sociology of the family or the economics of the local factories. Over the years, however, all the social sciences would be visited sufficiently to develop an understanding of their concepts.

In summary, this curriculum organization would provide continuity through three types of organizing centers: (1) the study of the human group, providing progressive understanding of group life; (2) the study of social science concepts, which would be developed toward adult application; and (3) the cooperative social climate, providing development toward open belief systems and interdependent relations with others.

PRINCIPLES OF SEQUENCE. The expanding-horizons approach is still the most prevalent means of giving curricula an easy, clearly defined sequence. The child studies life in what might be described as widening concentric circles—from school and family to community, to state, to nation, to hemisphere, to the world. The problems presented by this approach have already been suggested. Recalling the prescription stated at the beginning of this chapter—namely, that the curriculum should steer a course neither rigid nor directionless—we might further add that the expanding-horizons approach tends to err toward rigidity, particularly when the curriculum is geared strongly to a textbook series constructed on the expanding-worlds approach.

Occasionally at the other extreme is the principle of sequence that relies on the child's natural explorations. With his classmates the child attacks an interesting idea. Then another. Then another. The teacher helps him to become an increasingly better inquirer and to discover the concepts of learned men on the way. In the hands of the right teachers this strategy can be a powerful and effective means of providing sequential development of ideas, and all curriculum makers should consider it. However, the danger exists that such a program might lapse into something without direction or perspective.

Our earlier analyses of the organizing concepts of the social sciences may suggest an effective middle course—a sequential course of development which takes into account not only the abilities of the child and his fund of experience at succeeding ages but also his need to learn social ideas and methods for approaching a very confusing world reality. This sequence of development would rely on the *levels of concepts* described in Chapter 4:

> *Observed concepts*—those that can be perceived directly from available data.
>
> *Inferred concepts*—those that describe unseen conditions that can only be guessed at on the basis of more immediately observed data (*values*, for example, cannot be seen but have to be inferred).
>
> *Ideal-type concepts*—those representing broad categories and formed by classifying large quantities of data (*democracy*, *totalitarian state*, and *tundra* are ideal-type concepts).

Observed concepts are fairly easy to form, provided firsthand experiences are given as examples of the concept. One can identify *aldermen* by looking up public records or by meeting with aldermen and asking them what they do. An *extended family* or a *joint family* can be perceived directly, and children can grow *agricultural products*.

Ideal-type concepts can be formed after considerable experience with examples of one concept in comparison with examples of others. For example, after studying several *hunting-fishing* communities and several *agricultural* ones, a child is capable of making distinctions between the two types and to form the concepts. Similarly, after studying two or three *matriarchies* and two or three *patriarchies*, the child readily discerns the difference.

Inferred concepts are more difficult, because the hunch or inference lies between the data and the idea. To observe that population expansion followed waterways in the eighteenth century is as easy as seeing the population symbols grow on the map. To see that the frontier produced a kind of *character* involves several difficult inferences and long experience with people.

The sequence that could be derived from this analysis is as follows:

1. The early grades should stress observed concepts, and these concepts should be planned for every area in which ideal-type concepts are later to be developed.

2. The formation of ideal-type concepts can begin about the middle grades of the elementary school. Ideal-type concepts at the macrolevel (see p. 57) should be deferred until the upper grades or until senior high school.

3. Inferred concepts should be deferred until the upper grades

of the elementary school, and even then considerable attention should be paid to the process of making inferences.

Age of Child			
5	Observed		
6	concepts		
7	through	Ideal-type	
8	the	concepts	
9	program	formed	Inferred
10		from	concepts
11		observed	(with
12			attention
13			to inference
14			making)

The sequence based on these three levels appears to satisfy Jean Piaget's contention concerning the thinking abilities of children at different ages.

Some other characteristics of the social sciences are relevant to sequence. Since both anthropology and geography frequently use comparative approaches, the child might best learn the concepts of these disciplines by studying culture groups in pairs. The young child's need to form concepts out of direct experience might be satisfied by using the home culture as one of the pair. Thus the American home might be paired with the English home or the Mexican home. Bakeries in the United States might be compared with bakeries in Turkey or France. (Leonard Kenworthy has suggested that younger children should first be introduced to cultures somewhat similar to their own in order to reduce cultural shock and the danger of stereotyping the strange.[14] He would begin by comparing the Americans with the English, then with the French, then with the Germans— that is, with other cultures of the Western tradition. Only in the later grades—say, when the child reaches age ten—would there be a gradual introduction of non-Western cultures, Asian and African. Because Kenworthy's thesis is not entirely proved, however, each curriculum planner must himself decide whether primitive cultures and Eastern cultures can be studied in the primary grades.)

Something also needs to be said about the teaching of history to younger children. In history curricula one frequently finds that chronology provides the organizing principle. One starts as far back in time as neces-

---

[14] Leonard S. Kenworthy, *Introducing Children to the World* (New York: Harper, 1955).

sary and proceeds step by step to the present. Yet this runs counter to the evidence on child development, for the events farthest away in point of time are also the farthest removed from the experience of the child, and it is the very idea of chronology which has been so difficult to establish with children of elementary-school age. Some educators have therefore advocated that the younger child start with the community he finds around him and discover history by trying to explain how things became what they are.

THE DEPTH STUDY: SELECTING AND ORGANIZING UNITS OR TOPICS. The fourth task of the curriculum maker is to select topics or units of related subject matter around which instruction can be organized. In other words, principles have to be stated to guide decisions about what is to be taught. Some of the strategies for achieving continuity and sequence are also useful in developing topics. The comparative approach, for example, calls for studying culture groups in pairs. A sequential program proceeding according to the three levels of concepts also calls for topics that, in the early grades, are rich in observed concepts and that, in later grades, gradually introduce ideal-type and inferred concepts.

The chief strategy for developing content, however—the strategy which will be fully developed in the next two chapters—concerns the building of children's experiences and ideas through the study of *topics in depth*. Because young children need much concrete data on which to build ideas and because time is needed to build this fund of experience, it seems wise to have relatively few topics studied in any single year. Other facts support this strategy. Cooperative inquiry, essential if the concepts of the social sciences are to be learned, is time-consuming and should not be rushed. Organizing concepts themselves are complex in form and difficult to express; the vocabulary needs lengthy explanation and reexamination. Finally, an interdependent climate demands a checking of ideas, a swapping of viewpoints—everything that requires leisurely investigation. These observations lead to the following conclusions:

Relatively few topics should be studied in any school year and these topics should provide comparative analysis.

These depth studies should be arranged so that the organizing concepts of the several social sciences will be reexamined and extended periodically.

The studies planned for any one year should be few enough so that the teacher and children can build part of the program out of the study of current affairs and out of events affecting the class group itself or its interests. To the study of current affairs and the study of the class itself can be applied the organizing concepts learned in the depth studies of cultures and historical periods.

The depth studies should be selected so that the child acquires essential information about his society and the contemporary world. A certain number of depth studies should deal with governmental processes and the relation of government to society, because the adult needs to be well acquainted not only with the approaches of political science but with the facts of United States governmental structure. The major contemporary developments affecting the society, such as automation and urbanization, need to be introduced, although they will be the subjects of intensive study in the high school. The interdependence of nations and the nature of their interaction need to be introduced, as do some of the important current world movements, such as nationalism and communism.

Generally speaking, however, the basic core of curricular content should be selected to help the child explore the social world in such a way that he learns to think about it effectively. The approaches of the social sciences should be visited again and again in interesting ways and with varied content.

A curricular plan organized according to these criteria would therefore (1) identify the organizing concepts of the social sciences, (2) identify cross-cultural depth studies that will enable the child to study his society and others comparatively, (3) identify depth studies that will enable the child to probe his heritage, and (4) leave time for inquiries that the children and the teacher might wish to develop from their own classroom experiences or from current world events.

A Sample Curriculum Plan

Let us now apply the various principles advocated in this chapter and draw up a hypothetical curricular plan. In doing so, we can better illustrate how specific topics might be treated, using human groups as well as organizing concepts as the focus of study.

In the *first year* of school, these depth studies might be planned:

Our Home and the English Home
Our School and the French School
Music Around the World

Time would be left for the teacher and the children to develop one or two depth studies as their needs and interests or as contemporary events indicated. For example, an election year might well provoke a study of town officials and voting procedures. A local newspaper campaign might result in a study of recreational facilities. "Mapping Our Town" might develop into a study of businesses or transportation or ways in which citizens depend on one another.

In these four or five depth studies, the first-year student would begin to study the human group. He would for the first time be led to ask, in simple form, questions analogous to those the social scientist asks. What are the jobs different people do in English and American families? (*economics and sociology*). How do English (or American) mothers teach their children table manners? (*anthropology*). Who decides whether there should be a new French (or American) school? (*political science*). In this first year, observed concepts would be emphasized. Also, the relatively small units of society (the home and the school) permit the younger child to explore in greater depth than would larger units such as cities or nations.

For the *second year* of school, depth studies might include:

Our Town and a German Town
Our Leisure Life and Mexican Leisure Life
Folk Tales from Five Peoples

Once again time would be left for the children and the teacher to develop a collective inquiry or two as current events develop or as the teacher spots weaknesses in thinking.

Again in the second year, human groups can be identified in these topics along with the organizing concepts of the social sciences. Emphasis on economics and government could guide the study of the two towns, American and German. The study of leisure life might employ the sociological concepts "values," "roles," and "sanctions." The folk tales are well suited to introduce the interrelations between facets of culture that have to be identified if the idea of culture is to be understood.

The *third year* might include topics such as the following:

The Government of Our Town and of a Swiss Town
Our State and Japan
A New Mexico Pueblo and a Bantu Village

Although the comparison between the local and Swiss governments might emphasize the organizing concepts of political science, the interrelations between political life and other facets of life should also be noted.

Because the Pueblo and Bantu villages represent relatively small and simple societal units, their two cultures could be carefully examined in their totality. On the other hand, because Japan and one's own state are both political units on the macrolevel—that is, societies that are large and complex and thus demand lengthy, difficult analysis—perhaps their total cultures cannot be effectively studied by third-graders. On this first curricular venture into a macrostudy, perhaps only a few cultural elements seen from a circumscribed viewpoint should be studied. The concepts of economic geography could be useful, for they are chiefly observed concepts and are therefore easier to handle than inferred concepts.

The Chicago Board of Education has developed an interesting third-grade curriculum outline which suggests that the year's study compare the city of Chicago with New York and London. Such a plan would enable the children to study these cities thoroughly enough to extend their understanding of concepts from several of the social sciences.

The curriculum plan for the *fourth year* can begin to introduce inferred concepts and the processes by which they are developed. Consider the following topics as possibilities:

Religions and Their Origins
The Oil Industry and the Middle East
Biographies of Five Men from Five Nations
Current Issues in the United Nations

The study of religions involves inferred concepts (values), and a depth study of religion would permit sufficient attention to be paid to the process of inference. The study of the oil industry might emphasize economic concepts, but not necessarily exclusively. The study of biography changes the pace and follows up the studies of music, folk tales, and leisure life by concentrating on an art form. The focus on individuals balances the focus on large societal units in the other depth studies. "Current Issues in the United Nations" introduces international government formally but stresses events in the news so that the study is dynamic and does not lapse into a description of the divisions and agencies of the organization.

The *fifth year* might include the following topics:

The Modern Industrial State
A Technologically Underdeveloped Nation
The Art of the Southwest
Cultural Exchange, Worldwide

The study of one or two highly developed nations could introduce the study of macroeconomics and extend the concepts introduced in the oil study of the previous year. A contrast would be provided by a study of one or two less developed nations. The children and teacher might find it productive to follow these two units with a look at the Alliance for Progress or another example of international cooperation.

The art of the Southwest can be approached to identify cultural exchange. The four centuries of Southwestern art provide many examples of the mingling of Spanish, Indian, and Northern European culture. Today's Southwestern art shows the influences of all three. Following this unit, cultural exchange itself can be studied, providing a look at the ways in which Oriental, European, African, and Latin-American cultural ideas and products are currently being diffused over the world.

The *sixth year* might introduce the formal study of history with topics such as these:

> The History of the U.S. Government, 1776–1800
> The History of the United Nations, 1945–Present
> The History of Our Town, 1950–Present
> The Cold War

Concepts from every social science should be brought to bear on these studies. In the first two units, original documents should be used whenever possible. In the third unit, the techniques developed in the first two should be extended as the children explore local archives, newspaper files, resource persons, and actions of the town government. The study of the cold war similarly provides a look at history in the making and permits the children to study the behavior of our government in confronting and interacting with other governments.

It should be noted that nowhere in the six years did we suggest a sweeping study of history. The curriculum of the elementary school should prepare the children for later surveys of history. For most children, the mental maturity needed for chronological studies of history is not developed until the end of the elementary school years.

Any good curricular plan should be developed with special reference to the local situation. The curriculum for a lower-class neighborhood should provide extra firsthand experiences as well as many extra topics concentrating on the local community or city. In addition, every opportunity to further language development should be exploited to the fullest. No large city should engage in the development of a prescriptive curriculum that applies to all areas of the city.

Furthermore, children vary widely within each school and classroom. Less intelligent children need more concrete illustrations than brighter children do. Good readers can often use written references effectively while poor readers need more suitable materials and added instruction on their use. Likewise, although map skills will be developed in all studies, children differ greatly in their instructional needs and in their readiness for specific skills.

Both the curricular plan and the depth studies should allow for local differences and for variation among pupils. However, the emphasis for all should be on the development of the concepts of the social sciences. Then the years of secondary education can extend these concepts and apply them to the systematic study of world history (both Western and Eastern) and the study of contemporary societies.

Summary

Five criteria apply to the development of social studies curricula:

1. A limited number of clear objectives should be selected to give purpose to the program.

2. Organizing centers should be developed so that year by year ideas and behaviors are explored in increasingly sophisticated form and so that continuity is given to the program.

3. An educative sequence should be developed by a curriculum arranged so that organizing concepts are gradually unfolded in accordance with the maturity of the child.

4. The activities in the several curriculum areas should be coordinated to eliminate unnecessary overlap and to enable studies in the several areas to reinforce one another.

5. The study of the various social sciences should be balanced so that each receives adequate attention.

Most present-day programs are sequentially arranged to provide for an expanding-worlds approach, with places and events near to the child being studied early and faraway people and events being studied in the upper grades.

In this chapter a fourfold strategy for curriculum improvement has been developed:

1. A curriculum must state social studies objectives that take into

account the nature of the child, the nature of his society, and the nature of the social sciences.

2. Continuity in the curriculum must be established by repeated and gradually enlarged emphasis on the study of human groups, on the analysis of organizing concepts from the social sciences, and on the development of an interdependent atmosphere.

3. A curriculum should provide sequential development that places emphasis on observed concepts in the early primary grades and on inferred and ideal-type concepts in the middle and upper grades.

4. Instructional units in the curriculum should be organized into depth studies dealing with topics limited enough in scope to permit the thorough development of a child's experiences and ideas.

Every school district needs to take responsibility for the development of a curricular plan that provides clear-cut objectives and a plan for developing continuity and appropriate sequence in the learner's experience. The detailed plan in every school should be unique. The final decisions need to be made by the teachers, and the American scene should present an array of interesting, responsible curricular plans, the results of which are reported to teachers the country over. Teachers and schools should be distinctive in the same way doctors and hospitals are distinctive. The personalities differ widely, but the professional strategies have three elements in common: they are based on the best available evidence, they are exploratory and experimental in nature, and they are bound by a common humanitarian goal.

INQUIRIES

1. Collect several curriculum guides and textbook series from your educational materials center. Appraise them according to the criteria provided in the early section of this chapter.

2. Draw up a curricular outline for the social studies, defining your strategy and comparing it with the one presented here.

3. Draw up a curricular outline emphasizing a single subject discipline. Show how it could be used to introduce the strategies of the other social sciences.

---

4. It has been suggested that continuity in the program should be developed through the child's own inquiry without regard for the structure of the discipline. What do you think of this? What are the advantages and disadvantages of devoting the entire curricular effort to the problem-solving behavior of the child?

---

5. Emphasizing the organizing concepts of the disciplines has several advantages: it accounts for the structure of the discipline and provides for the development of the child's ability to inquire. What are the disadvantages of the emphasis on organizing concepts?

References and Readings

Association for Supervision and Curriculum Development. *Using Curriculum Developments.* Washington: National Education Assn., 1963.

DEWEY, JOHN. *The Child and the Curriculum.* Chicago: Univ. of Chicago Press, 1959.

EBENSTEIN, WILLIAM. *Totalitarianism: New Perspectives.* New York: Holt, Rinehart & Winston, 1962.

ELLSWORTH, RUTH. "Trends in Organization of the Social Studies," in *Social Studies in Elementary Schools.* (32d Yearbook of the National Council for the Social Studies.) Washington: National Education Assn., 1962.

HANNA, PAUL R., and LEE, JOHN R. "Generalizations from the Social Sciences," in *Social Studies in Elementary Schools.* (32d Yearbook of the National Council for the Social Studies.) Washington: National Education Assn., 1962.

HODGSON, FRANK MILTON. "Organization and Content of the Social Studies Curriculum." Unpublished Ed.D. thesis, Univ. of Southern California, 1953.

KENWORTHY, LEONARD S. *Introducing Children to the World.* New York: Harper, 1955.

MIEL, ALICE, and BROGAN, PEGGY. *More than Social Studies.* Englewood Cliffs, N.J.: Prentice-Hall, 1957.

National Council for the Social Studies. *A Guide to Content in the Social Studies.* Washington: National Education Assn., 1957.

National Education Association, Project on the Instructional Program of the
    Public Schools. *Deciding What to Teach.* Washington: National Edu-
    cation Assn., 1963.
————. *Planning and Organizing for Teaching.* Washington: National Educa-
    tion Assn., 1963.
————. *Schools for the Sixties.* New York: McGraw-Hill, 1963.
PRESTON, RALPH C. *Teaching Social Studies in the Elementary School.* New
    York: Rinehart, 1958.
TYLER, RALPH W. *Basic Principles of Curriculum and Instruction.* Chicago: Univ.
    of Chicago Press, 1950.

Chapter 10

THE DEPTH STUDY

In order to imitate the social scientist—in order to adopt his methods and style of approach to life—children must be able to analyze substantial quantities of facts and information about relatively limited topics. No child who is given only a sprinkling of facts or even a profusion of trivial information can possibly do any real hypothesis building or real testing and revising of ideas. Consequently, most instruction should be organized into depth studies which develop in the child a fairly thorough understanding of any human group under examination. The wealth of information that he examines should enable him to build well-founded ideas and to test out the organizing concepts used by the social scientist.

Some similarity exists between the depth study and the instructional "unit" that has been popular for many years. The chief difference is that the unit study has now often deteriorated into an organized but very superficial study of very broad topics (to study the entire continent of polyglot Africa in four weeks time is not uncommon today). Originally, however, a primary purpose of the unit method was to limit the range of a topic and hence to permit a thoroughgoing cooperative inquiry by the teacher and the children, to enable the children to acquire factual control, and to develop well-grounded answers to significant questions. In addition, it was designed to facilitate the practice of democracy in the classroom and to give every child some responsibility for decision making and planning for his own education.

The unit *as originally conceived* and the depth study may therefore be considered virtually identical. This original conception of the unit is what Ralph C. Preston had in mind in his recent definition:

A unit is a series of related learning experiences organized around a topic or problem. The unit method describes a process for systematically teaching a unit.

The unit method is one of the substantial contributions of the

educational experimentation which flourished during the last generation. Its success can be attributed to several factors. (1) It is flexible,
allowing the individual teacher to develop fully his own teaching
style. (2) It conforms to the psychology of childhood, permitting the
teacher to work with the child, rather than engage in a kind of tug of
war with him. (3) The unit method yields superior learning. Research
has demonstrated the superiority of many features of the unit method
over old-fashioned, routine recitation procedures in terms of both
the quantity and the quality of children's learning.[1]

Preston also provided a neat statement about the size and duration of
instructional units:

> A unit is built around as large a block of related subject matter as
> can be reviewed comfortably by the child prior to his study of it. It
> may be organized around any significant content.[2]

The Rationale for the Unit Method

The unit method was a child of the Progressive Era, especially of
the first forty years of the twentieth century. And although the unit
approach has been justified on several grounds, the earliest argument was
that it supplies opportunities for practicing democratic behavior in the
classroom. John Dewey's charge to the teacher was that he develop a
miniature democracy in the classroom and help children to formulate their
own aims and methods and to carry through their own problem-solving
activities, all in the democratic manner. To accomplish this, the teacher,
said Dewey, must himself have freedom of action and a voice in curricular
decisions. "The democratic principle requires that every teacher should
have some regular and organic way in which he can, directly or through
representatives democratically chosen, participate in the formation of the
controlling aims, methods, and materials of the school of which he is a
part."[3] Only if he has some degree of freedom can the teacher transmit
some freedom of action and decision to his pupils.

A second reason for the development of the unit method was the
apparent desirability of getting children involved in problem solving instead

---

[1] Ralph C. Preston, *Teaching Social Studies in the Elementary School*
(New York: Rinehart, 1958), p. 75.

[2] *Ibid.*

[3] John Dewey, *Intelligence in the Modern World* (New York: Modern
Library, 1939), p. 716.

of having them merely learn by memorization and recitation. Children would be able to view problem solving as a kind of democratic adventure that they would have some hand in organizing and that would end in their own evaluations of what they had learned. Dewey described this sense of achievement:

> The two limits of every unit of thinking are a perplexed, troubled, or confused situation at the beginning and a cleared-up, unified, resolved situation at the close. The first of these situations may be called pre-reflective. It sets the problem to be solved; out of it grows the question the reflection has to answer. In the final situation the doubt has been dispelled; the situation is *post*-reflective; there exists a direct experience of mastery, satisfaction, enjoyment.[4]

Dewey believed that the most effective and natural education resulted when this method of thinking was applied directly in the classroom. Thus the child's life in school would consist of his participation in a lively miniature democracy that would engage in cooperative attack on problem after problem and would lead the child to acquire the skills and values of democracy, the tools of effective thinking, as well as knowledge of subject matter.

The third reason for the development of the unit method has been essentially described in earlier chapters. Childhood is a state of limited experience. Thus, in order to think effectively about any new idea, the child must be preconditioned with a wealth of new experiences related to that idea. By proceeding in unit fashion, involving many kinds of activity, the child gains these experiences with which to reason out some generalizations, and he escapes ready-made conclusions that are easily forgotten.

The fourth reason for the rise of the unit study proceeds from the third. After or while acquiring experiences, the child must organize and evaluate them. According to Dewey, "finding the material for learning within experience is only the first step. The next step is the progressive development of what is already experienced into a fuller and richer and also more organized form, a form that gradually approximates that in which subject matter is presented to the skilled, mature person."[5] This advice of Dewey's may be rephrased in the terminology of earlier chapters: in analyzing observations, the child should progressively learn to ask the questions and use the organizing concepts of the scholar. For example, in studying children's attitudes toward their parents in the United States

---

[4] *Ibid.*, p. 855
[5] *Ibid.*, p. 674.

and in Japan, a pupil should be led to analyze his observations; he should describe the "roles" of various family members and infer the "values" held in each of these societies. Thereby his uncritical experiences are transformed into admittedly crude but nevertheless effective sociological ideas. Later these ideas are revisited, revised, and extended as the child progresses to new units or higher grades. This revisiting and amplifying of ideas is especially important. The child should never acquire a false sense of having exhausted a subject. So misled, he may think that knowledge is something learned once and for all, to be left unused and stored in the mind like coins in a box. Rather, he should perceive that what one learns at the conclusion of one study is the spur to new questions and future inquiries for information. A conclusion is merely another beginning. Said Dewey:

> It is a mistake to suppose that the principle of the leading on of experience to something different is adequately satisfied simply by giving pupils some new experiences any more than it is by seeing to it that they have greater skill and ease in dealing with things with which they are already familiar. It is also essential that the new objects and events be related intellectually to those of earlier experiences, and this means that there be some advance made in conscious articulation of facts and ideas. It thus becomes the office of the educator to select those things within the range of existing experience that have the promise and potentiality of presenting new problems which by stimulating new ways of observation and judgment will expand the area of former experience. He must constantly regard what is already won not as a fixed possession but as an agency and instrumentality for opening new fields which make new demands upon existing powers of observation and of intelligent use of memory. Connectedness in growth must be his constant watchword.[6]

Modes of Inquiry and the Depth Study

To accomplish this "leading on" of inquiry that progressively reveals to the child the organizing concepts of the social sciences requires that unit studies explore limited topics *in depth*. The child must not be confused and overwhelmed with a spread of facts in a subject too comprehensive for close study. The very nature of concept formation demands that the child concentrate on a limited topic, searching among data for answers to questions, finding tentative answers, then searching for new

---

[6] *Ibid.*, p. 675.

data to supply clearer and truer answers—and so on and on.

Consider, for example, a group of children embarking on a cooperative problem dealing with municipal government. Subtly teased into asking the probing questions used by the political scientist, the children first phrase their questions awkwardly, but gradually they are led to ask significantly, "What power does the mayor have?" Perhaps their first answer is quick and sweeping: "To make the laws." But soon, delving into more data, they may learn that the mayor's power, officially at least, is "to carry out the laws." Slowly, however, even this picture of affairs is revised and sharpened by more detail: the children come to see progressively that his presiding over the city council confers some authority not apparent in the city charter, that his position in a political party brings him power, and that his ability to make appointments and to supervise employees on the city payroll gives him a measure of control. Thus the children gradually learn to ask better questions, to squeeze hidden meaning out of data, and to find more appropriate information from more balanced sources.

This takes time. It requires contact with a lot of data about manageable topics. An enormous amount of information about a single Polynesian tribe on a single island is more useful for building modes of inquiry and developing the really big ideas in the social sciences than is the same quantity of information about all the peoples of Southeast Asia. When the child knows a great deal about a limited topic, the gap between his capacity and the adult's is narrowed.

Uninformed persons sometimes say, "All you can do with children is cover the main points." The really dangerous error in this kind of thinking is that main ideas are simply ways of thinking about all the details. An idea that is not seen in terms of concrete facts is no idea at all, but an empty verbal slogan.

One who sees, for example, the American Revolution simply as the time when the English colonies broke away from the oppression of the mother country has no idea about the Revolution at all. The economic and political struggle, the relation between events in America and other revolutions abroad, the rise of the commercial national state—all these factors, and more, denote relationships which, with supporting facts, nudge one toward a truer understanding of the American Revolution.

To do real thinking about real events, the child needs to pursue depth studies in which he can learn how the scholar assembles knowledge into ideas. The depth study is, in fact, a simulation of the conditions of scholarly inquiry. In the words of Jerome S. Bruner:

> Mastery of the fundamental ideas of a field involves not only the
> grasping of general principles, but also the development of an attitude

toward learning and inquiry, toward guessing and hunches, toward the possibility of solving problems on one's own. . . . To instill such attitudes by teaching requires something more than the mere presentation of fundamental ideas. Just what it takes to bring off such teaching is something on which a great deal of research is needed, but it would seem that an important ingredient is a sense of excitement about discovery—discovery of regularities of previously unrecognized relations and similarities between ideas, with a resulting sense of self-confidence in one's abilities. Various people who have worked on curricula in science and mathematics have urged that it is possible to present the fundamental structure of a discipline in such a way as to preserve some of the exciting sequences that lead a student to discover for himself.[7]

So that the child may learn to engage in discoveries simulating the scholar's investigations, the teacher therefore must—

Guide the child into asking interesting, exploratory questions.
Help him to gather quantities of relevant data.
Train him to build ideas out of the data.
Encourage him to check his ideas against the ideas of other children and against the concepts of scholars.

The Depth Study and Content Sources

Depth studies can draw upon all four sources of content in the social studies: (1) the class group, (2) contemporary American society, (3) other world cultures, and (4) history.

Even the study of current affairs can and probably should be pursued in depth. Although the teacher should probably touch upon all significant contemporary affairs in order to keep the children abreast of the times, the wise teacher selects a few headline events to be studied in greater detail. Such studies help to build the children's background and encourage them to apply the concepts learned in other scheduled units.

History also benefits by a study in depth. Of all instructional methods, the depth study is perhaps the most successful in bringing the past to life. The class that "lives in ancient Rome" for a few months can become familiar with Roman art and architecture, Roman laws and commerce, the very words of the senators. The child learns enough to be able

---

[7] Jerome S. Bruner, *The Process of Education* (Cambridge, Mass.: Harvard Univ. Press, 1960), p. 20.

to compare his life with that of the Roman child, the laws of Rome with the political system in his community. He can know the map of old Rome almost as well as the map of the nearest city, and, thanks to the color slide, he can gaze on the hills and houses where dwelled the Roman of two thousand years ago.

Curricula can contain depth studies drawn from history and the study of contemporary societies. Some studies, however, should be generated by the spontaneous interests of the children. The wise teacher plans the year so that part of the time is reserved for individual and small-group inquiry centered on special and personal intellectual interests. It is important that the child gradually develop the ability to select and carry on his own depth studies, making his own plans and judging his own progress.

Generally speaking, teachers should help children plan studies in which the content is deep rather than wide; that is, the subject should be narrowed as much as possible, so that time is allowed to gather information in quantity or in depth. The great temptation in the social studies is to let inquiry wander widely. "Communication" is an example of a topic that is too broad for easy management. It relates to government, culture, economics, and all other aspects of life. Consequently a study of "communication" can cover a lot of ground very loosely. However, "communication between the members of our class" or "communication in the United Nations" or "communication through packaging of goods" are more limited topics and subject to sharper intellectual analysis.

New teachers frequently wonder how large or how small a depth study should be. The answer is that there is no answer to that question. A unit should not wear on and on until it sickens. Nor should it be so short that it hinders really significant hypotheses from being formulated and tested, for every unit should be planned to develop scientific facility. Also, as the study develops, the children will start to shape it. They may ask really penetrating questions that extend what might have begun as a short study.

The Depth Study and the Social Climate

Depth studies directly influence the development of an interdependent training environment, particularly when the focus of study is on the class group itself—its nature, the behavior of its members, and their capacity for interdependence. In this study of themselves the children should, most importantly, be persistently led to examine and evaluate *standards* of behavior. The child needs to know what standards are, how they are formed, and why he should participate in forming them. At first the standards can relate to simple matters, such as the running of the class library. The children can decide on the criteria and procedures to improve performance. Gradually the standards can involve more difficult matters: "Were the questions we raised good enough? Did they involve the really important parts of the topic? Did we get good enough sources of data? Did we back up our ideas with facts?" The standards can also apply to interpersonal relations: "Did we take turns? Did our committee work well? Were we courteous to our resource visitors?"

At first, especially among the very young, many of the standards must be set by the teacher. However, by a combination of pressure and suggestion, the teacher can quickly get primary-grade children to learn how to judge performance and, indeed, can get them to be aware that they should help determine whether things are going well or not. By the time they reach the upper grades, children should be almost self-governing in their determination and evaluation of behavorial standards.

The development of procedures—planning, evaluating, and devising new ways of getting things done—should also be a part of life in school. Cooperative responsibility for establishing procedures should be encouraged in the first year of school and should mature in the upper grades.

Information and the ways it is handled also become objects of study. "Did the author back up that statement? What kinds of information were left out? Can we really say that from the evidence? Let's see if we can argue the other point of view." Statements like these should become the order of the day in a classroom which is learning how to handle information and ideas. In the really interdependent atmosphere, the class continuously examines its own thinking.

New teachers often ask, "How do I begin a depth study with children? What is involved in keeping it going?" There are no easy answers to these questions. Each teacher has to develop his own style—his personal answers. In general, however, it can be said that planning the study and continuously replanning it *with* the children offers maximal opportunity for smoothing out problems and developing a study with real drive behind it.

One can begin simply by asking the children what questions will help guide their exploration of the topic. Questions like "What do you want to know?" or "What do you think we should find out about Elizabethan England?" may start things off. The questions have to be justified (Why will that be important?) and shaped so that rich data will be unearthed and relationships found (Let's see also what religions are found in England and how they came there; I think this will help us understand the period). As the unit unfolds, problems arise and come up for discussion (What was wrong in the library yesterday? Were we confused or was it the way we worked together? Any ideas?). The teacher who sets out to develop cooperative studies—the team of teachers who set an example for the children—will find that the children increasingly take on the responsibility for planning and self-evaluation.

Summary

The depth study, cooperatively approached by children and teacher, has the following advantages:

1. It enables children, including the youngest, to gather enough information about a limited topic so that they can build their own general ideas and test them out.

2. It therefore provides a good vehicle for teaching the organizing concepts of the social sciences, for there are sufficient data available to explore ideas and sufficient time to refine question asking and to check ideas against those of other people.

3. The cooperative inquiry provides a training environment conducive to the development of open-mindedness and interdependence.

4. The depth study is useful in the study of contemporary affairs and cultures, historical periods, and the daily life of the class group. Hence it enables children to apply the concepts they are learning to topics either near at hand or far removed.

5. The depth study is suited to comparative cultural study, for it provides the time and the information to permit authentic comparison and to minimize stereotyping.

INQUIRIES

1. Identify some of the periods in world history that might be approached through depth studies. Rationalize your selection.

2. Examine some of the contemporary programs in elementary school science and mathematics. How are they utilizing depth studies to teach the central concepts of the disciplines?

3. Look up some of the research on children's interests. Identify some of these interests that might be good springboards for depth studies. See if you can devise an instrument for surveying the interests of the children you will teach.

4. Identify on the current scene a good topic for depth study by primary-grade children. You may find that current affairs in the local community and in the neighborhood will make better studies for them than national and international affairs.

5. You will have noticed that much of the intellectual debt of this book is owed John Dewey. See if you can trace the origins of one or two of his important ideas to philosophers and social analysts who preceded him.

6. In really cooperative inquiry, children, especially older ones, often disagree with the teacher about the conclusions to be drawn from data. In general, what should the teacher do when this happens? Particularly, what should he do when he is convinced the children are drawing an incorrect conclusion?

References and Readings

BRUNER, JEROME S. *The Process of Education.* Cambridge, Mass.: Harvard Univ. Press, 1960.

DEWEY, JOHN. *Intelligence in the Modern World.* New York: Modern Library, 1939.

PRESTON, RALPH C. *Teaching Social Studies in the Elementary School.* New York: Rinehart, 1958.

MATERIALS AND METHODS
FOR TEACHING
THE SOCIAL SCIENCES

Chapter 11

THE DEPTH STUDY
AND WORLD CULTURES

The development of effective depth studies requires that a wealth of interesting material be available—material that can be handled conveniently by children. In studying the neighborhood or local community, the children can find this material, of course, merely by going outdoors, making visits, and observing conditions firsthand. Nearly every other topic, however, requires books, magazines, films, and documents from which the facts can be reconstructed. One might, for example, wish to substitute a study of Birmingham and Leeds for a study of England, but unless one can assemble suitable materials dealing with these cities, the study will not succeed.

A serious problem is the lack of published materials especially designed for children yet containing the quantity of data necessary for depth studies. Most available reading materials that contain sufficient data cannot be read by elementary school children; the prose or the presentation is too sophisticated. Other materials, though readable, may lack an objective presentation of facts. Many organizations, such as chambers of commerce, though willing to share what they have written, cannot reasonably be expected to have an impartial view of their communities. Pressure groups pour out floods of material from the printing presses, but the materials are useful merely for the study of the pressure group itself as a phenomenon.

Even carefully constructed textbooks for the social studies often suffer from major limitations, when measured for their use in depth studies. Few of them, for example, treat racial and other minority groups effectively, and they have a tendency to picture the rosy side of things. We all know that the United States is not perfect in every way, but it is hard for the writers of books to say so directly to little children.

As the newer curriculum projects begin to make their materials available, the picture may change somewhat,[1] but at present effective

_____
[1] See the end of Chapter 12 for a list of current curriculum projects.

inquiry by children will depend on a school faculty's ingenuity in inventing effective learning devices.

The World-Widened Elementary School[2]

One easy and natural way to introduce children, even very young children, to the peoples of far-off lands is to "adopt" the school of another country.[3] It is not difficult to adopt a foreign school. Probably the most common method is to use the good offices of Americans who have lived abroad or people from other countries who have lived in the United States. However, some teachers have made arrangements by writing directly to school districts abroad. Occasionally exchanges of letters by pen pals have developed into such a close relationship that the schools of these correspondents have made a formal liaison.

The teachers and children of the two schools can arrange to exchange experience records, creative writing, drawings, studies of their communities, lists of questions to be answered, and pictures and maps. If the languages differ, an interpreter will be needed—perhaps an elementary school language teacher, a secondary teacher, or some bilinguist from the local community or college. For linguistic and other reasons, countries with a culture similar to ours are probably the easiest to set up relations with; but, with determination, language does not remain a barrier for long, and contacts with different cultures can be exceedingly productive.

Adoption of foreign schools has several advantages for both parties. In the first place, it facilitates the children's ability to collect honest, detailed information about the people of another country. To the children of a village in Normandy the children in a Pennsylvania town can address questions that would never be answered in a textbook or a commercial flier. The adoption of a faraway school can bring a realism to social studies that can come only from the consciousness that the respondent to one's question is actually on the spot. Whether the Pennsylvania sixth-grader asks, "Our trains run less often these days; do you have good train service?" or the French first-grader asks, "What did you have for dinner last night?" the answer that comes back has a ring of authenticity that no secondary

---

[2] Much of the material in this section has been adapted or taken directly from Bruce R. Joyce, "The World-Widened Elementary School," *Elementary School Journal,* LXII (April 1962), 343–45.

[3] See Chapter 8, p. 126–31, for an outline describing a unit of study for a school in Newark, Delaware, which has "adopted" as its twin city the French town of La Garde-Freinet.

source can inspire. There is also a freewheeling quality about a study that is not confined to the answers that can be found in the typical reference book.

Adoption establishes a real need to communicate information, together with an awareness of the problems and joys in human communication. A fifth-grader in Texas, trying to describe local industries and products to children in Liverpool, has a much more demanding job than if he were merely reporting to his classmates. Preparing a report takes on added dimensions when what one says becomes practically the whole source of ideas that someone else will possess. "Is this an honest description of our town?" "Are we saying what we really want to say?" These become crucial questions.

Amusing difficulties in language gently point out cultural differences. Our Texas students may find that when an English child says his family put their luggage and parcels into the boot and roared off for a fortnight at the seaside, he isn't referring to stuffing a shoe with anything.

Stereotypes will appear on both sides. "But we thought all Texans wore cowboy boots, and that you would surely carry a gun." "We thought the queen was your president." The children will have to learn to straighten out their thinking and, in so doing, will acquire some awareness of the extent of their own misinformation and overgeneralization.

Adoption of foreign schools enables children to double-check the information and ideas in reference works and textbooks. "We read that French towns are dominated by cathedrals. Can you send us a picture of yours?" "Our textbook says that nearly 25 percent of the Italian people voted Communist in the last election. Is that true? What does it mean?" Some difficult questions can also come from the other direction: "Our book says that it is not legal to be a Communist in the United States. How can that be if you have free speech?"

On the gentler side, the exchange of direct questions gives access to attitudes and emotions that are rarely encountered in standard reference works. "Our supermarket sells us food. The clerk got angry at me because I dropped a jar of peaches." "Our factory is on strike. We children wish they'd get together." Children can discover some of the homely emotions they have in common with children everywhere. "It was hot yesterday, but we weren't allowed to go swimming. My mother thought it was too cold. But it was *so* hot." Such contact reveals humanity to children in forms as charming as they are vivid.

In the course of several years of association with the children of another nation, children gradually see the part that culture plays in behavior. Discovered through concrete evidence, the understanding can and should begin early ("They wear Lederhosen like we wear slacks"), continue toward more abstract issues ("These Irish kids don't like Englishmen, but they've never met any. I guess they learned that from their parents"), and eventually proceed toward self-understanding ("I like the English because Dad does. I've never met an Englishman either").

The exchange between children, carried on in their own words, is likely to remain within the level of their understanding. First-graders can exchange pictures, experience records that they dictate to their teachers, tape recordings of stories, songs, and plays, pictures they take and pictures they draw, and many other things. Through these devices, a first-grader in Denver can exchange ideas and compare communities with a first-grader in Tokyo. "They have policemen too." "They use a different kind of stove." "Not always; the mother in that picture is using an electric stove." "They have churches too." The eyes of the children in the adopted school become extensions of the eyes of the children of the adopted nation. The first-grader in Denver studies economic interdependence in his community and division of labor in his family at the same time that he studies these concepts in relation to the community and families of his Tokyo friends.

Depth studies in the higher grades can also proceed on a comparative basis. "Please describe the political organization of your city. Here is our city charter. Do you have this kind of document? Can you send us a copy? We have included a tape recording of an interview with our mayor. He says the main issue in our city today is zoning to protect our recreation lands. What is the main issue in your town? Do you have good recreation facilities?"

The possibilities from this kind of association are limitless. The adoption, in itself, ensures that through the grades the children will have the constant opportunity for a comparative depth study of the local situation and the society of the adopted school. Leonard Kenworthy has stated the urgency of this sort of contact:

> It is no longer a question of whether we should prepare children to live in the world community; they will either live in a world community or not live at all.[4]

A SPY ON THE SCENE. Many young people are studying in armed forces schools abroad or traveling with their parents or living in another country where their parents are on lengthy business. Occasionally a class will have access to such a young traveler and can count on him for information. The following letters are from a fifth-grade child who spent a year

---

[4] Leonard S. Kenworthy, *Introducing Children to the World* (New York: Harper, 1955), p. x.

in the South African Republic. His class continued to correspond with him, and conducted a depth study of South Africa partly in order to take advantage of his presence and to prepare for his return.[5]
The following are excerpts from two of his letters.

I have just got back from Kruger Park. We had a lot of fun there except when we started seeing elephants and my six-year-old sister got scared. We saw only one lioness and no lions. It ran into the bush as soon as we saw it. We saw many impala and wildebeest, which looks like a bison. We saw a herd of about 400 water buffalo. We saw two crocodiles, one of which was far away, the other swimming about 15 feet away. We saw many elephants. The one that interested and scared me most was a male elephant with fairly large tusks, which trumpeted and came after us. There were some fairly large hippopotami which we always saw near the water.

There is a bad drought here. It is the worst in 70 years. The Limpopo River has run dry. The worst drought-stricken places are: Brits, Petersburg, Harmbaths, Messina, and Ohrigstad.

On November 5, 1963, and every other year, too, we will have a celebration called Guy Fawkes Day, where you shoot up fireworks. You can shoot as many fireworks as you want. (Guy Fawkes is a man who tried to blow up the houses of Parliament in London.) There is a field next to my cousin's house where we can set fireworks off. (Also it is the day after my birthday.)

Some of you have asked how come I have to pay 10¢ and you 11¢. We actually pay more than you. One cent is 40% more than yours. Some of you wanted to know if there were any black children in my class. People, they are so strict about that that they have special buses, train cars, benches, and places in post offices. Also, they probably couldn't afford a white person's school. So it would be impossible for a black to get into a white's school.

The flow of personal information, the ability to answer difficult questions about race relations simply and from direct observation, the ability to convey emotional atmosphere—all belong to our young observers.

Through Art and Literature

From many nations come folk tales, literature, music, and art which can be used in depth study of a culture. Folk tales in particular have been

---

[5] For these letters we are indebted to Mrs. Ruth Sutcliffe, teacher in Newark, Delaware.

translated, collected, and edited for children of all ages, and most nations and certainly every world region are represented. Literature can open up the study of a people's national values, their views of life, their reactions to plague and tyranny, and their ideas of pleasure or loyalty. Imagine children reading the following folk tale of India, prepared to find out what was important in the teller's message and what virtues were being extolled.[6]

The Golden Stag

An old hunter once saw a golden stag. He told no one till he lay on his deathbed. Then he told his son:

"It was up in the hills, far from the king's city. A rill ran over sands of silver. The golden stag led a herd of deer down to the rill, to drink."

The son was a hunter, too. He felt love for all things, and did not wish to kill. It was the wish of his heart to be a hermit and grow wise. But he was born a hunter, the son of a hunter; so a hunter he had to be.

One night, the queen of that land had a dream. In her dream, she saw a golden stag. The golden stag sat on a golden throne, to teach. The things he spoke of were so wise that as she awoke, she cried, "Catch that stag!"

Next day, the queen told her dream to the king.

"Did you ever hear of a golden stag in this land, Sire?" she asked.

"No," said the king. "But I will ask my hunters if they have."

Only one hunter had. "My father saw it, Sire," he said. "He told me of it on his deathbed. He saw it up in the hills, far from the city."

"Go and catch it," said the king, "and bring it to the queen."

The hunter went up into the hills, far from the city. He came to the spot his father had told him of, with a rill that ran over sands of silver.

Footprints of a herd of deer went down to the rill. So the hunter set a snare in the track and hid among the trees.

That night, he saw a herd of deer go down to the rill in the moonlight. The herd was led by a golden stag.

The golden stag set his foot in the snare. He cried the cry of capture. At that cry, the herd fled.

Then the hunter saw a thing he had never seen till now. Two of the herd came back to the golden stag. They tried to get his foot free. The thong cut his flesh to the bone, but he was still held fast.

"Go with the rest," cried the golden stag. "Go—you are still free."

---

[6] "The Golden Stag," from *The Golden Stag and Other Folk Tales from India,* © 1962 by Isabel Wyatt. Reprinted by permission of David McKay Company, Inc., and Margaret Christie, representative and author's agent.

Courtesy of Sara I. Fenwick, Graduate Library School, University of Chicago

The study of literature can lead children beyond an accumulation of factual data to an understanding of the qualities and values of human relationships. But an introduction to literature often succeeds best in a cooperative setting in which the teacher and children read, listen, and inquire together and in which the total atmosphere helps to develop interdependent attitudes and an appreciation of the views, needs, and contributions of others.

"We will not go," said the two stags. "We will stay and die with you."

The hunter felt his flesh creep with pity. He came out from among the trees with his knife in his hand. He stooped down, cut the snare, and set the golden stag free.

"Why did you snare me, hunter?" asked the golden stag.

The hunter told him of the dream the queen had had.

"Then why do you set me free?" asked the golden stag.

"Out of love and pity," said the hunter.

"Hunter, you are no hunter at heart," said the golden stag. "What is the wish of your heart?"

And the hunter told him:

"To be a hermit, and grow wise."

"Brush my back with your hand," said the golden stag.

The hunter did so. Golden hairs from the back of the golden stag clung to the palm of his hand.

"Keep them," said the golden stag. "When a man feels love for all things, hairs from the back of a golden stag can make him wise. Now look into my eyes."

The hunter did so.

"What I know, you know," said the golden stag. "Go back now to the queen. What to say to her will come to you."

So the hunter went back to the city. He came to the king and queen and told them how he had met the golden stag and how he had set him free. He told them all that the golden stag had said to him. Then new things came into his mind to say—wise things he did not know he knew.

When he came to an end, the queen cried, "But this is just how the golden stag spoke in my dream! Sire, give this man the wish of his heart. Let him be a hermit!"

"I will," said the king.

So the hunter got his wish and was a hunter no more, but a hermit. He grew so wise that even the king sat at his feet. And all his life he was able to help the king rule his land well, with the help of the golden hairs from the back of the stag.

The children will quickly find the value that Indians place on love for all creatures and on charity and mercy. The place of wisdom in the story, a place which might have been taken by riches, or security, or the hand of the princess, will be detected. The belief in destiny—the "wish of the heart"—will be examined.

As the children examine other folk tales, they will find some with similar themes. They will, as in "The Golden Stag," find the theme of magic and the use of magic to redeem life from an otherwise cruel fate. Gradually, they will also isolate those themes that many nations seem to share. Both common values and special values will be identified.

Perhaps the same unit, or perhaps a later study of India, will reveal to the children the tie between the wish to be a wise hermit and the tenets of the probable religion of the hunter. Much later, in senior high school or in college, the student will come upon these ideas again as he learns how Gandhi used the tales and religious ideas of the Indian people as he led them toward national independence.

Starting with a Book

Many publishers issue series of books about the countries and peoples of the world. Most of these are written for the upper grades and contain, unfortunately, only a brief survey of each country. Some do provide considerable information about a limited topical area—economic geography, for example—but most spread their coverage rather evenly over several areas. The Lippincott series includes some history, leisure activities, art, architecture, and literature; but the series comprises fairly short books and thus necessarily gives fairly brief coverage. Treating each nation very generally and providing very little data and illustration, such books are not good informational sources for an effective depth study. Nevertheless they do raise excellent questions and provide many general ideas which can be further investigated. The virtues and faults of these series become fairly evident when one reads the following passage from a book on Portugal:

> Elvas, on its steep hill overlooking the plain, is one of the largest, busiest, and most romantic of these old walled cities. Atop the hill is the castle. Below it are huddled the houses, glaring white, within the walls and moats that encircle the town. Inside the main gate one discovers a maze of narrow winding streets crowded with townfolk, peasants, and soldiers. From ramparts and towers there are splendid views across the plains which are brown, yellow, or green, depending on the season. In the churches is a wealth of sixteenth or seventeenth century tiles, paintings and images.
>
> The aqueduct built near the end of the fifteenth century brings to the town its supply of water. From the orchards outside the walls come the sweet green plums for which Elvas is famous. Out of season they can be had preserved in liqueur and coated with icing. The town is equally famous for its dried fruits and olives.[7]

---

[7] Raymond Wohlrabe and Werner Krusch, *The Land and People of Portugal* (Philadelphia: Lippincott, 1960), p. 71.

The passage above is all that is given about Elvas. The concept load is enormous, and the child is asked to accept many conclusions for which the underlying reasoning is not revealed. Hence his previous knowledge must be substantial if he is to comprehend such description. On the other hand, the passage could start a good deal of inquiry. The history and economy of the town have been hinted at. Its architecture and the suggestion that it is a feudal town are thought-provoking. The religion and some suggestion of the type of daily life could be checked out. The general ideas need to be made carefully explicit and then checked out, one by one. Highly motivated children with good reference books, a willing teacher, some writing paper, and the address of the Portuguese embassy could have a field day.

Some of the general discussions in the book on Portugal might be even better spurs to inquiry:

> The slump in the nation's economy meant less financial aid to poets and prose writers. Books were very expensive. A large segment of the nation was illiterate. Despite these conditions, outstanding work was produced, but not in so great a volume as in previous decades.[8]

Children of some sophistication might take this passage and embark on a general study of the subsidization of the arts and its effect on literary production. Iron-curtain countries, Western Europe, medieval times, the United States might all be explored. Perhaps not many youngsters would be likely to seize on this opportunity, but investigation of topics of like sophistication is not unknown by any means.

Careful depth studies, then, could use books of this sort as starters. Many titles will be suggested and reviewed for this purpose a little farther on. A reminder, however: an effective depth study must deal with a limited facet of a topic. To approach a country from the point of view of politics or economics is probably all the children should be expected to handle at one time.

One more note should be added before shifting to a slightly different subect. It happens that the "Lands and Peoples" Series published by Macmillan is also published in Great Britain, and some of the books have been written by Englishmen. In some cases the point of view is just different enough that an upper-grade class could make an interesting study of this aspect of the series. The English books could be compared with those of another series written by Americans and the clues to the points of view duly noted.

---

[8] *Ibid.*, p. 92.

Books on Seemingly Narrow Topics

In the last few years a very useful kind of trade book has appeared that takes a very small topic or even a small part of a small topic and develops it in some detail.

Such are the books by Sonia and Tim Gidal about villages in various (usually European) countries. *My Village in England* (Pantheon, 1963) is typical. In vivid black-and-white photographs accompanied by a workmanlike text, the book traces the life of a small boy in a village called Temple Grafton, a few miles from Stratford-on-Avon. The detail of daily activities is such that the reader begins to get some idea of the orientation of the people, even the sociology of the family. The continual references to historical events and figures bring out the sensitivity to heritage that characterizes the people; in particular, the continual and obvious forethought of the characters illustrates the thrifty, tidy culture of an English village. The daily lives of the children are painted in such detail that they can be compared point by point with those of American children. The profuse description of people face to face makes the material especially suitable for sociological analysis.

Books on limited aspects of many nations have begun to appear in increasing numbers. In the months and years to come, the depth study will no doubt have the published materials it needs.

Summary

The possibilities for depth studies dealing with the cultures of the world are as broad as the imaginations of the children and their teacher.

Adoption by the school of another land is a particularly effective means, for it ensures a continuing supply of authentic information and the need for clear expression about one's own culture. News from American visitors abroad is nearly as good, but it is difficult to find them staying in one place long enough to permit much exchange of information.

The art and literature of a people are doors to their minds, and collections of tales and excerpts from the modern literature of other lands are being published for children in greater numbers.

Many trade books for children make good bases for depth studies, even—or perhaps especially—those that concentrate on a single village, a single person, or a single aspect of life. They encourage children to seek a deeper knowledge of the total situation than do books having a broad topic.

In general, the "narrow-gauge" depth study is to be preferred, so that a single town, a single person, or a slice of life can be thoroughly studied.

INQUIRIES

1. Find a copy of the *Manchester Guardian*. Read its editorials. See if you can find an issue, problem, or incident that illuminates a facet of British life sufficiently to set off a depth inquiry.

2. Identify a contemporary primitive culture that could be the subject of a depth study. Select the social science from whose vantage point you believe the study should proceed. Identify materials from which children can get information about the culture. Identify references for your own background.

3. Identify a well-developed, "modern" nation with which to contrast the primitive society. Again identify the learning materials and the materials for your own informational background. How will you help children compare the cultures without their concluding immediately that the primitive one is "inferior"?

4. Leonard Kenworthy recommends that younger children study toys, dolls, fun, and music all over the world. Plan a resource unit for a depth study on one of these topics. Be sure to make provision for the use of the organizing concepts of the appropriate social science.

5. Identify an aspect of an American Indian tribe that would make a good depth study for a primary grade. Develop a teaching strategy that identifies the appropriate social science questions. Identify some materials that children can use to get information about the tribe.

6. With several other students, identify an aspect of a contemporary culture on which there is little information available in

books or films for children. Divide up the topic and, using adult sources, write some material that could be read in the primary grades. Try out the new materials with some children.

7. Familiarize yourself with the tales and stories of a foreign people. How might they be approached by children? Select one or two stories and build lessons around them. Try out the lessons with some children of elementary school age.

References and Readings

JOYCE, BRUCE R. "The World-Widened Elementary School," *Elementary School Journal*, LXII (April 1962), 343–45.

KENWORTHY, LEONARD S. *Free and Inexpensive Materials on World Affairs*. New York: Teachers College, 1963.

_____. *Introducing Children to the World*. New York: Harper, 1955.

_____. *Studying Africa in Elementary and Secondary Schools*. New York: Teachers College, 1962.

_____. *Studying South America in Elementary and Secondary Schools*. New York: Teachers College, 1962.

_____. *Studying the Middle East in Elementary and Secondary Schools*. New York: Teachers College, 1962.

_____. *Studying the World: Selected Resources*. New York: Teachers College, 1962.

PRESTON, RALPH C. *Teaching World Understanding*. Englewood Cliffs, N.J.: Prentice-Hall, 1955.

12

DEPTH STUDIES: TEACHING MATERIALS AND INDIVIDUAL DIFFERENCES

Instructional materials have two purposes. One is to give children access to data. The other is to help them draw meaning from the data. These two operations cannot, in practice, be separated effectively. It is clearly insufficient to present children with data (teach them the "facts") and conclude teaching at that point. It is clearly impossible for children to develop organizing concepts and methods of inquiry without dealing with data.

The depth study as an approach to teaching depends on leading children to rich data which they can be helped to analyze. When the children are studying their own groups—groups of which they are members—or local problems or processes, they have access to the direct collection of data. The local store or the government of the local town or city can be studied firsthand. People who are far away or events that happened long ago have to be studied with secondhand information. Books, pictures, recordings, and films then become critical ingredients of instruction.

One of the most important things to remember about a classroom is that it can easily become removed from most aspects of life. It teems with a life of its own (a life which needs to be studied by children), but the political and social life of the world, the commercial life of the city, the impact of changing technologies on society—these can easily remain outside the walls of the classroom.

It is to burst through these walls that we use instructional materials. Consider the first purpose of instructional materials: to give children access to data. Instructional materials should bring children the data of life as it is. The study of power, for example, requires examples of men wielding it, making decisions, defending their rights, making governments and overthrowing them. The study of the city requires examples of cities, and the materials of instruction have to be selected so that the child encounters the facts of city life. The study of ancient Greece requires the most concrete descriptions possible of life in ancient Greece.

Therefore the overriding criterion for the selection of instructional materials is that they provide authentic data about the most significant aspects of the subject of inquiry. When children are studying their own neighborhood, the crucial question about instructional materials is, What is the best way of revealing to the children the *real* neighborhood? When they are studying the American Revolution, the question becomes, How can the children obtain a realistic picture of the aspects of the Revolution that they are studying?

The second purpose of instructional materials is to help children draw meaning from data. Instructional materials can help the children to focus on the subject areas and the questions that the social scientist would emphasize. They can also be so arranged that the data offered can help the children to build concepts that explain the events or groups being studied.

The *arrangement* of instructional materials is crucial. One may present the children with a Japanese folk tale and follow it with an Irish folk tale because the contrast encourages the building of useful concepts. One may have the children visit local stores and factories and study them before they read much about economic life, because the data obtained from the local studies will make the readings more meaningful and because the readings help to tie together the information gained from the trips.

The *conceptual content* of the materials is also important. One may construct a map, for example, so designed that certain factors can easily be seen in relation to one another (such as the relation between the location of railroads and highways and the location of factories). Some books are written so that fact builds upon fact and are organized around a unifying idea (such as a book which describes the lives of New World explorers and then inquires into the motives that brought them on their adventures and conquests).

The aim of this chapter and the one which follows is to help the reader identify sources of instructional materials that can serve the two purposes we have outlined. The emphasis is on materials that are rich sources of information for the children. However, the application of a good teaching strategy must not be forgotten. Instructional materials can offer the child information and ideas, but only the instructional strategy can ensure that the children will interpret the data meaningfully, understand the concepts fully, and develop an ability to use the modes of inquiry of the social scientist.

We will begin with three considerations that should guide our exploration of instructional materials:

1. There is no simple, fixed strategy for teaching the social studies. Every teacher needs to develop a wide repertoire of approaches to be used in assisting and directing the inquiry of children.

2. Children vary enormously in almost every characteristic. Their common learning should increase their ability to communicate with one another about important problems, but without stifling their individuality or impeding their singular interests and aspirations.

3. Wide varieties of learning materials are necessary. Each individual approach to learning—and often each individual learner —requires a special use of material. A great supply of carefully chosen, creative material is essential to good teaching. Increasingly, such material will have to be collected and, oftentimes, written by creative teachers.

Materials from which children can learn, however, are often found near at hand. Because people—interesting people—can be excellent sources of information, can themselves be "materials" for inquiry, we shall first turn to a discussion of what are commonly called resource persons.

Resource Persons

In every community, no matter how small, there are people who have been somewhere, know something, or do something about which children should know. Every teacher should examine the accounts of the teaching units which were conducted at the Lincoln School of Teachers College, Columbia University, during the late nineteen twenties and the nineteen thirties. One of the distinguishing marks of these cooperatively planned, problem-solving units was the thorough and appropriate use of resource persons. For example, in the unit on Ships and Navigation one group of fifth-graders visited the liner *St. Louis* and interviewed the purser:

> The purser explained each important step in the mechanical operation of driving his ship through the water. The boys and girls inspected the motors while their guide explained how they were operated. He showed them where the oil flowed into the cylinders, and told them how compressed air ignited the oil, and how hot gas from this fire drove the piston. He also showed them the two great propeller shafts which are turned by the motors. Then the children followed these shafts aft through the bulkhead doors and saw where they emerged

at the stern of the ship to connect with the propeller. They already knew, of course, where the propellers were and that they pushed the ship through the water, so the story of the way that the *St. Louis* gets its power was complete, and the details sufficiently clear to satisfy them and meet their needs at this grade level.[1]

Somewhat later on in the tour of the ship there arose another question:

The children asked the purser to tell them how lifeboats were lowered. They grouped themselves along the taffrail while he explained that a place was reserved on one of the lifeboats for each person on the ship, how they would enter the boats in case of need, and how the davits would operate to swing the boats free of the ship and lower them into the water.[2]

This account of the purser is an excellent illustration of first-rate use of a resource person. It adheres to the following criteria for such interviews:

1. The children are well prepared beforehand with information derived from books and experiments.

2. They have questions to ask and are prepared to integrate the answers with other information. They are not dependent on the rehearsed tour or lecture.

3. The contact is planned so that there is room for spontaneous questions and ideas.

4. The inquiry is conducted so that the resource person has access to concrete examples of every point or idea he offers. By no means must children always be taken to the scene of the physical material (e.g., to the ship). An antique dealer, for example, either can be visited in his shop or can come to school, bringing along samples or pictures. But, in any case, without illustrative materials, very few adults can effectively lecture to children or answer their questions.

5. The use of the resource person (e.g., the purser) is a natural outgrowth of the study. The children *need* him as a source of information.

6. The resource person has control of his subject. He can speak with experience, and he can control events to the degree that

---

[1] Tompsie Baxter and Bess M. Young, *Ships and Navigation* (New York: Teachers College, Columbia University, 1933), p. 26.
[2] *Ibid.*, p. 27.

he can efficiently guide the children about on a tour and make sure they see the important things.

The same unit of study that dealt with the ship's purser also led to a study of imports from India, and another resource person appeared at the school:

> When Ben's mother, Mrs. Z, learned of the group's interest in Indian hand products she came to school, bearing a collection of these articles. The children examined each article with interest, and asked Ben's mother how it was made, what it was made of, and how it was used or worn. The boys and girls tried on the shawls and scarves, and Mrs. Z adjusted them in the native manner. . . .
>
> In a picture of a temple which Ben's mother displayed, the children saw with amazement that a cow "stood on the church steps!" Mrs. Z told them that the Hindus considered the cow a sacred animal, and gave them an idea of the various religions prevalent in India.[3]

Not long after the visit by Mrs. Z, still another visitor made an appearance:

> A day or two later, Ben's father appeared in the classroom, bringing with him a model of a houseboat that is typical of those used on the rivers in the hill country of India, and also a sort of sedan chair which he called a "dandy." With the models and through the children's questions and his answers the class gained an idea of these and other means of transportation in India. Mr. Z then placed a fez-like cap on Herbert's head and skillfully wound around it a silk cloth in the true Indian turban fashion.[4]

This use of resource persons again meets the criteria of good practice: the children were prepared; they had questions they wanted to ask; there was room for spontaneous conversation; the resource person had access to concrete examples; and the process was part of the natural inquiry of the children.

The potential use of resource persons is almost infinite. Industrial workers and executives, for example, can bring special knowledge to the children. As part of their public relations departments some business firms, such as telephone companies, maintain services providing experienced resource personnel. Local storekeepers, policemen, political officials, members of chambers of commerce, recreation workers—all have special knowl-

---

[3] *Ibid.*, pp. 35–36.
[4] *Ibid.*, p. 38.

edge about a local situation. In fact, it is inconceivable that a study could effectively concentrate on a local community without the involvement of resource persons. The teacher cannot possibly have the varied information and insights required to do an adequate job of instruction, and there are too few reading materials on community affairs written at an elementary school level. If the elementary child is to compare his culture with others on the basis of authentic data, the active citizens of his community must be involved.

The willingness of local citizens should really be an American legend. A few years ago, for example, one class in a Midwestern city undertook to build a combined playhouse and storage facility for younger children, a little house to stand on the playground. A local architect helped the children draw up plans and went into the intricacies of architectural planning and drawing. Local vendors of building materials discussed timberwork and carpentry and helped select the most suitable material. A local cement firm poured the foundation and explained its industrial operations in general. A PTA committee helped with the financing. The social world around the school had become the chief instructional resource for the unit.[5]

Realia

The Ships and Navigation unit discussed above involved first-rate use of Hindu and Indian realia, those things (such as costumes, tools, dwellings, and religious objects) that relate to the daily living of people. In general, when trying to picture a culture or society, children react with better understanding if they see real things, real activities. Watching a real train being moved by switchmen at a real railroad yard leaves a far more indelible impression than any picture. Better than any picture or story, a visit to the local airport supplies all the atmosphere generated by the travelers and airline personnel—the reality of human interaction.

Realia can lead to the formation of ideas and concepts—but only if, instead of being merely a "pretty" display, the realia are used as a means of inspiring inquiry. A context should gradually be woven about the realia; they should be accompanied by ideas gathered from books, movies, pictures, and resource people. Consider, for example, the kinds of ideas that could be inspired by the realia donated by our Mr. and Mrs. Z:

---

[5] This construction project was observed in the schools of Ferndale, Michigan. The exchange program between Newark, Delaware, and La Garde-Freinet, France, described in Chapter 8, is another excellent example of the use of resource persons.

These are a pair of vases that came from India. They are hand-made. First, they cut the design out of brass with a knife. The person that makes these gets only twelve or thirteen cents for his work.

In India men wear shawls, too. This is a Kashmiri shawl of Pash-mina wool. Notice the design. It is supposed to look like the Jhelem River which winds around the city of Arnagar.

This is a Buddhist prayer wheel. Inside is a roll of papers. When it is turned around one way a prayer has been said. When it is turned around the other way, a curse has been said.

This is a beggar's bowl. They attach a string in such a way that they can carry it over the shoulder. Many people spend most of their lives begging. It is part of their religion. Some beggars don't wear many clothes at all, some cover themselves with ashes.[6]

It is interesting to note that one of the offshoots of the depth study of Ships and Navigation was this depth study of India. The children had found that ships go somewhere, and they had begun to get interested in some of these destinations; new studies, generated by the children's interests, had begun to take shape. In the original unit, before the study commenced, the teachers had gathered many materials and many ideas for maritime resources. The inquiry into India, arising spontaneously, necessitated a hunt by children and teachers together for additional materials.

FIELD TRIPS. The field trip is the time-honored device for taking children to realia and resource people, but the sites visited should be chosen with discrimination. Often a site that may not at first seem most appropriate for a certain study will prove, on closer analysis, to be more suitable than a more obvious choice. For instance, a visit to a real farm is not necessarily the best way of studying agriculture or even "life on the farm." A "zoo farm" or a local green nursery may staff experts better qualified to discuss plant growth or food production with young children. Moreover, in studying farm production, a group of children may take special interest in or need more enlightenment on some particular phase of the food industry—processing, storage, or productivity. In such cases, a visit to a mill, grain elevator, or fertilizer plant may be preferable, depending on the nature of the inquiry. Probably the choice of the site for a field trip should not be made until the study is fairly well advanced, when interests and needs have become evident—*unless, of course, the trip is to be used as a stimulus to questioning.*

The field trip imparts a sense of realism and fixes information in the child's mind better than other media of study except possibly television

---

[6] Baxter and Young, p. 38

and, rarely, motion pictures. The field trip enables children to see spontaneous human interaction in the adult world. For example, to see a legislative body function is to see the interaction of its members. Only when congressional hearings or political conventions are televised does one see anything like it in the political sphere. One can read about a legislature, examine the laws it passes, look at the voting records of its members, follow issues in the newspapers, correspond with its members, and obtain a great deal of information and ideas about it. However, the essence of a legislature is the interaction of its members.

Politics is not the only sphere in which this is true. The interaction of workers in a factory, the excitement when a plane comes in at an airport, and the confusion in the city room of a newspaper are difficult to get from any source but direct experience. Of course, a sense of excitement should not be all that the child derives from seeing a legislature or newsroom in action. He should be carefully coached beforehand to look for certain subtle operations; he should, if possible, be accompanied by informed guides; his chaperons from school should be briefed sufficiently so that they can help him sort out the important information from the apparent confusion. If the child and those who aid him are not well prepared, he might assume, upon seeing the vote on a bill, that he is seeing the whole story of lawmaking; the caucus, the hearing, and the trading of votes will not become known to him. The field trip, while it can be an exciting stimulus to learning, can be really successful only if supported by many other learning activities.

Realia can be gathered and brought into the children's reach; buildings can be photographed; industrial processes can be pictured in films; and all these can be written about effectively. But human interplay needs to be perceived. The function of the field trip is to sharpen this perception.

MUSEUMS. Many museums in large cities maintain educational staffs which conduct lessons, distribute bibliographies, and in other ways provide instructional services—all of which can stimulate or further unusual inquiry.[7] For example, the Philadelphia Museum of Art provides combined lessons and tours, including one dealing with "The Woman in Art Through the Ages," conducted for third- or fourth-graders. The tour, which illustrates changing styles of art, might be used by a teacher to introduce a historical study of the relation of art to other areas of life.

The University Museum of the University of Pennsylvania pro-

---

[7] For a general description of museum collections and services, consult Erwin O. Christensen (ed.), *Museums Directory of the United States and Canada* (Washington: American Assn. of Museums, 1961).

vides, in addition to the museum exhibits, pamphlets that show children how to construct some unusually effective models and handicrafts. For example, their list of crafts for the unit "The History of Records" includes directions for making the buffalo-skin records of the Plains Indians, wampum belts, an Inca quipu, a Babylonian clay tablet, a wax tablet, a scroll, and papyrus paper (by the ancient method). In addition the museum sells, or provides without charge, directions for making a number of useful models. Included with a model of an Egyptian nobleman's house excavated at Tell el 'Amarna is a description of the estate so detailed that the daily life of the times might easily be dramatized or discussed by the children. Several other models of houses are available; thus, with the help of other sources, children could compare the home life of several peoples living in critical eras of Western civilization.

Many other museums offer tours, loans, and printed materials. The Commercial Museum in Philadelphia periodically devotes one floor or another to exhibits of a single nation or culture and provides a complete program of lessons, tours, and classroom exhibits. The Museum of Science and Industry in Chicago includes exhibits of modern industrial society, as do the Henry Ford Museum and Greenfield Village in Dearborn, Michigan, the Smithsonian Institution in Washington, the California Museum of Science and Industry in Los Angeles, and several other museums nationwide. Many other smaller museums are also exceptionally rewarding. For example, from the Henry Frances Dupont Winterthur Museum in Greenville, Delaware, the author has borrowed sets of slides on the American decorative arts, which have been used by his pupils to illustrate their study of life in colonial America.

A surprising number of small towns have historical societies which maintain small depositories of materials illustrating local history. Frequently one finds copies of the local newspaper going back a hundred years or more. Poems, letters, and other writings of early-day citizens will often be collected. Maps, the stories of early industries, the decisions of the town government, records of good times and bad—all these are available. In large cities the library or historical society frequently maintains a department which is an invaluable source. In small towns, the material is often tended by one or two interested volunteers.

Government Documents

The United States government, most foreign governments and their embassies and consulates, and many state and local governments provide publications which make good learning materials. The magazine *USSR* is available from the Russian embassy (the United States has the reciprocal privilege of distributing *Amerika* in the Soviet Union). The French embassy provides quantities of reading material, much of which is useful in the study of world affairs because its explanations of the French positions on international issues provide good comparisons with the U.S. positions.

Although the obvious disadvantage of governmental material is its bias, it would be a mistake to avoid these materials; for some interesting studies may arise because of the very differences in point of view. For example, imagine fourth-graders viewing a filmstrip from a South African information agency—"South Africa, the Other U.S.A." Identified in the film are industrial products, occupations, native welfare programs, and living conditions in the large cities. Then consider the same class subsequently viewing a filmstrip produced by *Life* magazine, which documents the policy of apartheid, again in terms of industrial conditions, occupations, government treatment of natives, and living conditions in the large cities. Soon the discussion is not about South Africa at all, but about the use of emphasis and language and photographic style to create an impression. It becomes plain that before inquiry devoted to South Africa can proceed, many materials from many sources must be found.

Our federal government produces documents, books, and pamphlets on an amazing range of topics, from driving a nail to congressional hearings. The wise teacher subscribes to the free *Biweekly List of Selected United States Government Publications*, distributed by the Superintendent of Documents, and periodically requests bibliographies and price lists related to particular government bureaus and topics.[8] A full and current listing of government books and pamphlets, of course, is always available in the issues of the *Monthly Catalog, United States Government Publications*,

---

[8] Special "Price Lists of Government Publications," each dealing with a specified topic or field, can be obtained free on written request from the Superintendent of Documents, Government Printing Office, Washington, D.C. 20402. A few of the price lists that can be particularly useful to the social studies teacher have the following titles and code numbers: 36 *Government Periodicals and Subscription Services;* 81 *Posters and Charts;* 31 *Education;* 71 *Children's Bureau* (publications relating to children and youth); 50 *American History* (Constitution of the United States, Revolutionary War, Civil War, World Wars I and II); 54 *Political Science* (government, crime, District of Columbia); 65 *Foreign Relations of U.S.* (publications relating to foreign countries, United Nations); 70 *Census* (statistics of population, manufactures, agriculture); 35 *National Parks* (historic sites, national monuments); 55 *Indians* (Smithsonian Institution, Fine Arts Commission, archaeology, ethnology); 25 *Transportation, Highways, and Roads* (railroad and shipping problems, postal service); 72 *Homes* (construction, maintenance, community development); 68 *Farm Management* (rural electrification, foreign agriculture, agricultural marketing); 44 *Plants* (culture, grading, marketing, and storage of fruits, vegetables, grasses, grain).

to be found in virtually every school and public library. Much of the material so listed is simply written and is easily adapted for the middle grades. The *Monthly Checklist of State Publications*, similarly useful, records those documents and publications issued by the fifty states and received by the Library of Congress.

Both the teacher (in order to improve his own background of knowledge) and the students should study primary sources of information whenever possible—that is, documents, diaries, tracts, and other firsthand accounts of events and policies. In this respect, various State Department pamphlets and bulletins are particularly interesting in their explanation and defense of current U.S. foreign policies: the pamphlet *U.S. Policy Toward Cuba* (May 1964) describes the assumptions on which U.S. actions in the Caribbean are based; *The United States and Africa* (July 1964) explains our problems in dealing with both the new African nations and the older regimes. Such pamphlets on current affairs help children to analyze causes and effects in politics and economics.

Various instructional or do-it-yourself manuals published by the federal government are useful in model building and other kinds of classroom construction. Farmers' Bulletin No. 1720 of the U.S. Department of Agriculture, for example, offers detailed directions on how to make adobe bricks and how to use the bricks in the construction of pueblo apartments, mission churches, and farm buildings—all very authentic in detail. Authenticity in constructing objects, of course, is extremely important; playthings from a make-believe world merely "give the student concrete ideas of the way things are *not* and discourage any effort to discover the truth."[9] Thus, in making dolls, buildings, masks, clothing, furniture, utensils, or any other objects simulating real life, the children should be led to use authentic construction materials and to follow accurate instructions and procedures.

Filmstrips and Slides

Inexpensive color photography has given rise to slide collections and filmstrips on almost every topic imaginable. Commercial film distributors have produced thousands of film packets, costing from about three to five dollars for thirty or so frames. In addition, many noncommercial organizations or commercial ones not ordinarily in the business of producing educational materials have collections which can be rented, purchased, or borrowed. Many industrial organizations—such as the Association of Ameri-

---

[9] Ernest Horn, *Methods of Instruction in the Social Studies*, Part XV: *Report of the Commission on the Social Studies*, American Historical Assn. (New York: Scribner, 1937), p. 421.

can Railroads and the Dairy Council—offer films which, though intended as advertising or as public relations media, often contain useful views and data. The same is true of films distributed by industrial firms such as airlines or automobile manufacturers. Museums and other repositories also usually lend audio-visual materials: Colonial Williamsburg, for example, has a large loan collection, and the Philadelphia Museum of Art's rental collection contains over 75,000 slides.[10]

Nearly all commercial filmstrips that describe the life of people in other lands suffer from two common defects: they overemphasize physical geography and man's adjustment to his natural environment, and they present scant data for children to reason about. Nearly all of them dictate conclusions about an economy and limit the data to facts in support of the given conclusions. Perhaps even less acceptable are the films distributed by foreign information agencies and travel bureaus—travelogue films that tend to emphasize the scenic and the quaint.

The slides produced by tourists, while they tend to focus on "landmarks," sometimes have an authenticity lacking in the governmental or commercial product. As his eye wanders, the tourist may record beggars and hovels and pretty girls; and although his snapshots may lack the coherence of a film specifically designed for a unit of study, they may still be serviceable. And such films are indeed available. Simply through the efforts of the parents of her students, one first-grade teacher in Chicago managed to gather slides photographed in over twenty different countries. Not every class would be so fortunate, but even in economically depressed areas some surprising collections can be borrowed from local ministers, recreation workers, teachers, and other professional people.

When all the film sources, commercial and noncommercial, are taken together, the clever teacher and the industrious student can squeeze quite good information out of existing slides and filmstrips. For example, a set of filmstrips dealing with a foreign country may be viewed for evidences of cultural change (What are the items that might have come from the United States?) or of advancing technology (One of these shows life in Charlestown, South Carolina, in 1825. The other shows a contemporary home. See what similarities and differences you can find. How can you explain them? What are the advantages and disadvantages of both styles of life? Justify your position). Studying the materials on economics produced by the Elkhart project, first-graders might view a filmstrip picturing a bakery or a colonial home and try to determine the division of labor in these eco-

---

10 Appendix B of R. Murray Thomas and Sherwin G. Swartout's *Integrated Teaching Materials*, rev. ed. (New York: McKay, 1963), lists nearly all the major distributors of filmstrips, slides, motion pictures, recordings, and other audio-visual materials.

nomic units. Third-graders might use a filmstrip on town government as a basis on which to compare the structure of their own municipal government.

The following criteria should be observed in the selection of filmstrips.

1. *Authenticity.* The ideal film maker secures scholarly advice in order to assure that his product combines accuracy and sufficient data for the building of important concepts.

2. *Appropriateness for children.* The text of a film needs careful scrutiny, particularly for the primary levels. Frequently, difficult terms and concepts are used without explanation.

3. *Balance of view.* A balanced presentation of viewpoints and data is a cruel criterion when applied to materials designed for advertising purposes. However, even a noncommercial filmstrip on city housing which shows mansions and pleasant subdivisions but ignores the slums is likewise unbalanced and misleading.

4. *Attention to concept building.* The sequence of frames (or the sequence of slides when the teacher is composing his own arrangement) should be arranged so that examples of a concept are presented before the introduction of the concept itself.

MAKING YOUR OWN. Polaroid and other hand cameras are the teacher's personal means of filming homelife, leisure activities, political affairs, and other local activities that may provide examples of the organizing concepts he wishes to teach his pupils. In fact, it would be well if the school staff together organized its photo taking and accumulated a shared collection of slides.[11]

Factories, commercial establishments, transportation centers, and the like make easy subjects. One teacher has collected Polaroid pictures showing the geography of her town's river valley and the local historic sites. Her children join in this photographic venture; each year a new class adds to the slide collections of the old.

Motion Pictures

All varieties of motion pictures are obtainable from the loan libraries of universities and state departments of education and from travel agen-

---

[11] Sections III and IV of Thomas and Swartout's *Integrated Teaching Materials* give detailed instructions for taking photographs, making filmstrips and slides, and organizing the materials for effective use in the classroom.

cies, embassies, state and federal governments, chambers of commerce, industries, and lobbyists. Again economic geography and the travelogue style tend to mar the accounts of foreign countries. One child's reaction to several such films was, "They all seemed the same. They all went to market in a horse-drawn cart, and they all bargained over prices in the market. Somehow I thought European countries had modern cities where people lived like we do." Nevertheless, motion pictures can animate and vitalize otherwise stock material, and even stereotyped descriptions can be used effectively with the right teaching strategy (Let's look and see what evidence we can find that religion is important to these people. Find all the objects which are kept around as reminders of the past. What are some of the things in the information agency film that the Encyclopaedia Britannica film covered differently? Is there any pattern to the differences?).

Moreover, many films produced by industrial firms or associations give good descriptions of industrial processes, and the art of industrial salesmanship itself makes an interesting object of study.

Some films originally shown on commercial television are now available to educational institutions. The Dupont Company's "Cavalcade of America" of a few years back offers a series of historical vignettes, each dramatizing human interaction well enough to be used as a data source for lessons using organizing concepts of several social sciences. (Radio scripts and recordings, incidentally, are also available from stations, networks, and sponsors.)

Many Hollywood-produced films are appropriate. *Shane,* for example, although the story is somewhat romantic, portrays authentic details in furniture, dress, housing, and tools and gives a vivid picture of the life of the old pioneering West. The movie, too, might lend itself particularly well to a study of values and loyalties.

To Kill a Mockingbird, a little difficult for children in some ways, shows the kind of family interaction that belongs in a social study. *How the West Was Won* uses beautifully authentic sets and brings out some of the American frontier character—though admittedly in a rather quaint or romantic fashion. *Johnny Tremain,* based on the children's book of the same name, portrays a boy's life in Boston at the time of the outbreak of the American Revolution. The historic figures come alive and make decisions, feel emotions, and reveal themselves in their homes and forums.

The strategies of sociology have been relatively neglected by the teacher, but they make the study of fictional interaction a respectable and productive enterprise. Children, studying the values and beliefs of Scout in *Mockingbird,* learn techniques they can apply to life situations. The norms evident among the people of Johnny Tremain's Boston are as fit subjects of study as the political attitudes of Americans today.

Television

Through the medium of television the panorama of current national and international events is now open to nearly on-the-spot study, and in view of the popularity of commercial television among children and its acknowledged influence on their thinking, every teacher should consider opportunities for using television to stimulate inquiry and focus the depth study of news events. Television obviously enlivens facts; from an early age, children can see kings crowned, rockets launched, and presidents discussing current events; an election coverage is history in the making. For children in the upper grades, the documentaries and depth analyses—such as *CBS Reports*, the *NBC White Paper*, and the *ABC News Scope*—are frequently superb sources of information and enlivened commentary. Even the nightly news broadcast can focus the study of current affairs. In the future, as more school systems acquire closed-circuit equipment, all commercial programs recorded on video tape will become potential educational aids to be used as needed right in the classroom.

One should not assume, of course, that children will transfer the rapt attention they give cartoons and action serials to news reports or televised lessons. Television (and the motion picture) must be integrated with other learning activities. Before listening to a newscast, a child must be prepared with questions relating to some specific classroom study, and he must have some measure of background knowledge in order to cope with the level of analysis employed by the professional commentator. Productive listening and watching are no accident; they are products of careful and vigorous preparation.

Closed circuits with taping facilities will also allow children to see and hear video recordings of their own discussions—their own "interaction." The playback of a parliamentary meeting, for example, can be analyzed by the participating children. A debate can be analyzed by a child to determine for himself how well he stated various arguments. A planning discussion can be reviewed for possible improvements in the techniques of planning. Role playing—in which children act out experiences, playing house or store or impersonating pioneers, trainmen, or legislators—can similarly be analyzed *post facto*. Play production may also benefit as the portrayer of Captain John Smith strives to make his words and gestures authentic.

Opaque Projections

Through the use of the opaque projector, a variety of opaque materials—printed pages, pictures, diagrams, maps, coins, and other graphic mat-

Courtesy of the Charles Beseler Co., East Orange, N. J.

On an ordinary screen or wall the opaque projector will reflect photographs, postcards, drawings, student papers, pages from journals and books, maps, plans, charts, and the like, and will even project solid objects such as coins, curios, and biological or geological specimens. In mapmaking, children can trace on a papered wall the reflected contours of an enlarged geographical area and, in the process, learn accuracy in scale, proportion, and outline features.

ter—can be reflected on a screen in a darkened room, thus permitting an entire class to examine an item together without its having to be passed about the room. A teacher possessing but a single copy of a book, for example, can project its pages for all the children to read. Or should an informational book be too difficult for independent reading by children, its pages can be projected and read to them; afterward they can repeat what they have heard in their own words, and the teacher can transcribe, organize, and polish these words and thus provide the children with materials they are capable of reading. Finally, the projection of maps, graphs, tables, and other illustrative materials makes the opaque projector a particularly valuable aid.[12]

The opaque projector is particularly useful whenever children wish to outline a map or mural on a chalkboard or papered wall. A small printed map or picture can easily be reflected, greatly enlarged, upon the desired surface and its outline traced by the children in pencil or chalk. For example, in drawing a mural depicting Bantu life, a group of children might be able, through use of the projected image, to achieve better artistic perspective or more authentic detail, say, in the drawing of huts or utensils. If direct tracing is thought to hinder the children's self-expression in art, perhaps the reflected image can be used merely as a model to be copied freehand.

Trade Books: Juveniles

Trade books—all the commercial fiction and nonfiction, including juveniles, designed for the general public or "trade" and not specifically for schools—are pouring from the presses in annually increasing numbers. In 1963 alone, 2605 *new* juvenile titles (out of a total of almost 25,000 new trade titles) were published in the United States—a 15 percent increase in juvenile output over 1962. Though blessed by this wide selection, the teacher nonetheless has the difficult task of sorting out from among the myriad publications those books most suitable for use in depth studies.

Fortunately, there are available a number of excellent bibliographical guides. *Children's Books to Enrich the Social Studies,* distributed by the National Council for Social Studies (Washington: National Education Assn., 1961), includes annotated lists of 618 books, for all grades, dealing with common social studies topics, and is a "must" reference for any school faculty. The annotations are detailed in their descriptions of content, of treatment of content, and of reading level. The *Children's Catalog,*[13] published with annual supplements and comprising thumbnail annotations of some 2500 children's books, might constitute a basic bibliographical guide for a small school. To be found in virtually any children's room of a public library and in almost every school library, this catalog is indexed by subject, author, and title, so that in a few minutes one can locate the recommended titles on any nation or topic (even such a topic as medieval weapons). May Arbuthnot's *Children and Books* (3d ed.; Chicago: Scott, Fores-

---

[12] Chapter 9 of Murray and Swartout's *Intergrated Teaching Materials* contains a thorough guide to the use of flat pictures as well as to the use of the opaque projector.

[13] 10th ed. (New York: Wilson, 1961); annual supplements, 1962–.

man, 1964) is a thorough guide to children's literature. Its sections on social education include discussions and lists of both fiction and nonfiction and offer several valuable teaching suggestions. Charlotte Huck and Doris Young's *Children's Literature in the Elementary School* (New York: Holt, Rinehart & Winston, 1961), another thorough analysis and guide, gives considerable attention to the social studies. Ruth Tooze and Beatrice Krone's *Literature and Music as Resources for the Social Studies* (Englewood Cliffs, N.J.: Prentice-Hall, 1955) is just what the name implies. A final important guide to children's books on all topics is the current book reviews in *Horn Book Magazine*.

For a number of years Leonard Kenworthy has provided references for materials (films, slides, and recordings as well as books) dealing with culture groups. The appendix of his *Introducing Children to the World* (New York: Harper, 1955) lists children's books (for both upper and lower grades) under headings such as "Fun Around the World" and "Pets Around the World." His regional World Affairs Guides, published by Teachers College of Columbia University, provide comprehensive references to everything from book titles to sources for contacting pen pals.[14] Kenworthy has also written resource units (lists of learning aids pertaining to a specified topic) on individual nations, and many of these are available from the World Affairs Center at Brooklyn College.

In addition, the teacher should become acquainted with the resource units found in curriculum guides published by many states and communities. One of the best guides to the books and other materials describing a particular city is frequently the curriculum guide written by the teachers of that city.

THE SELECTION OF BOOKS. On the matter of selecting quality books, May Arbuthnot offers this cautionary advice:

> Such stories, rich in social meanings but primarily good stories, are few and far between. So, too, good informational stories of the caliber of *Pelle* and *The Little House* are not plentiful. But mediocre or poor informational stories are coming from the presses in staggering

---

[14] The World Affairs Guides published by Teachers College, Columbia University, Bureau of Publications, include *Studying Africa in Elementary and Secondary Schools* (1962), *Studying South America in Elementary and Secondary Schools* (1962), *Studying the Middle East in Elementary and Secondary Schools* (1962), and *Studying the World: Selected Resources* (1962). Two other Kenworthy books containing resources are *Telling the UN Story: New Approaches to Teaching About the UN and Its Related Agencies* (Dobbs Ferry, N.Y.: Oceana, 1963) and *Free and Inexpensive Materials on World Affairs* (New York: Teachers College, 1963).

numbers. Most of them are written to fit a school unit or activity; food supplies in the city, safety, neighborhood stories. Too often these books are very dull reading. They have no sparkle, no element of surprise, no fun about them. Pedantically bent on informing and improving the young, they are examples of the didacticism of our day, and are almost as boring as their moralist predecessors. It is the age-old idea of sugar-coating with a story the informative pill a particular age or period believes in. Just now many writers apparently regard social studies as the pill which has to be overly sweet in order to be accepted by children, but the sugar coating results in just as arid reading as it did in the days when Morton and Sanford were paired in order to exhibit virtue and folly for the benefit of the young mind. To be convincing, children's stories in any field need a theme of sufficient strength to generate a good plot in which things happen and a climax is achieved. When both theme and plot are weak, neither beautiful pictures nor a utilitarian relationship to a unit in social studies can save a book from triviality.[15]

Books selected for the social studies influence a child's literary taste just as strongly as books selected primarily for the teaching of literature and language. Every social studies teacher, therefore, must develop a practical, sharp eye for literary quality. The contrived stuff criticized by Arbuthnot is not difficult to spot.

Our caution extends to other considerations. Despite the overall increase in the number of juvenile titles, there continues to be a serious lack in many subject areas. Communist China, for example, is represented by almost no useful book for children. Except possibly Japan, no Asian nation is represented by enough titles to make a depth study relatively easy. It takes nearly everything written about Africa for children to support even a superficial unit—and then only when the books are supplemented heavily with materials that the teacher has rewritten from adult sources. Asian and Latin American history have seldom been drawn on by children's authors, and many areas of European history are almost closed to children. Except for fictionalized biography, or histories that lean heavily on biography rather than on events and trends, even American history is neglected in many areas (there are, however, notable exceptions).

In short, there are many subject areas for which the teacher must himself write materials or help his children to adapt suitable materials. Nevertheless the picture is not all black.

For the selection of informational books, Huck and Young have suggested several criteria that we paraphrase as follows:

---

[15] *Children and Books* (1957). p. 559. Copyright © 1957 by Scott, Foresman and Company. Printed in the United States of America.

1. *Authenticity and accuracy.* The poor informational book overgeneralizes because its author believes that children cannot deal with the truth. The good books are not afraid of "sometimes," "usually," "apparently," and other words of qualification. The good informational book is also authentic. The author has done careful research on the topic and has checked his findings.

2. *Content and style.* The content should be presented without sugar coating, in a vivid style that does not stint detail. The book should relate to the child's everyday world so that he can easily sense the new information. Realistic fiction should also meet this criterion.

3. *Illustrations.* Pictures, maps, and other illustrations "should blend with the text. They should be accurate, large enough to show detail, and spaced so that the reader does not feel confused, and they should seem to flow with the text. Diagrams should be clearly explained. Photographs should illustrate one or two points instead of being general pictures."[16]

4. *Organization.* Paragraph and section headings, tables of contents, and indexes are all necessary as guides to inquiry; they are particularly necessary if children are to be properly taught reference skills.

In *Children and Books* Arbuthnot devotes over one hundred pages to an analysis of available books, many of which made ideal bases for little units of study.

These social-studies books begin for the youngest as his books begin in every field—with pictures. Big picture books of trains, planes, and farmyards are as beautiful to look at and informative as the four and five year old can comprehend. Then come such forthright narratives as *The Little Auto* and *Pelle's New Suit,* informational stories of unusual charm. When we use such books, we don't say to a child who is entranced with the sequential pictures of *Pelle,* "Now, this is a story about the evolution of wool cloth." We don't have to, because the child who lives with *Pelle* over the years and loves Pelle's blue suit as much as if it were his own will know that evolution by heart. Nor will the child who has pondered over *The Little House* ever see a small dilapidated dwelling in a crowded city street without wondering if it, too, was not once a little house in the country with apple trees by its side and a clear view of the stars. Has this young reader of *The Little House*

---

[16] *Children's Literature in the Elementary School,* p. 132.

learned about the evolution of the cities? Of course he has. He knows it well in terms of one small house made memorable in beautiful pictures and a significant text.[17]

The Fideler Company of Grand Rapids, Michigan, has published a series of books that blend the characteristics of the trade book and those of the textbook on human geography. Each book normally concentrates on a single nation and devotes an unusual amount of space to this limited subject. For example, Vincent H. and Ruth M. Malmstrom's *Norway* (1955) contains about 150 pages of text and vivid pictures, in contrast to a typical social studies textbook that relegates Norway to some ten pages. The coverage of economic geography is thorough—sufficient for a depth study from that point of view. However, the pictures and a portion of the text discuss Norway from other vantage points as well, so that some political and sociological exploration would be possible if supplementary materials were made available.

The American Heritage Publishing Company is issuing a series of American history books carefully researched by scholars and packed with information, illustrations, and excerpts from original sources. For example, Edouard Stackpole, curator of the Mystic Seaport Maritime Historical Association, was consultant in the preparation of *The Story of Yankee Whaling*, a book which includes technical descriptions of sailing and whaling, realistic descriptions of the recruitment of whalers, of their lives and the lives of their wives (the book does not shrink from informing the young reader that few whaling men shipped out more than once), and of shipwrecks and mutinies. The detail seems endless, and the richness of anecdote and the specificity of sources make these books well suited to serious research by the young scholar. Further, they are well balanced and realistic; they include the horrible as well as the gay. (Children, it should be remembered, come to trust books only when they find that there has been no censoring.) Some other titles in the series are *The California Gold Rush; Lexington, Concord, and Bunker Hill; Pirates; Men of Science; Steamboats on the Mississippi; Trappers and Mountain Men; Texas and the War with Mexico.* Six new titles are scheduled every year.

The American Heritage books can be read by upper-grade children or recited to younger and less able readers with help of the excellent illustrations. On a similar reading level are the *Life* magazine series dealing with various countries, religions, and the earth's environment. These books are spectacularly beautiful in illustration; the *Life* cameras have caught many interesting facets of life and art. But even more important, these

---

[17] *Children and Books* (1957), p. 559. Copyright © 1957 by Scott, Foresman and Company. Printed in the United States of America.

books provide excellent data for the building of organizing concepts in sociology and anthropology. Among the titles in the series are *The Arab World, Southeast Asia, Tropical Africa, Israel, Scandinavia,* and *Spain.* (What is still badly needed, however, are books of this sort written specifically for the younger child.)

Scholarly works that deal historically with arts and crafts and with the values they express, measured against life in action, are becoming more plentiful. Christine Price's little gem, *Made in the Middle Ages,* includes passages like the following, which help the child become aware of scholarly sources:

> Clothes do not last as well as armor. Linens, woolens, and silks worn in the Middle Ages have come down to us as fragments, and we have to look at Medieval pictures and statues to see how the people dressed and how fashions changed.[18]

In many little corners of her book lie opportunities for helping children examine human motives. Consider the following:

> Embroideries in threads of silk, gold, and silver were made richer still by the addition of jewels—rubies, sapphires, and pearls. Such clothes were ruinously expensive, and a nobleman might wear half his fortune on his back. Jewelry was an important item for the well-dressed person. Medieval people liked the sparkle of gems, but they valued jewelry for other reasons, as we shall see.[19]

Following through on this last sentence, Price gives the child the opportunity to examine the medieval European's conception of the world:

> Rings set with precious stones were supposed to have strong magic powers. This . . . was expected to cure eye diseases and protect its owner against poisoning. An opal, when wrapped up in a bay leaf, was supposed to make a man invisible. . . . This ring . . . has a secret charm engraved inside it which would not only cure toothache but also calm storms and tempests.[20]

Here in these quoted passages are found the essential characteristics of the truly useful informational book. Price does not simply report "Rings were believed to have magical powers." She presents a few particulars

---

[18] Christine Price, *Made in the Middle Ages* (New York: Dutton, 1961); p. 30.
[19] *Ibid.,* p. 36.
[20] *Ibid.,* p. 39.

from which the general principle can easily be induced.

With her companion book, *Made in the Renaissance,* the two ages, medieval and Renaissance, can be compared in terms of clothing, arms, and decorative objects—all interpreted according to the measure of human values. A child deceived by the notion, for example, that the supernaturalism of the Middle Ages was fully supplanted by the rationalism of the Renaissance might be better enlightened by the following information:

> Rings [in the Renaissance] were the most popular jewelry of all, and the hands of the rich were loaded with rings, almost to the fingertips. People still held to the old belief in the magic power of gems. The turquoise ring on page 30 was supposed to protect its wearer against a fall from his horse, while the rare toadstone, set in this curious ring of horn and silver, was highly valued for its power to guard its owner.[21]

Books, very obviously, continue to be the centrally important aid to learning. And, as we have seen, quality books are available and are discoverable by means of excellent bibliographical guides. Nevertheless, that more and better books are needed is equally obvious—especially, well-written informational books for the younger child and for the slower, poorer reader.

Trade Books: Adult

Though obviously useful for improving a teacher's own knowledge and background, adult trade books can often in some manner also be adapted as instructional materials for children.

Sometimes by simplifying the prose—the vocabulary and style— the teacher can use an adult book to guide his telling of a narrative; perhaps some excerpts might be read verbatim to the children. For example, Bruce Catton's vivid accounts of the Civil War evoke the grimness and bewilderment of battle largely through the words of soldiers writing letters home. Although such books in unaltered form are clearly beyond the grasp of elementary school children, the teacher with a display of battle maps can effectively recite and interpret the complex story of battles —indicating step by step the advances, the flanking movements, the retreats —and he can vivify some of the action by quoting the simple letters of a Yankee or a Reb. At Petersburg, as the coal-miner-turned-soldier crawls

---

[21] Christine Price, *Made in the Renaissance* (New York: Dutton, 1963), p. 33.

through the tunnel to see whether the fuse is still burning toward the explosives, all the children will follow, and they will learn about courage, fear, and rejoicing, and a little more about real life. In the course of such a narrative, children can take notes for later reference and for integration with other materials. One must remember, of course, that the study of a few battles is worth more than any superficial account of an entire war and that anecdotes (*real* anecdotes) of actual events have the most telling effect on children.

Numerous histories, descriptions of contemporary cultures, stories of current events, and many government reports on industry, internal affairs, and foreign affairs can be used in a similar manner—especially if some of the information has been translated into maps, charts, graphs, tables, and other illustrations.[22]

Textbooks

Many textbook series that are designed as the core around which to build a social studies program are accompanied by teachers manuals providing advice on the handling of children, on the arrangement of classroom furniture, on background reading for the teacher, as well as on the use of the texts themselves and other learning materials. Every teacher of the social studies should examine these texts and their manuals for their often excellent suggestions for teaching. The following criteria for judging texts are based on the teaching strategies earlier described.

1. A social studies textbook should include examples of the central organizing concepts of the social sciences. The descriptions of actual events and places should contain sufficient data, and in sufficient detail, so that the children can build these concepts.

2. The textbook should only rarely make a flat, unsupported statement of a general idea or conclusion. The child should be required to construct the important concepts himself after analyzing the available data. The emphasis of the textbook should be on helping the child to learn how to analyze data in the fashion of the social scientist.

---

[22] As we go to press, the McCormick-Mathers Company is beginning a new series of books, each book dealing with a single nation. The first, Seymour Fersh's *The Story of India* (Wichita: McCormick-Mathers, 1965), contains chapters describing many aspects of Indian life, chapters filled with data that can be analyzed with the organizing concepts we have emphasized. Better readers in the upper elementary grades will be able to handle this series.

3. The textbook should confine itself to relatively few topics, each thoroughly explored. One primitive culture studied well is more beneficial than six studied superficially.

4. The textbook should identify sources of data and indicate the presence of bias. Arguments and counterarguments should be presented on all important issues. Similarly, the confusion and perplexity of human relations should not be glossed over. If the data are true and honest, the child can live with perplexity. The notion that a child can grasp only the "big" ideas and not the details runs counter to the evidence on child development.

5. The content of the textbook should be balanced among the several social sciences. If economic data are included to the neglect of political data, for example, the teacher should be warned so that he can compensate.

Original Documents

For developing organizing concepts in the classroom, few current textbooks are instructionally as efficient and informationally as complete as original documents or primary sources. Documents offer a fund of data from which children can build their own concepts. Textbooks usually verbalize ideas and conclusions, and much of the teacher's instruction consists of straightening out the meaning of words.

The depth study of original documents provides the experiences needed by the child to reason out for himself the conditions of life. It does not leave him dependent on a textbook writer's choice of facts in support of a general opinion. The child can engage in the same activities as the behavioral scientist who seeks data for the development of concepts.

The study of urban renewal, for example, succeeds best if children concentrate on a single renewal project and explore all the arguments, pro and con, given in the very words of the protagonists. Examining not only the physical and sociological benefits of urban renewal but also the saddening breakup of human attachments that comes with the destruction of an old neighborhood, children will begin to realize the complexity of human problems—problems that a few simple generalizations cannot possibly explain. They will better understand the sentiments expressed in a feature article in the *New York Times:* "For eight years they have seen it coming, but until last month they hoped some miracle would prevent it. To these residents of Bellevue South, the death of their neighborhood will be excruciating. To an outsider, the seven-block area bounded by 23d and 30th Streets and First and Second Avenues presents a dreary prospect. Yet those who dwell there say it possesses the warm human qualities of a fine neighborhood."[23]

At the school of education of the University of Chicago, one graduate student has assembled pamphlets, editorials, and stories on urban renewal at Lake Meadows on Chicago's South Side—all the materials selected, adapted, and arranged for use by elementary school children.[24] The children's study begins with the basic arguments in favor of urban renewal:

> The construction of Lake Meadows by the New York Life Insurance Company at a cost "in excess of $35,000,000," has produced a vital influence-for-good on the near southside area where it replaced some of the city's worst slums. . . .
>
> The real impact . . . results from the development of a first-rate housing project on an interracial basis. If it's successful, and it is, it could lead to other developments throughout the city.[25]

This report from a Negro community newspaper proceeds to discuss problems and successes in the history of the Lake Meadows housing project. (Petty crimes, for instance, are shown to have decreased in the improved area, while on the other hand crimes like grand larceny that feed on middle-class neighborhoods have become more prevalent.) However, if the children studying this report tend to leap to the conclusion that the old residents of the neighborhood were generally delighted with all the social and economic uplifting encouraged by urban renewal, they are soon led to revise their opinions. They read more arguments—counterarguments of community groups that have desperately resisted urban renewal. In the course of their study the children also get involved in planning and architectural problems, such as those described in pamphlets distributed by the Department of Urban Renewal of the City of Chicago.

A sixth-grade class at the University of Chicago Laboratory School has also utilized original documents in its study of the muckrakers of the early twentieth century. As a guide to inquiry, they use two questions, one derived from political science (What were the types of power which were used to control the workers, as the muckrakers saw it?), the other from economics (What were the conditions of food and shelter that the

---

[23] John Sibley, "A Wrecking Ball Casts a Shadow," *New York Times*, November 12, 1964, p. 35.

[24] Credit is due Miss Jean Paulson, education student at the University of Chicago in 1964.

[25] A. S. Young, "Common Crime Goes Down in Project Area, Police Report," *Chicago Defender*, November 15, 1962.

muckrakers objected to?).[26] Studying Upton Sinclair's *The Jungle*, the writings of Jacob Riss, and the Grissom Report, as well as articles from *Collier's, Everybody's,* and other periodicals, the children attempt to catalog information that answers these questions. The reconstructed picture of the times that results from these muckraking tales is that of the interlocking power of business, government, and news media. They also receive a good idea of the economic conditions about which the muckrakers complained. And just as important, they perceive the journalistic techniques used to rouse public opinion.

A teacher, it should be noted, need not rely solely on journal articles and official documents. Many trade books include what might be called authenticated data (often in quantity) and reprint original source material. The American Heritage books mentioned earlier contain old pictures and excerpts from diaries and other primary sources—all useful to the child engaged in depth studies.

In summary, *the closer the child can be brought to the real people and conditions that he is studying, the more facts he will learn, the better reasoner he will become, and the more thoroughly will he absorb the organizing concepts of the social scientists.* Each depth study requires that the teacher find authentic materials, rewrite them or cast them in a form suitable for children, and carefully guide the child's fumbling first steps through the data. The child will make a good many mistakes, but he must be allowed to, and he must be given the time and the guidance to learn to right himself.

Programed Instruction

The programed-instruction approach analyzes a subject into its component parts and arranges the parts into a sequential learning order. (For example, to teach latitude and longitude, programed materials would begin by exploring contributing ideas such as "sphere," "scale," and "axis" —each idea presented in some kind of logical, pedagogical sequence.) At each step in his reading or listening, the child is expected to make a response and is immediately informed of the correctness or incorrectness of his answer; however, the program is supposedly so constructed with sufficient clues that incorrect answers are held to a minimum. The resultant high percentage of correct answers is thought to encourage the child's

---

[26] Credit is due Miss Barbara Hughes, education student at the University of Chicago, for selecting the materials and teaching the unit. The cooperating teacher was Mr. John Patrick.

progress, to give him a continual feeling of success. The dependence on correct answers is thought to ensure that a child will fully understand one component idea before proceeding to the next and that in the end he will understand all the ideas that contribute to a general conclusion or a general concept. Programed material may take the form of workbooks, textbooks, cards, or separate worksheets, or it may be presented in a variety of so-called teaching machines.

Programed instruction does not confront the child with a difficult problem and help him to fumble toward a solution. It rather feeds him little questions that are easy to answer and that gradually build up to the solution of what might have been a difficult problem. Because the program is designed so that the child can proceed in steps, it is well suited for independent instruction—each child proceeding at his own rate. If a child moves slowly, no harm is done, because he is working by himself and faster workers are independent of him. Consequently, programed instruction may be important for helping children of different abilities to learn verbal material that all are expected to learn in the same form. Concepts such as "latitude" and "longitude" might be examples of suitable material for this kind of instruction, for they are useful to all and difficult to teach by conventional methods.

To date there are few programed materials available in elementary social studies. However, teachers should keep posted on the publications of the Center for Programed Instruction at Teachers College, Columbia University, and should consult the publications of the U.S. Office of Education,[27] which provides guides to new materials and reports on their effectiveness.

Differences in Learning Ability

The individual responses to any single teaching strategy differ widely among children. Some first-graders will be able to do things that sixth-graders cannot. In any one classroom there will be different reading rates and comprehension levels and differences in ability to make practical use of concepts. Everyone should be grateful that this is so. The purpose of instruction is not to homogenize the abilities of the children but to help each to sharpen the critical tools in his own way and to the best of his ability.

---

[27] Center for Programed Instruction in cooperation with the U.S. Department of Health, Education, and Welfare, *Programs '62: A Guide to Programed Instructional Materials Available to Educators by September, 1962* (Washington: Government Printing Office, 1962).

The cooperative planning of instruction, therefore, should allow different children to play different roles according to their ability and needs. A child unable to summarize information should be given practice in analyzing details and collecting main ideas. A child unskilled in the use of encyclopedias or other reference works might be assigned to work with a child who is proficient and can offer help. A child with reading problems—in structural analysis, comprehension, retention, "word attack," or whatever—should receive added reading instruction focusing on the specific deficiency, perhaps even special remedial instruction.

Occasionally children may be temporarily separated into small groups to pursue individual inquiries. Sometimes the grouping may be determined on the basis of academic ability, the three or more groups being charged with tasks of different levels of difficulty. Sometimes children of different intellectual or scholastic abilities can be brought together if they all share a common and specific problem, such as an inability to take notes well or an inability to comprehend spatial relationships on a map or globe. Sometimes children can be joined merely because they share a common interest. In any event, these groupings should indeed be temporary. The interdependent climate should enable each child to feel respect from his peers and from the teacher; perhaps more than anything else this respect and consequent self-respect will help to lift the slow and the shy.

The climate of the classroom should not embarrass or discourage the slow learner (the sixth-grader, for instance, who must rely on a picture book for information); rather it should provide him with important questions and challenge his thinking. On the other hand, no one should ridicule —and thereby possibly stifle—the energies of the bookish child who digs through original documents and scrambles for the truth until he finds it. Teaching teams and other organizational devices help to care for individual differences. Basically important, however, is the point of view of the teacher. If one loves human diversity and works to increase it, then the "problem" of individual learning rate melts into insignificance.

Summary

All varieties of instructional materials and activities are useful in social science education—field trips, resource persons, realia, models, television, motion pictures, slides, filmstrips, books, and original documents. Nevertheless, the teaching materials obviously must be appropriate to the requirements of the chosen teaching strategies. Depth studies employing the organizing concepts of the social sciences must give children access to quantities of data about which they can reason—and to which they can later apply acquired concepts. One of the teacher's major tasks thus is to familiarize himself with the great quantity of available trade books, texts, pictures, maps, and other documents.

Different levels of intellectual and scholastic ability must also be considered in selecting materials and organizing children into groups. For example, the slow learner is often stimulated by devices such as the opaque projector; the more inventive and quicker child by original documents.

INQUIRIES

1. Select a topic that you feel would be suitable for the first grade, such as the comparative study of an American family and a family of another country or culture, perhaps an Eskimo family. Using sources such as the *Children's Catalog* and *Children's Books to Enrich the Social Studies*, locate and review the appropriate trade books.

2. Similarly develop a resource unit for another topic, such as "Games Around the World," using, especially, the bibliographical works by Leonard Kenworthy and by Ruth Tooze and Beatrice Krone.

3. Suppose you were to help your fifth grade study a battle of the Revolutionary War. Find an adult book describing the battles, select one, and prepare the maps and the narrative you will deliver.

4. Assemble tables of data concerning the development of the iron and steel industries in the United States. What strategies could be used to analyze the data?

5. Select a filmstrip that could be used to detect the "values" of a people. Plan a lesson using that concept.

6. Find a motion picture that exhibits some idea about government. Evaluate it for use with children and develop a strategy for its use.

7. In a curriculum guide, find the recommended units for a second-grade curriculum. What resource visitors would be useful? How?

References and Readings

ARBUTHNOT, MAY HILL. *Children and Books.* 3d ed. Chicago: Scott, Foresman, 1964. (Quotations appearing in this chapter are from the revised edition, 1957.)

BARNES, EMILY. *Children and Architecture.* New York: Teachers College, 1932.

BAXTER, TOMPSIE, and YOUNG, BESS M. *Ships and Navigation.* New York: Teachers College, 1933.

Center for Programed Instruction in cooperation with the U.S. Department of Health, Education, and Welfare. *Programs, '62: A Guide to Programed Instructional Materials Available to Educators by September, 1962.* Washington: Government Printing Office, 1962.

Children's Catalog. 10th ed. New York: Wilson, 1961. Annual supplements, 1962–.

EAKRIGHT, JESSIE B., and YOUNG, BESS M. *Adventuring with Toys.* New York: Teachers College, 1933.

HUCK, CHARLOTTE S., and YOUNG, DORIS A. *Children's Literature in the Elementary School.* New York: Holt, Rinehart & Winston, 1961.

HUGHES, AVAH W. *Carrying the Mail.* New York: Teachers College, 1933.

KENWORTHY, LEONARD S. *Introducing Children to the World.* New York: Harper, 1955.

———. *Studying Africa in Elementary and Secondary Schools.* New York: Teachers College, 1962.

———. *Studying South America in Elementary and Secondary Schools.* New York: Teachers College, 1962.

———. *Studying the Middle East in Elementary and Secondary Schools.* New York: Teachers College, 1962.

———. *Studying the World: Selected Resources.* New York: Teachers College, 1962.

National Council for the Social Studies. *Children's Books to Enrich the Social Studies.* Washington: National Education Assn., 1961.

THOMAS, R. MURRAY, and SWARTOUT, SHERWIN G. *Integrated Teaching Materials.* Rev. ed. New York. McKay, 1963.

TOOZE, RUTH, and KRONE, BEATRICE PERHAM. *Literature and Music as Resources for the Social Studies.* Englewood Cliffs, N.J.: Prentice-Hall, 1955.

WRIGHT, LEILA B. *A First Grade at Work.* New York: Teachers College, 1932.

Current Social Studies Projects

New materials for elementary social studies are being prepared at a good rate. The individuals listed with the following ongoing projects may be contacted for information. (Credit for this listing is due John U. Michaelis of the School of Education, University of California, Berkeley.)

ANTHROPOLOGY CURRICULUM STUDY PROJECT. Malcolm C. Collier, Department of Anthropology, Univ. of Chicago, 5632 S. Kimbark Ave., Chicago, Ill. 60637.

BASIC CONCEPTS IN HISTORY AND SOCIAL SCIENCE. Edwin C. Roswenc, Dept. of American Studies, Amherst College, Amherst, Mass. 01002.

DEVELOPMENT OF A SEQUENTIAL CURRICULUM IN ANTHROPOLOGY FOR GRADES 1–7. Wilfred Bailey, Dept. of Sociology and Anthropology, Univ. of Georgia, Athens, Ga. 30601.

ELEMENTARY SCHOOL ECONOMICS PROGRAM. Robert Lee, Dept. of Industrial Relations, Univ. of Chicago, Chicago, Ill. 60637.

ELKHART, INDIANA, EXPERIMENT IN ECONOMIC EDUCATION. Joseph A. Rueff, Coordinator of Economic Education, Roosevelt School, 215 E. Indiana Ave., Elkhart, Ind. 47901.

IDENTIFICATION OF MAJOR CONCEPTS FROM THE SOCIAL SCIENCES. Roy A. Price, Dept. of Education, Syracuse Univ., Syracuse, N.Y. 13210.

THE LINCOLN FILENE CENTER FOR CITIZENSHIP AND PUBLIC AFFAIRS. Franklin Patterson, Tufts Univ., Medford, Mass. 02155.

A PROGRAM OF CURRICULUM DEVELOPMENT IN THE SOCIAL STUDIES AND HUMANITIES. Elting E. Morison, Educational Services, Inc., 108 Water St., Watertown, Mass. 02172.

SERVICE CENTER FOR TEACHERS OF HISTORY. Walter Randall, Jr., American Historical Assn., 400 A St., S.E., Washington, D.C. 20003.

A SOCIAL SCIENCE CURRICULUM FOR GRADES EIGHT–TEN FOCUSING ON THE ANALYSIS OF CONTROVERSIAL PUBLIC ISSUES. Donald Oliver, School of Education, Harvard Univ., Cambridge, Mass. 02138.

SOCIAL STUDIES CURRICULUM GUIDES AND MATERIALS FOR GRADES K–14. Edith West, College of Education, Univ. of Minnesota, Minneapolis, Minn. 55414.

SOCIOLOGY IN ELEMENTARY SOCIAL STUDIES. Bruce Joyce, Dept. of Education, Univ. of Chicago, Chicago, Ill. 60637.

Chapter 13

SKILLS FOR HANDLING SYMBOLS: MAPS, CHARTS, GRAPHS, AND WORDS

Man has learned to communicate using language and visual symbols that refer to objects, qualities, processes, and ideas. In the social sciences, as in all branches of knowledge, we find both a specialized language—represented by words like *norms, values, power,* and *culture*— and a variety of visual symbolic systems called maps, charts, and graphs. Both means of communication enable man to represent information about economics, politics, and other facets of life compactly and meaningfully. In his education the child must learn to recognize these special words and symbols, to analyze them, and to understand their referents or meaning. In addition, as in any worthwhile use of language, he must acquire an ability to use words accurately and fluently and to create maps, charts, and graphs that organize the data and concepts he wishes to communicate.

Maps, graphs, and charts are *systems* or arrangements of visual symbols. Thus, to understand and use them, the child must learn not only the meaning of each symbol (that is, each cartographic symbol representing a hill, a city, or a species of vegetation) but also the meaning presented by these symbols in combination (in other words, the conventions we employ in combining these symbols in a map).

The vocabulary of the social sciences may be taught using a number of strategies. One may proceed inductively, in the manner outlined in earlier chapters: the children are led to work with data first, exploring examples of a concept like "sanction" before the concept itself is actually discovered by name. Another strategy, deductive in nature and useful particularly in presenting geographic concepts, is to present a word like *peninsula* and then illustrate it with pictures and with its symbol or outline on a map. Finally, of equal importance is the strategy that gets children into the habit of using dictionaries and other reference works upon encountering unfamiliar words in their reading.

A note of caution: many textbooks and other books for children introduce new words and concepts at a rate far too rapid for the intended audience; studying such books can therefore become merely a confusing journey through verbalisms and meaningless words. Teachers must become sensitive to this large symbol load in many reading materials. In developing a topic like the American Revolution, for example, a teacher must prepare his children for their encounter with words like *Whig* and *Tory* and phrases like *taxation without representation* and *economic causes.*

Maps

MAPMAKING. Perhaps no means of acquiring an understanding of maps is quite so effective as the actual making of maps. From the child's first year in school—when he learns to map the room, the school, and the neighborhood—to the day when he can make a series of map overlays showing how various factors affect, say, agricultural production in Italy, the child learns through mapmaking to represent reality in a more compact and symbolic form. He learns scale, legend, orientation, and the other cartographic principles as they serve his needs to handle data and ideas.

For children aged eight to twelve, Harold Tannenbaum and Nathan Stillman have recently authored a kit for mapmaking that includes a compass, a transit, a protractor, and other measuring devices.[1] Of particular interest is the accompanying instructional booklet that teaches the child to make picture maps and landmark maps, to orient a map according to the compass directions of north and south, east and west, to draw maps to scale using measuring cords, to interpret scales on various maps, to use graph paper in mapmaking, to employ protractor and transit, to use triangulation to measure hills, and to translate these measurements into contour maps. All these self-instructive guidelines involve simple and pleasant activities that can be adapted to a thousand personal and classroom needs. Geographic and geometric knowledge—such as knowledge of direction, projections, and triangulation—is instilled in the child as he progresses through the experiments. In other words, the cartographic method is employed to teach the child geographic concepts; the child actually learns scientific mapmaking. With a minimum of help, even the child aged six or seven can do many of the lessons; the older child can use the material with considerable independence. The teacher, incidentally, would do well to

---

[1] *Science Book-Lab: Map-Making* (New York: Science Materials Center, 1963). See the illustration on page 228.

A globe, in approximating the curvature of the earth, is the only true representation of the surface of our planet. That a flat map must in some way distort this curved surface can be demonstrated to children by attempting to flatten a slit tennis ball—an impossible feat without stretching or tearing the rubber out of shape. Only a globe can show simultaneously the correct <u>shape</u> of surfaces, all <u>areas</u> in true proportion, accurate <u>distances,</u> and true <u>direction.</u> (The various projections used in flat maps can accurately represent one or two of these properties, but only at the expense of severely distorting the others.) Thus a

globe should be used in every classroom as a basic reference to assure the development of accurate concepts of physical geography—especially such concepts as the equator and the poles, latitude and longitude, the great circle routes, the change of seasons and of night and day, and the directions of the compass. The construction of globes—as depicted in this series of photographs of fifth-graders—is important because it compels children to put geographic concepts to practical use; the concepts do not remain mere verbal abstractions but rather become working tools, visually conceived.

Courtesy of Betty Ann Cacioppo and the University of Chicago Laboratory School

examine the arrangements of activities in the book, for the sequential programing that builds one idea on another is excellent.

Among other aids to mapmaking are the elementary atlases that explain map concepts simply enough to guide the young cartographer. "Conservation trays" are also helpful teaching aids. Modeled into hills and valleys and other natural features, the soil in these waterproof trays is subjected—by means of water pumps—to simulated rain and streams in order to show the effects of erosion, the patterns of drainage, and the techniques of soil conservation. Because the experimenter himself must mold the soil into topographic features, every child learns skills and devices similar to those used in making a relief map.

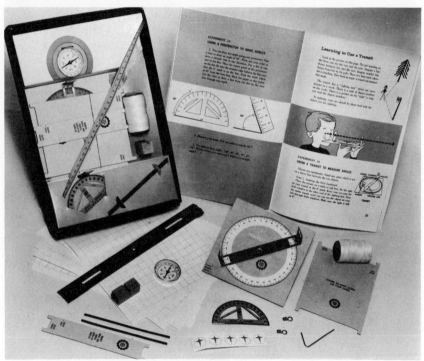

Courtesy of Science Materials Center, Inc., New York

Mapmaking kits—such as this Science Book-Lab: Map-Making, *prepared by Harold E. Tannebaum and Nathan Stillman—teach the child not only how to practice the elementary principles of surveying and cartography but also how to read and interpret maps. Teaching the child concurrently how to interpret maps and how to construct maps is an extension of the inductive teaching strategy urged elsewhere in this volume.*

The principle, simply stated, is that *learning how to interpret maps and learning how to construct maps (that is, how to translate data into graphic symbols) should proceed concurrently.* For example, a group of first-graders may first use a published map to locate the sites of churches, stores, and railroads in their community, but they must immediately begin construction of their own map, using some kind of symbolic representation of churches, stores, and railroads. Or the sequence may be reversed: map-making may slightly precede map interpreting. After measuring a local hill by means of triangulation, a group of fourth-graders may symbolize that hill on their own relief map; then they may study a contour or relief map of the United States to learn how elevations are represented by the professional cartographer. The possible teaching strategies are limitless: for example, the map kits available from many airlines offer excellent descriptions of cartographic projections, air routes, and climatology; these kits could be studied by children who wish to draw polar projections showing water surfaces, ice formations, or climate.

FLOOR MAPS AND MODELED RELIEF MAPS. For very young children in the primary grades, realistic three-dimensional maps are perhaps the most easily understood of all types of graphic representations. Using blocks, boxes, and cardboard, children can make a simple floor layout of box houses, paper trees, and wooden automobiles, all simulating a map of their neighborhood. Similarly, they can lay out a farm with farmhouse, barn, silo, fences, trees, and animals. Airports, harbors, railroad yards, zoos—almost any identifiable locale can be represented in a floor map. Sand-table maps decorated with miniature cutout buildings are realistic and possess the added advantage of topographical representation—indented lines for roads, mounds for hills and mountains, depressions for bodies of water.

The making of modeled relief maps and globes—constructed from materials like papier-mâché or burlap and patching plaster—comes closer to true cartography. In such maps the elevation or vertical scale is almost always highly exaggerated relative to the horizontal scale. But aside from this inevitable distortion, authenticity can be achieved if the children are so encouraged, and in the process of construction many map and globe skills come into play.

COMPARING MAPS IN THE SEARCH FOR INFORMATION. In an earlier chapter we noted how a map showing waterways on the Atlantic seaboard and a map showing the distribution of population in the American colonies might be compared to determine the importance of water transportation to people living in a wilderness before the advent of modern technology. In an interpretation of this kind we are using maps not necessarily for the

PROBABLE LOCATION OF NATIVE INDIAN PEOPLES
BEFORE COLUMBUS DISCOVERED THE NEW WORLD

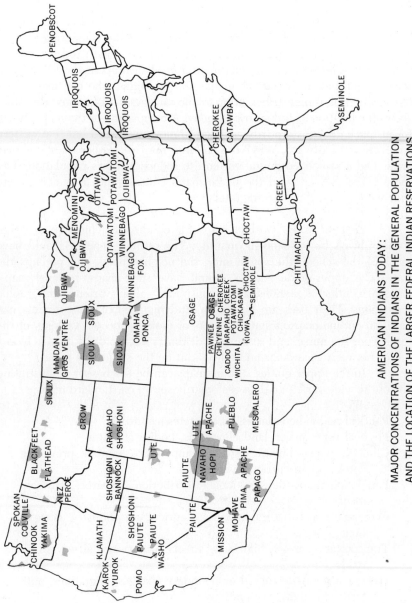

AMERICAN INDIANS TODAY:

MAJOR CONCENTRATIONS OF INDIANS IN THE GENERAL POPULATION

AND THE LOCATION OF THE LARGER FEDERAL INDIAN RESERVATIONS

specific purpose that the cartographer had in mind; rather we are comparing two or more maps and using them for our own purpose.

This particular use of materials, of course, is characteristic of any kind of imaginative, scholarly inquiry. For example, by comparing the two maps on the preceding pages and adding information gathered from documents and other sources, one can learn a good deal about the history and sociology of Indian migrations in the United States. The one map shows the location of Indian tribes prior to the voyage of Columbus; the other shows the location of Indian tribes today. A comparison of the maps shows, for instance, that eastern tribes tended to move westward but few western tribes moved eastward. Why? the children may ask. Other questions may arise: Did a prolonged migration tend to reduce a tribe's population? Did those tribes that adopted the white man's culture tend to remain where they were or did they also migrate?

OUTLINE MAPS. Outline maps for children to complete in detail should always be on hand in quantity. The primary teacher should have maps of the school, the community, the neighborhood, and perhaps the state. The upper-grade teacher should have state maps, regional maps, maps of continents, nations, and hemispheres—all in various cartographic projections. Their uses are legion. In studying "school," first-graders can paste on outline maps various pictures—of desks, of people walking, of the teacher, of the nurse, and so forth. Exit routes for fire drills or merely any routes between classrooms and offices can be the subject of maps.

In the upper grades, outline maps can be the bases for illustrating any of the wide variety of data customarily shown on standard maps:

Political maps—boundaries, cities, states, countries
Physical relief maps—land elevations, bodies of water
Climatic maps—climatic regions, temperature, rainfall, prevailing
    winds, ocean currents, vegetation
Population maps—density, racial distribution, resources, environment
Economic maps—natural resources, agriculture, industry, occupations
Transportation maps—highways, streets, waterways, airways, railroads
Historical maps—territorial or boundary changes, migrations, military campaigns, explorations
Ideational or cultural maps—distribution of religions; locales of works of literature, music, and art; locales of native sports
Sightseeing maps—historic sites, scenic places

Using the opaque projector, the children through tracing can transfer the information from individual outline maps to one large mural map, thus combining political, topographical, climatic, cultural, and other data and permitting an analysis of the relations between the data. Or perhaps the individual maps can be retraced on separate sheets of cellophane or polyethylene in order to create overlay maps, which can also be used for analyzing relations.

LEARNING THE VOCABULARY AND SKILLS FOR USING MAPS. Because maps are symbolic representations employing many geometric and geographic terms and concepts, children must gradually develop the language of maps. Almost every general map requires the user to comprehend such spatial concepts as latitude, longitude, scale, compass direction, elevation, and sea level. Also necessary is the vocabulary of land forms, such as archipelago, peninsula, alluvial fan, inlet, gulf, plateau, and strait. For his own information and for instructional techniques, a teacher might consult these two reference works on cartography: Ruby M. Harris, *Handbook of Map and Globe Usage* (Chicago: Rand McNally, 1959); Ervin Raisz, *General Cartography*, 2d ed. (New York: McGraw-Hill, 1948). The first contains suggested activities for the classroom. In the second work, the section on the history of cartography could provide the teacher with background for an interesting classroom study.

The school faculty must identify the essential concepts and skills to be learned and then arrange them in the curriculum in some kind of sequential order, putting first things first. (On pages 234–240 are printed two skill-development charts—one distributed by the Chicago Public Schools, the other published by the Denoyer-Geppert Company.) Next, diagnostic tests must be prepared so that each teacher can easily identify the vocabulary, the skills, and the concepts that the class members have and have not learned. Each teacher should plan instruction on the basis of the test and keep progress records (to be passed on to the teacher in the next grade level). Obviously learning rates differ so greatly from child to child that grade placement of map skills (the determination of the grade levels at which specific skills should be introduced) cannot be exact and inflexible, but a sequential chart will permit a teacher to measure the relative progress of his class and to differentiate instruction for individual children. To repeat a note of caution: to concentrate on a very few concepts, words, or skills at any one time is the wisest course—particularly in dealing with the slow learner, who is the very one we are tempted to rush so that he will be brought up to the class average. The slow learner, however, achieves better progress and feels more confident when he is not overwhelmed with learning tasks.

SUGGESTED SEQUENCE CHART FOR MAP AND GLOBE SKILLS
BOARD OF EDUCATION, CITY OF CHICAGO

The grade placement of the map and globe skills suggested in the following table is flexible. With each group of pupils, the teacher will find it necessary to make adjustments according to individual abilities, previous learnings, and topics of interest. Any selection should be based on the specific need for this skill and the immediate, practical use which can be made in understanding the problem or topic under study. The skills should begin with simple concepts and understandings, and the experiences should progress successively to include more complex understandings and broader generalizations at each grade level.

	K	1	2	3	4	5	6	7	8
ABILITY TO EXPRESS SELF ON MAPS	▷————————————————————————→								
MAKING AND CONSTRUCTING MAPS									
Reading and making maps	▷————————————————————————→								
ABILITY TO ORIENT AND NOTE DIRECTIONS USING MAPS									
Using maps and globes to learn directions and map orientations									
Left and right	▷——————————————————————→								
Up and down	·····	▷———————————————————→							
North and south	·····	▷———————————————————→							
East and west	·········		▷————————————————→						
The 4 main in-between directions				▷——————————————→					
ABILITY TO LOCATE PLACES AND TO EXPRESS RELATIVE LOCATION ON MAPS AND GLOBES									
Using maps and globes to locate key places									
Continent	·····	▷——————————————————→							
Country	·········		▷————————————————→						
State	·············			▷—————————————→					
Province	·········				▷————————————→				
City	·············			▷—————————————→					
Capital	········			▷—————————————→					
Historical places	········			▷—————————————→					
Points of interest	········			▷—————————————→					

······· Readiness

▷ Formal introduction

————→ Simple to more complex understandings

	K	1	2	3	4	5	6	7	8

Understanding the use of map grids for specific location

North Pole and South Pole

Equator

Tropics of Cancer and Capricorn

Arctic Circle and Antarctic Circle

Great circle routes

Latitude and longitude—degree

Low, middle, and high latitudes

Understanding the relationship between surface features and man's ways of living

Elevation

Relief

Slope

Mountain

Hill

Plateau

Plain

Valley

Moraine

Canyon

Using globes to understand man's exploration into space

ABILITY TO READ MAPS AND NOTE DISTRIBUTIONS

Using map symbols and reading the map legend

Color and pattern

Relief symbols

Pictorial symbols

Semipictorial symbols

Abstract symbols

Identifying land forms

Continent

Island

Coastline

Harbor

Delta

Peninsula

Isthmus

Cape

Identifying water forms

Ocean

Sea

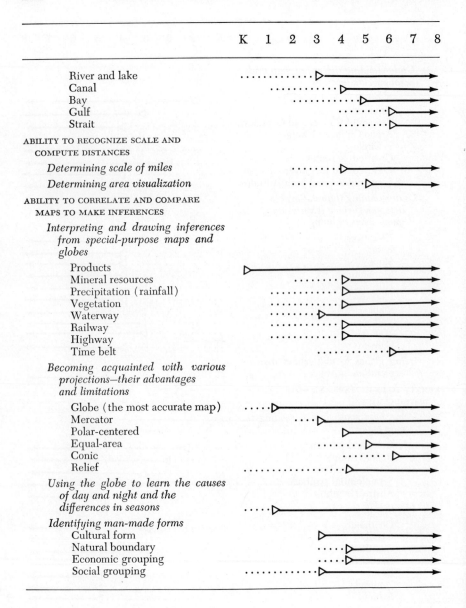

	K	1	2	3	4	5	6	7	8

River and lake

Canal

Bay

Gulf

Strait

ABILITY TO RECOGNIZE SCALE AND
COMPUTE DISTANCES

Determining scale of miles

Determining area visualization

ABILITY TO CORRELATE AND COMPARE
MAPS TO MAKE INFERENCES

*Interpreting and drawing inferences
from special-purpose maps and
globes*

    Products

    Mineral resources

    Precipitation (rainfall)

    Vegetation

    Waterway

    Railway

    Highway

    Time belt

*Becoming acquainted with various
projections—their advantages
and limitations*

    Globe (the most accurate map)

    Mercator

    Polar-centered

    Equal-area

    Conic

    Relief

*Using the globe to learn the causes
of day and night and the
differences in seasons*

Identifying man-made forms

    Cultural form

    Natural boundary

    Economic grouping

    Social grouping

Service Publication #M44   *Denoyer-Geppert Company, Chicago, Illinois 60640*

Suggested Sequence for Globe and Map Skills
Grades 1-6, Jan. 1958, P.S. 116, Queens, New York City

DIRECTIONS AND DISTANCES	LOCATING PLACES	READING AND INTERPRETING SYMBOLS ON MAPS	DEVELOPING CONCEPTS	GEOGRAPHICAL TERMS ON GRADE LEVELS
GRADE 1				
Developing sense of direction, e.g., left, right. Use of further, nearer, etc. Number of blocks to a specific store.	Placing objects in proper relationships when building with blocks. Observing surface features on neighborhood trips.	Representing objects by blocks, e.g., automobiles, boats. Representing hill on sandbox. Large floor map with aid of teacher.	Observing pictures and drawing conclusions. Understanding that information can be summarized on charts.	bridge water river
GRADE 2				
Near enough to walk. Number of blocks to different stores. North, East, South, West. Position of sun during day.	Neighborhood walks. Map of school block.	Large floor map with aid of teacher, using pictures as symbols. Dramatizing bridges, rivers, etc.	Studying and interpreting pictures to determine significant relationships between man and his environment. Understanding that pictures or symbols may represent objects.	ocean mountain lake shore north east south west

Review of Previous Grade Work

DIRECTIONS AND DISTANCES	LOCATING PLACES	READING AND INTERPRETING SYMBOLS ON MAPS	DEVELOPING CONCEPTS	GEOGRAPHICAL TERMS ON GRADE LEVELS

GRADE 3

Blocks to a mile. Time needed to travel distance. Using directions (N,E,S,W) in games in reference to schoolroom.	Map of community with special reference to places of interest. Floor map of classroom and/or school.	Picture symbols on maps, developed by class. Land and water masses on globe.	Earth is round like a ball. Understanding that a large area may be shown on a small map.	sea island forest waterfall globe earth
Cardinal directions in relation to rising sun.	Table maps of clay etc. Maps of class trips.		Understanding there is a greater water area than land area. Understanding sun may be used to determine direction.	

Review of Previous Grade Work

GRADE 4

North and south lines on globe and map. East and west lines on globe and map.	On globe to show where child lives, places read about, places studied. Use of outline maps to label places of interest in N.Y. City.	Globe points north. Simple globe and map language, e.g., ocean, country, river, lake. Using maps to plan trips.	Understanding similarity between globe and earth. Understanding map hung on wall does not change directions of north and south. Understanding earth spins in space (like globe). Earth's rotation causes day and night. Understanding map is really a diagram.	country bay continent desert oasis harbor valley volcano reservoir dam glacier iceberg city state borough
	More detailed school community maps, using symbols.			
	Position of Jamaica with with respect to Queens, of Queens with respect to N.Y.C., of N.Y.C. with respect to N.Y. State.			

Review of Previous Grade Work

DIRECTIONS AND DISTANCES	LOCATING PLACES	READING AND INTERPRETING SYMBOLS ON MAPS	DEVELOPING CONCEPTS	GEOGRAPHICAL TERMS ON GRADE LEVELS

GRADE 5

DIRECTIONS AND DISTANCES	LOCATING PLACES	READING AND INTERPRETING SYMBOLS ON MAPS	DEVELOPING CONCEPTS	GEOGRAPHICAL TERMS ON GRADE LEVELS
Directions of north and south toward poles. Directions, e.g., NE, SE, etc. Directions from equator.	Use of grid system to locate places. Source and mouth of rivers. Position of N.Y. State with respect to U.S. Locating land and water masses on globe and map. Locating the four hemispheres. Locating North and South Poles. Making maps in connection with class trips. Zones on maps and globe. Use of outline maps. Locating places studied. Position of U.S. in relation to other countries affecting our historical development.	Reading and interpreting legend on map, e.g., colors on maps. Recognizing different types of symbols on map. Knowing some symbols represent real places, e.g., oceans; others represent imaginary places, e.g., equator.	Rivers flow downhill and land may slope toward north; therefore rivers may flow to north on maps. Map represents part of globe. All land and water areas are not alike. It's hottest near the equator. Climate becomes colder as we go toward the poles. A hemisphere is half of our earth.	mesa peninsula canal slope mountain range strait cape prairie upland lowland rapids swamps plateau plains gulf hemisphere rotation equator North Pole South Pole Arctic Circle Antarctic Circle Tropic of Capricorn prevailing winds

Review of Previous Grade Work

DIRECTIONS AND DISTANCES	LOCATING PLACES	READING AND INTERPRETING SYMBOLS ON MAPS	DEVELOPING CONCEPTS	GEOGRAPHICAL TERMS ON GRADE LEVELS
		GRADE 6		
Understanding and expressing distance in terms of time as well as by miles. Measuring distance by scale. Prime meridian relationship of longitude to time; of latitude to miles. Great circle routes as shortest distances between two points on globe.	Use of outline maps to note historical and geographical information. Position of U.S. in relation to other countries studied and to bodies of water. Earth is slanted on its axis. Earth revolves around sun. Meridians and latitudes. Using them to locate places studied. The continents.	Reading and interpreting symbols and keys on different kinds of maps, e.g., rainfall, population, political, etc. Color and shadings on map, e.g., surface features. Use of maps for reports. Use of world map to show relationships. Use of relief maps.	Flat map distorts (flatten orange peel to prove). There are different kinds of maps for special purposes. Man's natural environment will influence his activities, e.g., kind of houses lived in. Longitude is related to time. Latitude is related to temperature. Oceans influence weather on continents. Mountains influence rainfall. A city to be large must be accessible. Revolution of earth causes change of seasons.	isthmus water shed reef irrigation altitude meridian latitude tributary axis revolution continent longitude

Review of Previous Grade Work

NOTE: Experience with globe and floor and table maps should precede experience with wall maps.

This chart is neither prescriptive nor exhaustive. The teacher may introduce geographical terms and map skills as the need arises regardless of grade level. This chart is suggested as a guide. The teacher may add to it as she sees fit.

Suggested Sequence for Globe and Map Skills, reprinted by permission of Denoyer-Geppert Company.

MAPS AND THE STUDY OF HISTORY. The study of history relies heavily on the extensive use of maps. First, chronology—which young children often find hard to comprehend—can sometimes be pictured by a series of maps. The growth of American railroads, for example, can be illustrated chronologically by a series of maps, showing the total rail mileage in 1840, 1850, 1860, and so on into the present century. Advancing settlements or territorial expansion can likewise be mapped serially by time units. Second, maps can indicate the conditions of geography strongly influencing the course of history of a nation or a people (this geographic influence is an important consideration even if one rejects pure environmentalism and rightly brings cultural attitudes, dynamic leadership, and mere historical chance into account). Obviously no study of military campaigns, for example, can neglect ridges, hills, open country, or naturally protected flanks. No study of migrations or advancing settlements can overlook either the obstacles of terrain or the natural avenues of easy movement. The American westward movement, for example, might initially be studied in terms of the successive obstacles to migration west—the Fall Line, the Appalachians, the vast forests of the Ohio-Mississippi basin, the semiarid plains, the Rockies, the Sierra Nevada.

Less obvious but no less important uses of maps in historical study are conceivable. A map like that on page 242, showing the ground plan of a California mission village, can be used to develop concepts dealing with the social and economic uses of land; the concepts learned could be applied to present-day conditions. Or possibly land use in this Spanish settlement could be compared with land use in nearby Indian villages or in the pueblos located near other Spanish missions in the Southwest. An additional map pinpointing the sites of Franciscan missions up and down the California coast would be helpful in determining the extent of the commingling of Spanish and Indian cultures.

Reproductions of antique maps can have more than curiosity value. Pre-Columbian conceptions of the world or seventeenth century notions of a Northwest Passage reveal a great deal about our predecessors' attitudes, values, and aspirations. Even old geographical terms that have survived to the present—terms like West Indies, Near East, and Far East—are handy indicators of European ethnocentrism.

Finally, maps of medieval towns, ancient Rome, the Acropolis, Revolutionary Boston, colonial Williamsburg, and the like are necessary if the child is to visualize life and events from the past.[2]

---

[2] To obtain inexpensive maps on various historical subjects, the teacher may write the National Geographic Society and the U.S. Geological Survey. The U.S. Geological Survey distributes aerial maps of the United States which make good outline maps for tracing in historical information.

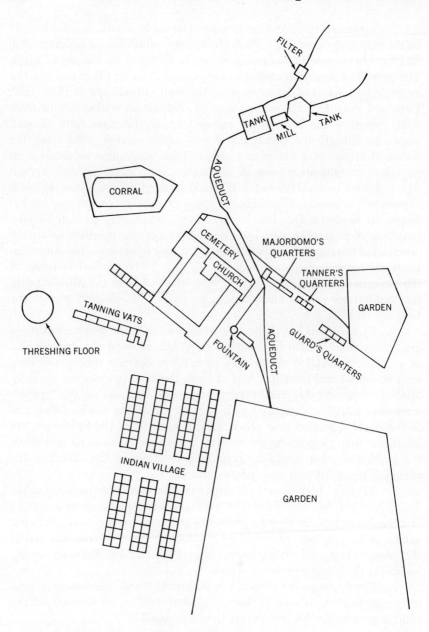

MISSION SANTA BARBARA

Gertrude Stephens Brown, with Ernest W. Tiegs and Fay Adams,
California: Story of Our Past (Boston: Ginn and Company, 1963), p. 96.

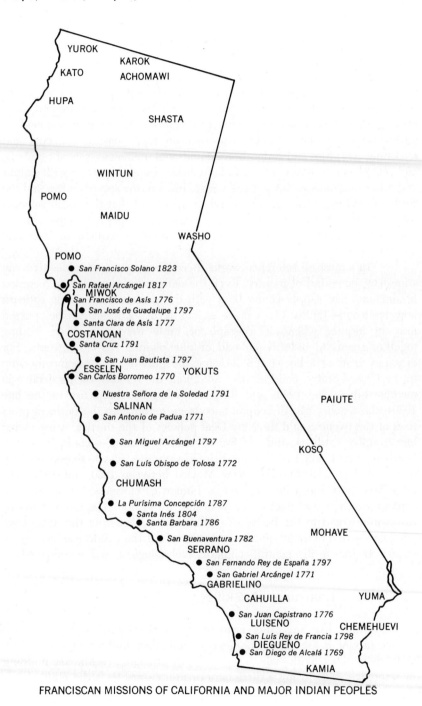

FRANCISCAN MISSIONS OF CALIFORNIA AND MAJOR INDIAN PEOPLES

Graphs, Charts, and Tables

Learning how to decode material compactly represented in charts, graphs, and tables should proceed concurrently with learning how to encode data in such forms—for the same reasons that map reading and mapmaking should go together. However, because the trend in elementary arithmetic is to place greater emphasis on mathematical concepts and reasoning—on ratios and proportions, equational unknowns, sets of numbers, and sets of points—the child nowadays should be able to cope with graphs and other diagrams with far greater ease. Indeed, the social studies and the study of arithmetic can be integrated to the extent that the social sciences use such concepts as the number line (in line graphs), volume (in bar graphs and many pictographs), and percentages (frequent in statistical tables).

In almost all reference works there are graphs and tables that can stimulate some kind of inquiry. Even the data on sporting events recorded in almanacs can supply young boys with the personal motivation to learn how to decode tables. On a more serious level, children can be spurred into an inquiry whenever a graph or table they have been reading together seems to indicate an odd or unexplained trend of events. For example, reading a line graph showing the growth of union membership in the United States, children may ask about the reasons for the decline in membership in the 1920s and the extraordinarily sharp rise in the late 1930s; the teacher can thereupon encourage search into the business practices of the twenties and the New Deal policies of the thirties. A somewhat less complex study—a study of fire control, for example—could be stimulated by a table such as the one printed opposite, which shows the incidence of destructive fires in New Mexico between 1950 and 1957. The table lists those forest fires caused by human carelessness, but it does not explain the degree of man's success in fire prevention. The table shows no discernible trend to the better or to the worse. Pondering the data, however, can generate many questions that can lead the children to search for various factors in fire control—climatic, technological, and sociological.

The Learning of Skills

Skills, like any other element of social science education, should not be taught in isolation, unrelated to any ends but the mastery of the skills themselves. Skills—whether they be mapmaking, vocabulary building, or reference skills (using a dictionary or index)—are tools the child should

DESTRUCTIVE FIRES IN NEW MEXICO, 1950–1957

Year	Man-Caused Forest Fires	Percentage of All Fires
1956	164	13.7
1955	89	23.3
1954	106	14.2
1953	86	12.9
1952	53	11.6
1951	107	17.2
1950	161	24.4

learn to use in the course of a depth study; he uses these tools to get at information that tells him more about human groups or that leads him to the development of the organizing concepts of the social sciences. Even in using Tannenbaum and Stillman's mapmaking kit, the child should be engaged in some depth study—in, say, political science or economics—the resultant map being employed to objectify certain ideas or data in the study.

On rare, brief occasions the focus of classroom instruction may need to turn directly on a skill, particularly if the skill itself is acquired only if one understands some difficult concept. "Projection" in cartography, for example, is a geometric concept that may need to be studied independently before one can begin to acquire the skills of map reading. In general, however, skills can be learned in the course of social science inquiries, for the very simple reason that the whole range of diagrammatic materials—maps, globes, graphs, and tables—are found everywhere in the social sciences, there to be used.

Summary

The teaching strategy recommended in this chapter can be summarized in seven points:

1. Maps, globes, charts, graphs, and tables are all systems for representing information and ideas compactly and symbolically. The skills necessary to use them should be understood as keys which unlock ideas.

2. The child must learn both how to decode information from these symbolic forms and how to encode information for storage and use by other people. These two processes are best learned simultaneously, inas-

much as the processes involved are complementary.

3. The development of concepts and skills for handling data is best carried on in the context of depth studies. There are ample opportunities to teach skills in every social studies unit. Special "skills" units are necessary only rarely and should be primarily mathematical in nature.

4. A good skills program depends on constant diagnosis, measuring a child's progress against the progress levels of a developmental chart. The variation in progress among children will be large.

5. Many abstract concepts relating to maps and globes are difficult to teach to the elementary school child, including key concepts such as latitude and longitude.

6. The young child, nevertheless, can make and interpret maps and globes within certain limits. Skill development may depend greatly on beginnings that are made in the primary school.

7. All elementary school children need rich illustration of concepts. The sixth-grader, for example, needs to make maps of his local community as well as maps showing the distribution of religions around the world. A good principle is to combine experience with local phenomena with experience with faraway things.

INQUIRIES

1. Identify the ways in which first-graders might use maps in their study of the community. What are the terms they should know? What skills should they develop?

2. Globes and maps are now available with chalkboard surfaces to write on. How might these serve fifth-graders who are studying the early explorers of America?

3. Plan a series of experiences designed to teach fourth- or fifth-graders how to use triangulation to measure elevation.

4. How might maps, charts, and graphs be used by third-graders comparing recreation in their own town with recreation in an English town?

5. Examine the skills charts from a number of curriculum guides. Is there any major disagreement about the sequence of

concepts? Can you use the charts to develop a sequence chart of your own to use for diagnosis?

6. How might first-graders studying dolls around the world use a globe in ways that would enhance their study without involving the use of concepts such as latitude and longitude?

7. Assume that many elementary children will not learn how to use the concepts of latitude and longitude effectively. What are the limitations this places on their use of maps and globes? What are the uses that are not affected?

References and Readings

CARPENTER, HELEN McCRACKEN (ed.) *Skill Development in Social Studies.* (33d Yearbook of the National Council for the Social Studies.) Washington: National Education Assn., 1963.

HARRIS, RUBY M. *Handbook of Map and Globe Usage.* Chicago: Rand McNally, 1959.

RAISZ, ERVIN. *General Cartography.* 2d ed. New York: McGraw-Hill, 1948.

————. *Principles of Cartography.* New York: McGraw-Hill, 1962.

SCHINDLER, ALVIN W., and others. "Developing a Sense of Time and Chronology," in *Skills in the Social Studies.* (24th Yearbook of the National Council for the Social Studies.) Washington: National Education Assn., 1953.

TANNENBAUM, HAROLD E., and STILLMAN, NATHAN. *Science Book-Lab: Map-Making.* New York: Science Materials Center, 1963.

Chapter 14

EVALUATION

The purpose of evaluation is to determine what the child can do, what he knows, what skills he can practice, how well he can think, and what he feels and values.

The basic method for finding out about the behavior of an individual is to ask him to behave. If one wants to see whether he can make a map, he should be asked to make a map. If one wishes to learn whether he can draw conclusions from evidence, he should be presented with evidence and asked to draw conclusions. If the object is to discover what facts he knows about something, then he should be asked to recall facts or to associate facts with ideas. When one wants to know how he attacks problems, problems should be presented and his strategy of attack observed.

The Basic Characteristics of Evaluation

Because of past associations, most persons entering teaching think of evaluation as the measurement of factual retention or the memorization of someone else's ideas. This is not at all the limit of measuring devices. Indeed, many devices that measure other things do not look like traditional tests at all: they are opportunities to practice behaviors that would not be elicited in conventional test situations.

TYPES OF QUESTIONS. James Gallagher has described teaching styles in terms of different types of questions that teachers put to their pupils. (The examples that follow draw upon a study of the relation between the defeat of the Spanish Armada and the English colonization of America.)

One teacher approach could be styled *cognitive-memory*: . . . "Can someone tell us what he has read about the Spanish Armada?" This requires no thinking ability but merely the ability to remember.

An alternative approach might stress *convergent thinking;* . . . "Give an explanation of why the Spaniards lost." While this could be *cognitive-memory* also, it may test the ability of the student to put facts in a logical and sequential order.

Or the teacher could tap *divergent thinking:* . . . "Suppose the Spaniards had won, what sorts of things might be different about our country today?" Here we have multiple possibilities and the student is encouraged to range over many dimensions without concern for the one right answer.

Finally, there is *evaluative thinking;* . . . "Do you suppose we would have been better off if the Spaniards had won?" This type of question demands the application of some value dimension to the problem and the judgmental relationship regarding the item in question and that value dimension.[1]

Although Gallagher's typology was constructed to guide the teacher in forming discussion questions, the classification applies equally well to test construction and shows that it is possible to measure four quite different abilities.

Most written or oral tests should be balanced among the four types —the emphasis depending on the objectives of the unit or depth study being evaluated. For example, a group of first-graders who have completed a comparison of Navaho and Eskimo family life might be tested by the teacher with questions like these:

Cognitive-memory: What weapons and tools were used for hunting in the two families? What did the women in each family do as their daily chores?

Convergent thinking: Why do you suppose their clothing was so different? Why was wood scarce in both places?

Divergent thinking: Suppose you went to live with these families. In what ways would your life be different from what it is now?

Evaluative thinking: How would you like spending some time in these families? What are some of the things you would particularly like? What are some of the things that bother you about the idea?

The responses to these questions would clearly provide a measure of four very different kinds of behaviors or abilities. No testing that relies

---

[1] James J. Gallagher, "Research on Enhancing Productive Thinking," in *Nurturing Individual Potential* (Washington: Assn. for Supervision and Curriculum Development, National Education Assn., 1964), pp. 52–53.

merely on memorization of facts and ideas can show a student's progress as adequately as this diversified evaluation.[2]

MEASURING TWICE. Ordinarily the object of evaluation is either to diagnose what needs to be learned or to determine what behaviors have changed during a period of instruction. In order to measure change, two measurements are obviously necessary—and sometimes more than two. Clearly, if a teacher measures behavior only at the completion of a unit of study, he will not know whether the behaviors practiced have been acquired during the unit of study or whether the children already possessed them before study began.

One problem in testing a child twice is that his second performance is likely to improve simply because of the practice provided by the first attempt; on the second time around, he may already sense the nature, formula, or direction of the questions he will be asked. Hence it is frequently wise to make two distinct versions of the test or of the testing situation. Sometimes two questions may deliberately approach a problem or behavior from a different angle, and one question of these pairs may be put into each test. This is good testing policy, but its accomplishment is admittedly arduous.

VARIABILITY. Every measurement of group behavior is described in terms of two characteristics: (1) the *central tendency* of the scores, or their tendency to group around the average or median score (that point in the distribution of scores that is exactly in the middle—half the scores being higher and half lower), and (2) the *variability* of the scores, or the extent of their dispersion around the average or median. Hence, when we describe how children scored on a test, we describe the average or middle score and the range or spread of the scores on either side of the average.

Because different children respond differently to content, teaching methods, and materials and because they vary widely in interest and adaptability, one of the results of instruction is to increase the variability or the spread of behavioral adequacy.

As an example, the table on the opposite page shows the scores on tests given before and after a unit on colonial America. The median score was 28 points higher on the second administration of the test; only seven pupils received a score lower than the median established on the first test. This rise in the median score and in scores in general indicates overall gains

---

[2] An inexpensive paperback that offers a guide to the making of tests for most purposes and describes some simple statistics that can aid in interpreting test results is John A. Green's *Teacher-Made Tests* (New York: Harper & Row, 1963).

in knowledge and skills. On the other hand, the range—difference between the highest and the lowest score—widened from 64 to 89 points. This increase in variability is normal; gains should not be expected to be uniform. If the variability does decrease—if *all* the scores improve and draw closer together—then either many students did not learn as much as they might have or the test did not measure all the things it might have, so that many students learned behaviors that the test did not tap.

TESTS ON COLONIAL AMERICA UNIT

PRETEST		POSTTEST	
Number of Pupils	*Score*	*Number of Pupils*	*Score*
1	71	1	98
1	66	2	97
2	58	1	94
2	57	2	91
2	56	1	90
3	55	3	88
3	54	3	87
4	53	4	84
4	51	5	79
5	50 (median)	4	78 (median)
4	49	3	77
3	48	2	71
2	47	2	69
1	46	1	62
2	41	2	60
2	36	2	59
1	22	1	52
1	14	1	46
1	7	2	33
		1	27
		1	18
		1	14
		1	9

Testing for Organizing Concepts

PROBLEM SOLVING. The ability to analyze problems effectively involves an understanding of organizing concepts and the ability to use them—an understanding and an ability that need to be tested in problem situations. The teaching strategy for this testing is to identify clearly the organizing concepts that are to be observed and to invent a problem or setting that demands the use of these concepts. As an example, let us take a class that has studied factors associated with agricultural production and confront them with the following testing problem:

Create a map of an island in the Pacific Ocean which is likely to have a climate suitable for the production of cacao, rubber, and tropical fruits. Indicate latitude and longitude, elevations, and other data related to these products. Show what parts of the island would be best for each of the three kinds of plants.

With such a problem, we soon determine whether the children have learned the general concepts that apply and whether they are able to apply them in relation to one another. This type of problem is often most revealing when solved collectively by a group that is allowed to debate the reasons for its choices and conclusions. Also, in a group discussion the teacher can feed specific information at appropriate times if the children themselves have forgotten or cannot locate the information easily.

Another problem question could begin with a map such as the one on the opposite page and with a set of related statements and questions:

This map shows an island in the middle of a lake. The island is connected to the shore by a causeway made from stones piled on the bottom of the lake until the pile reached the surface. Then smoothed stones were laid down to make a road. The lake is surrounded by mountains, and the only flat land is near the lake. The island is covered with buildings whose walls are still standing although the roofs are now gone. It is completely uninhabited. What do you think happened to the people who lived there? What caused the place to become empty of human beings? Relate your reasons to the conditions for human life and the kind of life you believe was being lived there.

The teacher stands by and is prepared, when asked, to provide information about such things as climatic conditions, possible evidence of a war or other struggle, and the existence of lake fish suitable for food. By observing how the children's queries are phrased, the teacher can fairly well measure their ability to apply the concepts they have learned. How they seek information about soil fertility and the fish population, for example, could indicate to what degree they have mastered economic concepts. What they ask about certain natural phenomena like earthquakes or climatic changes could reveal their ability to apply geographical concepts or even related concepts from the natural sciences. And if they ask whether the large central building had been a temple or whether the government had been theocratic, they could be revealing their understanding of political concepts.

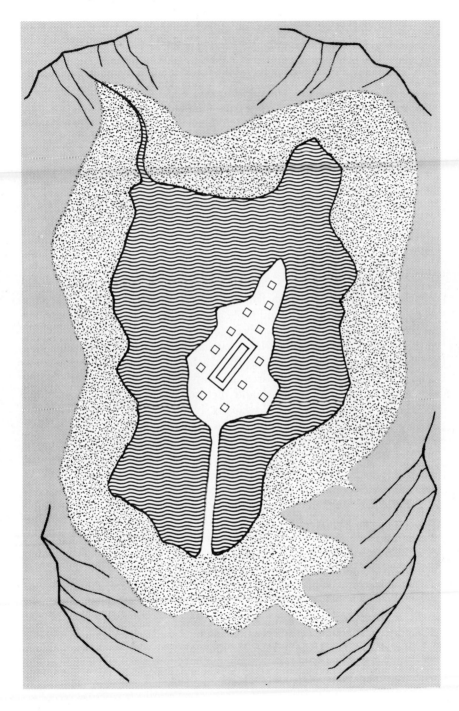

Such hypotheses raised by the children show *where* they have learned to look for information and *how* they go about it: "Their houses covered the whole island and there wasn't much land around the lake that they could grow things on. I think they just ran out of food and had to leave." "Maybe there was an earthquake and the priests thought it was a sign; so they left." "I think another tribe guarded the causeway so that they ran out of food and had to surrender. Then they burned the town—that's why the roof is gone—and took them away."

The conditions pictured, stated, or implied can be varied in order to determine the children's ability to cope with other factors and concepts. Perhaps a condition can be added: "Suppose the primitive people you've just been studying suddenly get electricity (or automobiles). How will it affect their lives?" Or perhaps some condition or factor can be taken away: "Suppose there was only one house in Congress"; "What would happen if the big factory in our town were to close?"

MODELS AND MURALS. Similar problems can be posed using relief models or murals rather than flat maps. For example, in the course of a study of colonial Virginia a sand table might be used to model a plantation on the James River. Merely by observing what items the children include in the model, what items they leave out, and what explanations they give for their inclusions and exclusions, the teacher can fairly well measure the children's progress. If the children are truly developing an understanding of plantation life, the model should picture certain important social and economic factors: the fields and wharves should indicate Virginia's reliance on staple crops for export, particularly tobacco; the activities of the people should demonstrate a division of labor and a social system somewhat divided by class lines; the ships, wharves, and homes should show the imports from England, particularly the manufactured products; and, in general, the model should measure the accuracy of the children's knowledge of clothing, housing, and other physical characteristics. This kind of evaluation can extend to models of airports, harbors, railroads, medieval manors, wagon trains, or any other identifiable economic or social units. The model of a town or a school may tell more about the perceptions of first-graders than anything said in classroom discussion.

Murals may be similarly employed for evaluation. Children who create a mural comparing life in their town with life in a French town must organize their knowledge and make decisions pinpointing what they believe is important. A mural constructed on some kind of time line is invaluable in measuring the children's grasp of chronology.

EVALUATING AT PLANNING SESSIONS. Whenever the teacher and the children get together to plan a new unit of study, the teacher has an excellent opportunity to discover whether the children have understood the organizing concepts developed in the previous unit and whether they have been influenced by the preceding unit to ask pertinent questions regarding human groups and concepts. It was pointed out in Chapter 5 that "when teachers repeatedly stress certain sides of topics, children come to regard those sides as the important ones, the ones to be looked for in new topics." Thus, if the children have properly absorbed the knowledge offered in a previous unit, then for a new unit they should logically pose questions and problems that draw upon this knowledge. For example, if in the earlier unit the teacher emphasized questions involving "evaluative thinking," then the children in the planning session should be expected to frame topic questions calling for value judgments. If the previous depth study leaned heavily on the organizing concepts of political science, then the children's new questions should be gauged for their effectiveness in applying these political concepts. In sum, the questions that children ask when planning a study are one index of the effect of past instruction.

EXPERIENCE RECORDS. Younger children can be tested on their ability to summarize stories, reading materials, films, or ideas they have encountered or "experienced." In recounting a particular event or series of impressions, have they given the facts accurately? Have they identified the important ideas? Have they drawn their own independent conclusions? The answers to such questions can be analyzed by the teacher to determine the children's grasp of organizing concepts or information in general.

Testing for Attitudes

Attitudes can be evaluated through either observation or interrogation. By the observation method the teacher merely watches children at work or play—perhaps in situations especially set up to expose degrees of either fair play or antisocial behavior—and then tries to infer or estimate each child's attitudes. By the interrogation method the teacher candidly asks each child how he feels about this situation or that. Of course, the child's answers to such direct questions may not themselves be direct, but the degree of defensiveness or lack of self-understanding can reveal a great deal about his attitudes. By either method the teacher is compelled to make careful inferences and to employ some psychological insight.

OBSERVING ATTITUDES. In order to observe specific attitudes, the teacher can usually set up a situation that will evoke their expression. An unsociable child, for example, can be placed in a work group or a team so that his behavior and the behavior of his associates can be observed. This setting is particularly useful if a teacher wishes to determine whether over a period of time the other children have come to accept the child or whether their hostility toward him has increased. Naturally a sensitive situation like this must be carefully, if unobtrusively, controlled.

Role playing is frequently advocated for diagnosing attitudes. For example, shown a film or photograph depicting some kind of conflict, such as the bullying of one person by another, a group of children can discuss the situation and then act it out. Every child may assume each role in turn, that of the bully and that of the bullied. In short, a problem has been set and the children can all be observed acting out aggressions or defensive plays. The skillful teacher can use this technique as both an instructional and an evaluational tool.

Dramatics has a similar usefulness. Does each child properly simulate the attitudes demanded by a particular role in a story or play? Have the children singly and collectively considered the dramatic parts in the light of the purposes set by the playwright? In short, have they understood or sensed the proper attitudes?

QUESTIONING FOR ATTITUDES. Hilda Taba has recommended that children be directly questioned on their attitudes:[3] "What are some of the things you would like to change in your neighborhood?" "What are some of the things you like (or dislike) about your school?" The children's answers to such questions can be in the form of drawings, written prose, or oral statements.

In 1960 children in four schools in Wilmington, Delaware, were administered such a test of attitudes with the single topic "What I dislike about my neighborhood." The purpose of the inquiry was to determine the children's feelings about living in communities undergoing rapid racial and economic change, to determine specifically whether they felt "accepted" in their neighborhoods. The results of this test are classified in the table opposite. Note that in their responses none of the children mentioned race directly. Rather, they concentrated on the noise, the dirt, the drunkenness, the squabbles among neighbors—the same conditions about which their parents were complaining. Significantly, too, nearly all the responses dealt with people. It was people the children liked, people they disliked, people they loved, people they thought they hated. The children needed a warm and human school environment, especially during this time of unsettlement

---

[3] Hilda Taba and others, *Diagnosing Human Relations Needs* (Washington: American Council on Education, 1955).

Children's Responses to the Survey Question "What I Dislike About My Neighborhood" Wilmington, Delaware, 1960

CLASSIFICATION OF RESPONSES

PERCENTAGES OF THE CHILDREN WHO INDICATED SPECIFIC DISLIKES *

SCHOOL	NUMBER OF CHILDREN SAMPLED	Bothersome Neighbors and Friends	Noise and Drunkenness	Animals	Poor Housing Conditions	Lack of Neighborhood Cleanliness	Poor Paving on Sidewalks and Streets	Miscellaneous
George Gray	58	22%	72%	26%	5%	5%	17%	79%
Williams	56	34%	50%	13%	11%	30%	18%	66%
Shortlidge	37	48%	5%	3%	5%	0	8%	46%
Washington	20	25%	5%	10%	30%	0	0	55%
Total	171	32%	43%	15%	10%	12%	13%	65%
GRADES								
1–3	20	25%	5%	10%	30%	0	0	55%
4–6	151	33%	48%	15%	7%	13%	15%	66%

*Percentages total more than 100% because most children gave more than one response.

in their neighborhood. Seeing his pupils milling about, making demands, squabbling, getting things dirty, even the most even-tempered teacher sometimes needs the kind of reminder that came from the little girl who said, when asked to tell what she liked about her neighborhood: "The park is a place I take my troubles to."

Analyzing Discussions

To make tape recordings of discussions and to play them back for analysis is an easy and effective means of measuring children's progress. By recording one class discussion per month, the teacher can keep a record of the number of the children's relevant and irrelevant statements and over the course of the year can determine whether his instruction has improved their ability to keep to the point (at least when they know their words are being recorded). One year's results could look like this (percentages of relevant contributions), indicating marked improvement:

October	48%
December	60%
March	65%
May	85%

Analyzing the same tape recordings, the teacher could measure many other factors. For example, did the children understand causation in human affairs? A count of their questions that probe for causes could help— even if the teacher were faced with poor and indeterminate results such as the following (percentages of questions involving causation):

October	7%
December	9%
March	8%
May	9%

Standardized Achievement Tests

From among the available standardized tests, each school or school district should select one or more that clearly relate to the objectives of the overall curricular plan and that will help the teachers to plot the children's progress from year to year. However, because selecting, administering, and scoring standardized tests are such difficult and professional tasks, a committee of experienced teachers should study the problem and avail itself of expert advice from consultants in universities or state departments of education. Some technical know-how in measurement and statistics must guide both the selection and administration of tests.[4]

The test publishers in the following list issue detailed catalogs (as distinct from mere price lists) and usually also offer free technical advice to teachers of the social studies:

Acorn Publishing Co., Rockville Centre, Long Island, N.Y. 11570

Bureau of Educational Measurements, Kansas State Teachers College, Emporia, Kan. 66801

Bureau of Educational Research and Service, State University of Iowa, Iowa City, Iowa 52240

Bureau of Publications, Teachers College, Columbia University, 525 W. 120th St., New York, N.Y. 10027

California Test Bureau, Del Monte Research Park, Monterey, Calif. 93940

Cooperative Test Division, Educational Testing Service, Princeton, N.J. 08540

Educational Test Bureau, 720 Washington Ave., S.E., Minneapolis, Minn.

Educational Testing Service, Princeton, N.J. 08540

Harcourt, Brace & World, Tarrytown, N.Y. 10591

Houghton Mifflin Co., 2 Park St., Boston, Mass. 02107

Ohio Scholarship Tests, State Department of Education, 751 Northwest Blvd., Columbus, Ohio 43215

Psychometric Affiliates, Box 1625, Chicago, Ill. 60690

Public School Publishing Co., Test Division of Bobbs-Merrill Co., 1720 E. 38th St., Indianapolis, Ind. 46206

Scholastic Testing Service, 3774 W. Devon Ave., Chicago, Ill. 60645

Science Research Associates, 259 E. Erie St., Chicago, Ill. 60611

Western Psychological Services, Box 775, Beverly Hills, Calif. 90210

Keeping Records of Individual Progress

To be able to classify and analyze the continuing inflow of information regarding each child's progress, the teacher must devise some convenient bookkeeping system—perhaps one using file folders. The information should be separated into at least eight categories (the teacher making

---

[4] Some aid can be found in Henry E. Garrett's *Testing for Teachers* (New York: American Book Co., 1959), which contains simple, clear explanations of terms commonly used in testing and evaluation. Of course, every teacher should be acquainted with Oscar Krisen Buros' (ed.) *The Fifth Mental Measurements Yearbook* (Highland Park, N.J.: Gryphon Press, 1959) and with Buros' other reference work, *Tests in Print* (Highland Park, N.J.: Gryphon Press, 1961).

sure that information is indeed received for each category):

1. Copies of corrected tests, both standardized and teacher-made, with an indication of the child's relative class standing.

2. A record of the types of thinking of which the child seems capable (a record, that is, of his ability to develop and test out generalizations and hypotheses, to detect flaws in arguments, and to identify relevant information).

3. A list of books read, reports delivered, projects completed, and projects under way.

4. Inventories of vocabulary, especially vocabulary related to depth studies either completed or contemplated.

5. A checklist of research skills.

6. A checklist of map skills (and skills related to graphs, charts, and tables).

7. An inventory of social adjustment and participation.

8. Indications of the child's attitudes, values, and interests that are important to instruction.

Summary

Evaluation or testing must be guided by several principles.

First, it must be a cooperative endeavor on the part of both teacher and pupil. To be measurably aware of a child's progress (or lack of it) is just as important to the child himself as it is to the teacher. Not only must the child continually know how he is doing but also, after each evaluation, he must join with the teacher in planning for corrective instruction or intensified pursuit of certain interests.

Second, evaluation should be closely related to the objectives of the curricular program.

Third, evaluation, to be effective, must define behavioral changes in such a way that teachers can recognize means of improving or refocusing their instruction.

Fourth, evaluations must be made not just once but twice, both before and after a period of instruction, in order to determine accurately the effect of the instruction.

Fifth, formal tests and problem questions should measure not only the child's fund of factual information but also his ability to use organizing concepts and his ability to evaluate information, make inferences, and draw conclusions.

Sixth, evaluations must further measure not only knowledge and thinking ability but also attitudes, which seem to be best determined simply by observing each child in group activities, in role playing, or in dramatic play.

Because there is an ingrained notion that the purpose of evaluation is merely to measure a child's store of facts and generalizations, most new teachers must commit themselves to a reeducation or reorientation; they must experimentally learn how to assess thinking abilities and attitudes. To this end some methods of evaluation have been suggested in the preceding pages, but ultimately it is the creative teacher who must devise his own means of measuring a child's creative achievements.

INQUIRIES

1. Look in Buros' *The Fifth Mental Measurements Yearbook* and locate tests of map skills and tests of knowledge of democratic principles or institutions. Are there any tests at the elementary school level? What do the reviewers think of them?

2. Read *Making the Classroom Test* and see whether you can put some of the suggested principles to work yourself. Select a passage in a social studies text and make up a few test items, using the ideas you have found.

3. How would you determine whether second-graders realize how modern communication systems make us increasingly inter-dependent?

4. Make a test to determine whether elementary school children can understand and apply the concepts of "latitude" and "longitude." Trading ideas with other teachers, you may be able to invent a useful test.

5. What can be done so that a poor writer can take a general test that reveals some of the same things measured by an essay test?

6. Consider that, in the course of a unit dealing with colonial America, you have failed to establish the concept of "colony." What are some of the other concepts contributing to an understanding of "colony"? How can you detect that your students have or have not gained control of these concepts?

7. What are some of the devices that will reveal whether first-graders understand the concept of "role" as applied to the family?

References and Readings

Buros, Oscar K. (ed.). *The Fifth Mental Measurements Yearbook*. Highland Park, N.J.: Gryphon Press, 1959.

————. *Tests in Print*. Highland Park, N.J.: Gryphon Press, 1961.

Gallagher, James J. "Research on Enhancing Productive Thinking," in *Nurturing Individual Potential*. Washington: Assn. for Supervision and Curriculum Development, National Education Assn., 1964.

Green, John A. *Teacher-Made Tests*. New York: Harper & Row, 1963.

Making the Classroom Test. Princeton, N.J.: Educational Testing Service, 1959.

Taba, Hilda, and others. *Diagnosing Human Relations Needs*. Washington: American Council on Education, 1955.

Chapter 15

SOCIAL STUDIES FOR DISADVANTAGED CHILDREN

In the inner part of big cities, in certain rural areas, and in small pockets of little towns throughout the nation there are children who have not developed fully because their social environment has not been a nurturing one. Sometimes they have been called the culturally deprived.[1] The term has meaning, for in vocabulary, in ability to use language flexibly, and in certain other ways critical for education and life, these children have not been able to participate fully in society. Wise men have pointed out, however, that part of the disadvantage results from being deprived of the "middle-class culture" so essential to American economic success.

Sometimes these children have been called the products of depressed areas,[2] and if by this one means that economic resources are spread more thinly in their homes and neighborhoods, this is true. If by this one means that most people, including the residents of such areas, find many parts of the inner city depressing, then it is still true.

Some observers have pointed out that few school administrators, teachers, and lay people, even behavioral scientists, understand slum children or have been able to teach them with obvious success.[3] Some careful research has indicated that educators generally, in small cities as well as large, have difficulty finding the means for teaching lower-class children. Hollingshead found that teachers in one town spent more time tutoring the children of middle-class parents, gave them more privileges, and made them feel more welcome in school than they did the children of lower-class parents.[4]

---

[1] Frank Riessman, *The Culturally Deprived Child* (New York: Harper & Row, 1962).

[2] A. Harry Passow (ed), *Education in Depressed Areas* (New York: Teachers College, 1963).

[3] James B. Conant, *Slums and Suburbs* (New York: McGraw-Hill, 1961).

[4] August deB. Hollingshead, *Elmtown's Youth* (New York: Wiley, 1949).

In some areas of the big cities, three-fourths of the children who entered the first grade twelve years ago will not graduate from high school this June. Even in the country as a whole, only in recent years has the number of graduates equaled half the number of those who entered school a dozen years before. Many of those who dropped out came from impoverished homes, especially in the concentrated slum areas at the edges of the city center. Other deprived children were not so much children of poverty and its related conditions as of homes that are rigid-minded and uncommunicative, that lack a father, or that suffer from other psychosocial difficulties.

Furthermore, even in school the academic ability of lower-class children, though it improves, tends to lag farther and farther behind the rapidly expanding ability of middle-class children. The gap in ability, wide at the beginning, widens through the school years—even though these are the very years when children are under the influence of trained teachers dedicated to the steady improvement of academic ability.

The primal cause of this increasing lag in school is probably the lack of preconditioning in the preschool years—years blighted and empty, years that psychologists now perceive to be critical in promoting a subsequent ability to grow and develop. Those who have studied intellectual growth believe that the environmental influence that results in mature intelligence is perhaps strongest in the very early years of life.

> What we have hypothesized is that extreme environments can have far greater effects in the early years than they can have in later years. That is, deprivation in the first four years of life can have far greater consequences than deprivation in the ten years from age 8 through age 17.[5]

Because a poor home environment apparently does arrest a child's intellectual development, the New York City schools, the University of Chicago Laboratory School, and other districts and institutions have experimented with nursery schools specially designed to give children from depressed areas sufficient "experiences" to quicken their intellectual awareness. Such provision seems desirable and overdue. However, we are concerned here with the social studies during the primary and intermediate years of school. What special provision should be made for children who have already suffered cultural deprivation?

---

[5] Benjamin S. Bloom, *Stability and Change in Human Characteristics* (New York: Wiley, 1964), p. 72.

A growing child becomes a private replica of his social environment. If the values, experiences, and patterns of action that he finds about him are not varied and socially nourishing—if, in particular, his experiences are few and restricted—then he is apt to suffer intellectual deprivation as well. The classroom must aid in supplying the enriching experiences and cooperative atmosphere that the disadvantaged child needs in order to establish responsible relations with other human beings.

Experience with Interdependence

Applying the theory of conceptual systems discussed in Chapter 6, David E. Hunt has found that junior high school students in depressed areas can be distinguished by their degree of socialization. Some of the children appeared to be in an almost "presocialized state"; they appeared to lack the internalized standards, the conceptual development, or the easy ability to communicate with people that are thought to be normal for their age.[6] To thrust these children immediately into a complex interdependent environment, with cooperative planning of standards, goals, and procedures,

---

[6] David E. Hunt, "A Conceptual Systems Change Model and Its Application to Education" (unpublished paper, Syracuse University, 1964).

would be disastrous. At the other extreme, to treat this unruly group in an authoritarian, extremely military manner would deprive them of the gentle interaction they must experience in order to form standards and learn how to relate to others. More appropriate for these children would be a kindly environment, filled with clear and fairly simple tasks requiring not necessarily *close* cooperation but some degree of interaction with others.

Hunt also found that many of the children were arrested at a "docile" stage, characterized by extreme conformity to standards and by exaggerated competition for achievement rewards such as grades. These children became very upset when left on their own, without clear guidelines handed down from above. They urgently desired definite, simple instructions uncomplicated by ambiguity. To place these children in an extremely interdependent environment would therefore tend to bewilder and demoralize them. Yet to continue to treat them in the unilateral way they crave would probably stifle their future development. The wisest compromise seems to be to give them tasks requiring them to share in the making of some standards and decisions but at the same time to provide them with some structure that gives them a feeling of security.

Hunt found still a third category in the depressed areas, those children who were "rebellious," who actively resisted authority. Although as difficult to handle as the "presocialized" children, this third group tended to be the most socialized group—children who had internalized the norms of society and were now actively rebelling against them. Again an interdependent environment is inadvisable, while a completely unilateral one would probably foment even more active rebellion. These children will most likely respond to an environment which places emphasis on warm, human ties, an environment in which cooperation is prized and required by the appointed tasks and which encourages them to reestablish ties with other human beings.

Hunt's research appears to suggest that problem children in slum areas should not all be viewed as one and treated identically. Nor should the other children, those who show academic promise, necessarily be removed and given a different education. Hunt's work suggests that the culturally deprived differ widely in their degree of socialization and in their responses to an environment. Some are neglected so much that they fail to become socialized. Others are as docile as lambs—and, because of their quiet, dutiful nature, their academic ability may be rated higher by the unwary than their achievement warrants. Finally, there are the rebellious ones, who in spite of their restiveness may be closer to interdependence than either of the other groups.

The teaching strategy, then, should be adapted to the degree of socialization and conceptual development manifested by the children.

Essential in all cases is a warmly human environment that allows the child
to explore himself without reproach. Says Herbert A. Thelen:

> Consider the child whose range of experience has been so narrow
> that he has simply not had the opportunity to try to cope with very
> many aspects of life. It is fashionable to think of "lower class" children
> in this way, and to refer to them as "culturally deprived." I would in-
> clude under this term, in addition, children whose families have been
> so preoccupied with making a living, achieving social status, being
> intellectual sophisticates, maintaining piety, etc., that the child has
> never had the chance to recognize, let alone explore, the possibilities
> of any other way or kind of life. Such children often appear to have
> no goal or direction in their own lives, for they have not had to make
> choices, and therefore they have not had to think through "who they
> are" and where their commitments lie. . . . The culturally deprived
> child simply needs participant-observer experience in families, groups,
> and organizations whose existence he could not have dreamed of.[7]

The child needs genial, sympathetic relations with other people
under conditions that require his asking questions, giving information,
making decisions, and otherwise performing in ways that permit him to
learn about groups and to be part of them. As he becomes part of a group,
the unsocialized child will acquire socialization, the docile child will reach
out and find support among his peers, and the rebellious child will reestablish cooperative relations with other human beings. The processes of
growth will be slow, and patience is necessary. But *calm and determined
teachers may yet find a way to overcome, in the years from eight to eighteen,
the disadvantages that accrued in the years from one to four.*

Experience with Words

The narrowed world of the deprived child requires widening. It
is not unusual to find youngsters living in depressed areas on the edge of the
city center who have never walked down the main streets. The child has
often missed contact not only with people but with many of the arts and
products of contemporary society. Accompanying this narrow experience
with things has been a relatively narrow experience with words and the
ways to use words. And, finally, the child of the slums has had little opportunity actually to use his experience or his words meaningfully—at least,

---

[7] Herbert A. Thelen, *Education and the Human Quest* (New York:
Harper, 1960), pp. 78–79.

not as much opportunity as middle-class children have had. He has not been encouraged to explore as much, to question as avidly, or to talk about his experiences.

Clearly the school program in depressed areas must provide explorations in which the child gradually acquires experience with those common things previously denied him that give him cause to reason and talk about life. In other words, helping the child to explore the city and the country, taking him places, showing him films, helping him to interview people, letting him see how factories operate and ships are built—these are more important in the long run than helping him to read about the early explorers of North America. Massive doses of firsthand experiences, taken under conditions of guided group inquiry, are the prescription. And as he explores, he must learn to talk about what he sees. He must record his talk and listen to the playback and work on more effective modes of expression. He must dictate his experiences and observations to the teacher until he is able to write independently. And what he dictates he must read until he has learned to read independently.

In many cases this kind of child will have trouble reading books dealing with topics of interest to him. Thus, in all grades the old tricks of the first-grade teacher are brought into play: the teacher reads; the children then repeat what they have heard; and their versions are recorded in written form to become part of the reading lesson.

Overcoming the Child's Feeling of Helplessness

Living in a financially uncertain home environment, deprived of intellectually stimulating experiences, missing warm personal relationships, and growing increasingly aware of these disadvantages, the child of the depressed area tends to fall into a feeling of helplessness. Therefore, even more than other children, he needs to join with others in cooperative projects—projects in which he can personally feel that he is identifying with a group and making common cause for purposeful ends. He must see himself actually doing something, getting something done.

This kind of cooperative atmosphere is found in so-called community-action projects: in the early grades, planting trees, framing pictures, putting on plays, and painting scenery; and in the upper grades, serving on safety patrol, supervising other children on the playground and in the lunchroom, and earning money for class trips. To create further opportunities for productive volunteer work, the teacher can enlist the aid of community agencies such as choral societies, art museums, social welfare offices, and police and fire departments. The deprived child simply must have successful cooperative experiences in order to overcome his feelings of helplessness; if he does not acquire these personal attachments in school, he may easily, soon after leaving elementary school, make the decision to leave school altogether.

Studying the Faraway

The study of the faraway and the long ago, however, does have a place in a program for the deprived child. For one thing, faraway places are interesting for their very novelty and help arouse his interest. For another, topics removed in time or place provide a respite from the here and now. The adventures of the explorers, the ways of life in faraway lands can have high interest. The content, however, should be designed chiefly to provide an entry into the study of the child's own society about which he knows so little. During the elementary school years culturally deprived children need not study France, or India, or any other place far removed from their lives, unless the topic provides some interesting focus for a study already under way or some comparative base for the study of their own society. They may, for example, find the study of the Japanese family less traumatic than the study of their own family, but the things they learn may help them to improve their lives.

A final point: learning to view things from the vantage point of the social scientist is as important for the deprived child as it is for other children. His economic life needs the illumination of the economist's questions, and cooperative political action will be essential in his later life.

Summary

Clear knowledge of the problem of the culturally deprived is still very limited; we do not know how the mental damage suffered by a child in his early years can be remedied or adequately overcome in his later years. For this reason the teaching strategies for such children must, for the time being, necessarily be experimental. However, there is evidence in support of certain principles and procedures:

1. Culturally deprived children differ markedly in their degree of socialization and conceptual development. Some are almost "presocialized" and may lack internalized norms or an ability to communicate, even in their early teens. Some are "docile" and extremely dependent on cultural norms and rules. Still others are

"rebellious" and resist rules and authority. Different strategies must be applied to each type of child.

2. The deprived child needs contact with groups of warm, sympathetic people who can become important to him and can accept him into their fellowship. The absence of these attachments has damaged his aptitude for school and therefore must be pointedly considered in planning a teaching strategy.

3. The deprived child needs especially heavy doses of firsthand experiences. Because his world has been limited, his school must plan for a deliberate extension of his knowledge of his community. To become acquainted with his immediate environment is more critical to him than to learn about foreign cultures and history, especially during his elementary years. However, occasionally and with proper application, the study of faraway places and times can be motivating and therapeutic, and may be essential to the child's understanding of his own situation.

4. How to help the depressed-area child to organize this experience into ideas and to learn words for what he sees and thinks must also be carefully considered. He must learn to talk about what he sees, write about what he sees, and reason about it as well. A vigorous intellectual atmosphere is essential.

5. The deprived child must be led to join in cooperative social action, in and out of school, in order to overcome his sense of helplessness and to build his sense of optimism about individual and collective action.

INQUIRIES

1. Automation is reducing the number of jobs at the lower end of the economic scale more rapidly than at the upper end. Find some expert opinion on the future prospects of dropouts.

2. Because of the high dropout rate in depressed areas, the elementary and junior high schools must provide terminal education for many young people. How can this be accomplished?

3. Acquaint yourself with one of the big-city projects for the culturally deprived. Find out what is being done for young people in and out of school.

4. Vocational education was once recommended as the cure-all for children who had academic difficulty. It is now recognized that most kinds of vocational training require superior academic ability. What do you see as the alternatives?

---

5. Imagine that you are to teach the first grade in the inner city. In what ways would you have to modify the teaching strategy suitable for a middle-class community in order to adapt it for the less advantaged children?

---

6. What are the ways in which the social studies program can be organized and taught so that heavy emphasis is placed on language development for children requiring this added instruction.

References and Readings

ASHTON-WARNER, SYLVIA. *Teacher.* New York: Simon & Schuster, 1963.

AUSABEL, DAVID P. "A Teaching Strategy for Culturally Deprived Pupils: Cognitive and Motivational Considerations," *School Review,* LXXI (Winter 1963), 454–63.

BLOOM, BENJAMIN S. *Stability and Change in Human Characteristics.* New York: Wiley, 1964.

CONANT, JAMES B. *Slums and Suburbs.* New York: McGraw-Hill, 1961.

HOLLINGSHEAD, AUGUST DEB. *Elmtown's Youth.* New York: Wiley, 1949.

PASSOW, A. HARRY (ed.). *Education in Depressed Areas.* New York: Teachers College, 1963.

RIESSMAN, FRANK. *The Culturally Deprived Child.* New York: Harper & Row, 1962.

THELEN, HERBERT A. *Education and the Human Quest.* New York: Harper, 1960.

THE PROSPECTS
OF A SOCIAL SCIENCE
EDUCATION

Chapter 16

A MEMORANDUM ABOUT THE FUTURE

Where are we heading in elementary school social studies? What kinds of innovation promise to lead to better strategies of curriculum and instruction? What materials should be created to advance our technology and to involve children in more exciting encounters with ideas and social movements?

Diversity of Curricula and Instructional Patterns

For the past twenty years curricula have been dominated by the expanding-worlds principle described in Chapter 9—the principle that demands that the child be led gradually from a study of his immediate neighborhood in the early grades to a study of his national and international environment in the upper grades. Because most textbook series have been organized on this pattern and because instruction has tended to be oriented around such texts, the expanding-worlds approach has become entrenched in the majority of the American schools—almost to the exclusion of all other approaches. Indeed, the lack of other materials has hampered experimentation with other approaches. The college "methods books," while advocating that a teacher and his children plan their inquiries together in a democratic fashion, have nevertheless restricted this planning within the confines of the expanding-worlds approach. However, if the current curriculum projects in the social studies are carried vigorously to the point of implementation, they should result in the development of a much wider range of curricular plans and instructional strategies and materials.

In some schools we may see future attempts to build curricula organized around the individual social sciences. For example, the Anthropology Curriculum Study Project at the University of Chicago is preparing study units organized around anthropological concepts. Two projects —the Elkhart Experiment in Indiana and the Elementary School Economics Program at the University of Chicago—have developed plans for centering curricula on economics.[1]

In other schools we should see a variety of attempts to blend the several social sciences into a coherent curriculum framework. The approach described in this book is designed for a curriculum in which concepts from all the social sciences are systematically explored by children.

Some curricular patterns should appear in which the child's problems, interests, and experiences determine the content to be explored. In such a curriculum the teacher and his pupils jointly draw their study topics from contemporary events in the child's life, the life of his community, and the life of his nation and the world. As the studies proceed, the teacher becomes responsible for helping his children to identify and apply the organizing concepts of the social sciences.

Still other curricular patterns could provide a great deal of independent study by individual children. In the Valley Winds Elementary School in Riverview Gardens, Missouri, teachers are experimenting with highly individualized instruction in which individual students identify and pursue their own projects. Sometimes the student uses highly sequenced materials, such as programed materials and specially prepared autoinstructional aids. In other cases the student pursues his study through recordings, books, and other more conventional materials. A good many curricula in the future will probably include this kind of individual inquiry along with cooperative group inquiry.

The topics chosen for study can be phrased in terms that are not quite conventional. Instead of a familiar study of a nation, a government, or a political or economic process, children might be persuaded to pursue an interdisciplinary study, one that concentrates on what might be called the "decision areas" of group life—aesthetic decisions, decisions about collective responsibility, educational decisions, career decisions, and the like.

Curricula could be developed to focus on social and ideological movements that are shaping the future world. Urbanization, nationalization, communism, democracy, totalitarianism, and other such topics could serve as pivots for studying the organizing concepts of the social sciences.

If we are to see strong schools develop, we *should* see a variety of plans emerge. Some of these plans should reflect local conditions; the big city school in a changing neighborhood should have a different educational plan from that of the school in a country town or in a suburb.

---

[1] See the list of "Current Social Studies Projects" on page 222.

Other plans should reflect differing attempts to use the organizing concepts of the social sciences. Still others should represent attempts to individualize instruction. Some should reflect explorations into new content areas.

Instructional Strategies

Currently there are several exciting experiments in instruction which can change educational strategies radically. One of these is teaching through "simulation." At the college and secondary school level, Harold Guetzkow and others have experimented with what they call inter-nation simulation, in which international games are played in order to illustrate processes of international relations.[2] In this simulation groups of students play the roles of nations. One group is given information about a hypothetical nation, its economic resources and processes, its government, and so forth. Other groups are given similar information about other hypothetical nations. Then problems are posed (should country A form a trade agreement to sell sugar to country B?), and the groups consider the ramifications of various solutions to the problem (How will the agreement affect relations with country C?).

Although the sophisticated kind of inter-nation simulation that can be practiced by secondary school students may not be suitable for elementary children, nevertheless simulation techniques can possibly be put to some use in elementary schools. For example, because real cities are complex and therefore difficult to study adequately, children could be introduced to urbanization by simulating a mythical city whose activities are reduced to a very few urban processes. Children studying the simplified mythical city could learn concepts that later they could employ in studying the real thing. Similarly, governmental processes could be simulated. It might be possible to develop a hypothetical urban government confronted by problems requiring city council decisions and so forth—all tailored to the experience and capacity of the young child. (The author and his wife have developed a strategy whereby children study cultural change in a society simulating the Indian pueblos of the Southwest.)

Another new and exciting instructional technique attempts to help children learn the processes by which the social scientist builds concepts

---

[2] See Cleo Cherryholmes, "Developments in Simulation of International Relations in High School Teaching," *Phi Delta Kappan*, XLVI (January 1965), 227–31.

and makes inferences. For example, children might arrive at some ideas about cultural diffusion by studying art in the Southwest under Indian, Spanish, and American occupation. By comparing samples of Spanish art of the Renaissance, Navaho and Pueblo art of the nineteenth century, and present-day art in the American Southwest, children can be led to analyze how one culture borrows ideas and styles from another and refines and develops them. Archaeological case studies and original documents could be used in studies of this sort that attempt to reconstruct history.

A third interesting instructional strategy applies "training group," or "T-group," techniques in the elementary school. Throughout the United States the National Education Association has set up a number of temporary and permanent National Training Laboratories (the first in Bethel, Maine, in 1947) for the purpose of bringing groups of adults together to explore group dynamics and, more particularly, to study their own individual adjustments and reactions to group situations. Teachers have formed some of the groups; others have been composed of production managers, judges, business leaders, or military personnel—that is, people faced with similar administrative and organizational problems in their professions. Although, observed by a trained monitor or psychologist, each group does attempt in its sessions to discuss problems common to its members, the real focus of study becomes their attempts to organize their discussions and "to create a productive and viable organization."[3] In these attempts some members become natural leaders and others become followers; indeed, behaviors range from the overaggressive to the oversubmissive. In the beginning sessions there may be a certain aimlessness or disorganization, but as leaderships develop, there arise antagonisms or even aggressions. Guided by the monitor, the group tries to work toward a state of harmony and collective action. In the process, individuals come to understand themselves better psychologically and learn how to cope better with group situations and how to stimulate and support one another. In other words, the group studies its own behavior as a miniature society. At the Valley Winds Elementary School several teachers have explored means of adapting these T-group techniques for elementary school children.[4] The positive results seem to show that children can increase their ability to make decisions and to cope with interpersonal discord in group situations.

Another possible instructional innovation has originated in Syracuse, New York, where psychologist David Hunt and educator Gerald Weinstein have helped teachers to plan social environments suitable for

    [3] Leland P. Bradford and others, *T-Group Theory and Laboratory Method: Innovation in Re-education* (New York: Wiley, 1964), p. 1.
    [4] Charles Mansfield, the principal, and Belden Hare, a teacher at Valley Winds, deserve credit for much of this work with T-groups.

improving the personalities of culturally deprived children. Their work has wide implications: perhaps there are various classroom environments or climates that can be accurately defined and applied so that children of all types can achieve interdependence in groups and autonomy as students.

Planning for the Future Society

We must search for an education that prepares children to cope with a social world radically different from the one that exists at present. We have at hand a great quantity of knowledge and educational media whose potential has barely been realized. The successful society of the future will be the one that has been bold enough and inventive enough to anticipate the currents of change. Such a society must prepare its children to comprehend their world and to become adults who are not confined in the mold of the present but rather are able to develop and fashion an ever improving society.

APPENDIXES

Selected List of Catalogs, Guidebooks, and Handbooks for Social Studies Methods and Materials

The bibliography below supplements the references and readings listed at the end of Chapter 12. A classified directory of distributors and manufacturers—a directory that the teacher will find worthwhile—is *Patterson's Source Guide for Educational Materials and Equipment*, published annually by Educational Directories, Inc., 410 East Northwest Highway, Mount Prospect, Illinois 60058. For annotated listings of free instructional materials, the teacher should consult the following catalogs, revised and published annually by Educators Progress Service, Randolph, Wisconsin 53956:

> *Educators Guide to Free Films*
> *Educators Guide to Free Filmstrips*
> *Educators Guide to Free Guidance Materials*
> *Educators Guide to Free Science Materials*
> *Educators Guide to Free Social Studies Materials*
> *Educators Guide to Free Tapes, Scripts, and Transcriptions*
> *Educators Guide to Free Teaching Aids*
> *Educators Index to Free Materials*

ADAMS, RUTH J. *The Kindergarten How-to-Do-It Book*. Minneapolis: Denison, 1962.

BETTS, VICTORIA B. *Exploring Papier-Mâché*. Worcester, Mass.: Davis, 1955.

BROWN, JAMES W., and others. *A-V Instruction: Materials and Methods*. New York: McGraw-Hill, 1959.

Bulletin Boards for Teaching. Austin: Univ. of Texas, Visual Instruction Bureau, 1954.

BURGER, ISABEL. *Creative Play Acting*. New York: Barnes, 1950.

COX, DORIS, and WARREN, BARBARA. *Creative Hands: An Introduction to Craft Techniques*. 2d ed. New York: Wiley, 1951.

DALE, EDGAR. *Audio-Visual Methods in Teaching*. Rev. ed. New York: Holt, Rinehart & Winston, 1954.

DAVENPORT, MILLIA. *The Book of Costume*. New York: Crown, 1948.

Drama with and for Children. Washington: Government Printing Office, 1960.

DURLAND, FRANCES CALDWELL. *Creative Dramatics for Children*. Yellow Springs, Ohio: Antioch Press, 1952.

EAST, MARJORIE. *Display for Learning: Making and Using Visual Materials*. New York: Holt, Rinehart & Winston, 1952.

ENDICOTT, ROBERT F. *Scrap Wood Fun for Kids: 100 Easy-to-Make Projects for Boys and Girls*. New York: Association Press, 1961.

The Feltboard in Teaching. Austin: Univ. of Texas, Visual Instruction Bureau, 1955.

FLETCHER, HELEN JILL. *The Big Book of Things to Do and Make.* New York: Random House, 1961.

FRANKEL, LILLIAN and GODFREY. *Creating from Scrap.* New York: Sterling, 1962.

GREEN, ARTHUR S. *Arts and Crafts Activities for Primary Grade Children.* Minneapolis: Denison, 1962.

GRISWOLD, LESTER E. *Handicraft: Simplified Procedure and Projects.* 9th ed. Englewood Cliffs, N.J.: Prentice-Hall, 1952.

HALLEN, JULIENNE. *How to Make Foreign Dolls and Their Costumes.* Baltimore: Ottenheimer, 1961.

HUNT, W. BEN. *Golden Book of Crafts and Hobbies.* New York: Golden Press, 1957.

————. *Golden Book of Indian Crafts and Lore.* New York: Golden Press, 1954.

————. *Indian and Camp Handicraft.* Rev. ed. Milwaukee: Bruce, 1945.

ICKIS, MARGUERITE. *Folk Arts and Crafts.* New York: Association Press, 1957.

————, and ESH, REBA SELDEN. *Book of Arts and Crafts.* New York: Association Press, 1954.

IRELAND, NORMA OLIN. *The Picture File in School, College and Public Libraries.* Boston: Faxon, 1952.

JOHNSON, LILLIAN. *Papier-Mâché.* New York: McKay, 1958.

KENWORTHY, LEONARD S. *Free and Inexpensive Materials on World Affairs.* New York: Teachers College, 1963.

————. *Introducing Children to the World.* New York: Harper, 1955.

————. *Studying Africa in Elementary and Secondary Schools.* New York: Teachers College, 1962.

————. *Studying South America in Elementary and Secondary Schools.* New York: Teachers College, 1962.

————. *Studying the Middle East in Elementary and Secondary Schools.* New York: Teachers College, 1962.

————. *Studying the World: Selected Resources.* New York: Teachers College, 1962.

————. *Telling the UN Story: New Approaches to Teaching About the UN and Its Related Agencies.* Dobbs Ferry, N.Y.: Oceana, 1963.

KINDER, JAMES S. *Audio-Visual Materials and Techniques.* 2d ed. New York: American Book, 1959.

KRAUS, RICHARD G. *Folk Dancing: A Guide for Schools, Colleges, and Recreation Groups.* New York: Macmillan, 1962.

LEEMING, JOSEPH. *Costume Book for Parties and Plays.* Philadelphia: Lippincott, 1938.

LOVELL, ELEANOR COOK, and HALL, RUTH MASON (eds.). *Index to Handicrafts, Modelmaking, and Workshop Projects.* Boston: Faxon, 1936. Supplements, 1943, 1950.

LUMSDAINE, A. A., and GLASER, ROBERT (eds.). *Teaching Machines and Programmed Learning.* Washington: National Education Assn., 1960.

LYSAUGHT, JEROME P., and WILLIAMS, CLARENCE M. *A Guide to Programmed Instruction.* New York: Wiley, 1963.

MEEKS, MARTHA F. *Models for Teaching.* Austin: Univ. of Texas, Div. of Extension, 1956.

MOORE, FRANK C., and others. *Handcrafts for Elementary Schools.* Boston: Heath, 1953.

NEWKIRK, LOUIS V., and ZUTTER, LAVADA. *Crafts for Everyone.* 2 vols. New York: Van Nostrand, 1950.

NORBECK, OSCAR E. *Book of Indian Life Crafts.* New York: Association Press, 1958.

ROBINSON, ARTHUR H. *Elements of Cartography.* 2d ed. New York: Wiley, 1960.

SANDS, LESTER B. *Audio-Visual Procedures in Teaching.* New York: Ronald Press, 1956.

SHAFTEL, GEORGE and FANNIE R. *Role Playing the Problem Story.* New York: National Conference of Christians and Jews, 1952.

SMITH, MOYNE RICE. *Plays and How to Put Them On.* New York: Walck, 1961.

THOMAS, R. MURRAY, and SWARTOUT, SHERWIN G. *Integrated Teaching Materials: How to Choose, Create, and Use Them.* Rev. ed. New York: McKay, 1963.

WANKELMAN, WILLARD, and others. *Arts and Crafts for Elementary Teachers.* Dubuque, Iowa: Brown, 1954.

WARD, WINIFRED. *Playmaking with Children.* 2d ed. New York: Appleton, 1957.

WILLIAMS, GUY R. *Instructions to Young Model-Makers.* New Rochelle, N.Y.: Sportshelf & Soccer, 1960.

WITTICH, WALTER A., and SCHULLER, CHARLES F. *Audio-Visual Materials.* New York: Harper, 1957.

ZECHLIN, RUTH. *Complete Book of Handcrafts.* Newton Centre, Mass.: Branford, 1959.

Publishers of Textbooks and Other Reading Materials for Elementary and Junior High Social Studies

The publishers in the following list usually distribute catalogs and brochures upon request. Before writing, the teacher may wish to consult *Textbooks in Print, Including Teaching Materials,* a catalog and price list published annually by R. R. Bowker Company, 1180 Avenue of the Americas, New York, N.Y. 10036.

Allyn and Bacon, Inc., 150 Tremont St., Boston, Mass. 02111
American Book Co., 55 Fifth Ave., New York, N.Y. 10003
American Heritage Publishing Co., Inc., 551 Fifth Ave., New York, N.Y. 10017
Association Press, 291 Broadway, New York, N.Y. 10007

Benefic Press, Publishing Div. of Beckley-Cardy Co., 1900 N. Narragansett Ave., Chicago, Ill. 60639

W. S. Benson & Co., 109 E. Fifth St., Austin, Tex. 78766

Bobbs-Merrill Co., Inc., Subsidiary of Howard W. Sams & Co., Inc., 4300 W. 62d St., Indianapolis, Ind. 46206

Cambridge Book Co., Inc., 45 Kraft Ave., Bronxville, N.Y. 10708

The Caxton Printers, Ltd., Caldwell, Idaho 83605

Childrens Press, Inc., 310 S. Racine Ave., Chicago, Ill. 60607

Coronet Instructional Films, 65 E. South Water St., Chicago, Ill. 60601

Thomas Y. Crowell Co., 201 Park Ave. S., New York, N.Y. 10003

Doubleday & Co., Inc., Garden City, N.Y. 11530

Encyclopaedia Britannica Press, Inc., 425 N. Michigan Ave., Chicago, Ill. 60611

The Fideler Co., 31 Ottawa Ave., N.W., Grand Rapids, Mich. 49502

Follett Publishing Co., 1010 W. Washington Blvd., Chicago, Ill. 60607

Franklin Publishing & Supply Co., 2134 N. 63d St., Philadelphia, Pa. 19131

Garrard Publishing Co., 1607 N. Market St., Champaign, Ill. 61820

Ginn & Co., Statler Bldg., Back Bay P.O. 191, Boston, Mass. 02117

Globe Book Co., Inc., 175 Fifth Ave., New York, N.Y. 10010

Golden Press, Inc., 850 Third Ave., New York, N.Y. 10022

Graflex, Inc., Program Learning Publishing Div., Box 101, Rochester, N.Y. 14603

Grosset & Dunlap, Inc., 1107 Broadway, New York, N.Y. 10010

C. S. Hammond & Co., Inc., Maplewood, N.J. 07040

Harcourt, Brace & World, Inc., 757 Third Ave., New York, N.Y. 10017

Harper & Row, Publishers, 49 E. 33d St., New York, N.Y. 10016

Harvey House, Inc., Publishers, Irvington-on-Hudson, N.Y. 10533

D. C. Heath & Co., 285 Columbus Ave., Boston, Mass. 02116

Holt, Rinehart & Winston, Inc., 383 Madison Ave., New York, N.Y. 10017

Houghton Mifflin Co., 2 Park St., Boston, Mass. 02107

Laidlaw Brothers, Div. of Doubleday & Co., Inc., Thatcher & Madison Sts., River Forest, Ill. 60305

J. B. Lippincott Co., E. Washington Sq., Philadelphia, Pa. 19105

Lyons & Carnahan, Affiliate of the Textbook Div. of Meredith Publishing Co., 407 E. 25th St., Chicago, Ill. 60616

McCormick-Mathers Publishing Co., Inc., 1440 E. English St., Wichita, Kan. 67201

McGraw-Hill Book Co., 330 W. 42d St., New York, N.Y. 10036

The Macmillan Co., Div. of the Crowell-Collier Publishing Co., 60 Fifth Ave., New York, N.Y. 10011

Melmont Publishers, Inc., Subsidiary of Childrens Press, Inc., 310 S. Racine Ave., Chicago, Ill. 60607

Charles E. Merrill Books, Inc., 1300 Alum Creek Dr., Columbus, Ohio 43216

Noble & Noble, Publishers, Inc., 67 Irving Pl., New York, N.Y. 10003

Platt & Munk, Inc., 200 Fifth Ave., New York, N.Y. 10010

Prentice-Hall, Inc., Englewood Cliffs, N.J. 07632

Rand McNally & Co., 8255 Central Park Ave., Skokie, Ill. 60680

The Reilly & Lee Co., Subsidiary of Henry Regnery Co., 114 W. Illinois St., Chicago, Ill. 60610

Scholastic Book Services, Div. of Scholastic Magazines, Inc., 50 W. 44th St., New York, N.Y. 10036

Science Research Associates, Inc., wholly owned Subsidiary of International Business Machines Corp., 259 E. Erie St., Chicago, Ill. 60611

Scott, Foresman & Co., 433 E. Erie St., Chicago, Ill. 60611

Charles Scribner's Sons, 597 Fifth Ave., New York, N.Y. 10017

E. C. Seale & Co., Inc., 1053 E. 54th St., Indianapolis, Ind. 46220

Silver Burdett Co., Subsidiary of Time Inc., Park Ave. & Columbia Rd., Morristown, N.J. 07960

The L. W. Singer Co., Inc., Div. of Random House, Inc., 249-259 W. Erie Blvd., Syracuse, N.Y. 13202

The Steck Co., Box 16, Austin, Tex. 78761

Teachers Practical Press, Inc., 47 Frank St., Valley Stream, N.Y. 11580

United Educators, Inc., Tangley Oaks Educational Center, Lake Bluff, Ill. 60044

The University Publishing Co., 1126 Q St., Lincoln, Neb. 68508

Vanguard Press, Inc., 424 Madison Ave., New York, N.Y. 10017

The Viking Press, 625 Madison Ave., New York, N.Y. 10022

Harr Wagner Publishing Co., 609 Mission St., San Francisco, Calif. 94105

Henry Z. Walck, Inc., 19 Union Sq. W., New York, N.Y. 10003

Warp Publishing Co., 325 N. Colorado Ave., Minden, Neb. 68959

Albert Whitman & Co., 560 W. Lake St., Chicago, Ill. 60602

Publishers of Maps and Globes

Aero Service Corp., 210 E. Courtland St., Philadelphia, Pa. 19120

American Map Co., Inc., 3 W. 61st St., New York, N.Y. 10023

The George F. Cram Co., Inc., 730 E. Washington St., Indianapolis, Ind. 46206

Denoyer-Geppert Co., 5235 Ravenswood Ave., Chicago, Ill. 60640

Encyclopaedia Britannica, Inc., 425 N. Michigan Ave., Chicago, Ill. 60611

Farquhar Transparent Globes, 3724 Irving St., Philadelphia, Pa. 19104

Hagstrom Co., Inc., 311 Broadway, New York, N.Y. 10007

C. S. Hammond & Co., Inc., Maplewood, N.J. 07040

Hearne Bros., National Bank Bldg., Detroit, Mich. 48232

McKinley Publishing Co., 809-811 N. 19th St., Philadelphia, Pa. 19180

National Geographic Society, 17th & M Sts., N.W., Washington, D.C. 20036

A. J. Nystrom & Co., 3333 N. Elston Ave., Chicago, Ill. 60618

Rand McNally & Co., 8255 Central Park Ave., Skokie, Ill. 60076

Replogle Globes, Inc., 1901 N. Narragansett Ave., Chicago, Ill. 60639

Weber, Costello Co., Div. of Benefic Press, 1900 N. Narragansett Ave., Chicago, Ill. 60639

Manufacturers and Distributors of Films and Filmstrips

Association Films, Inc., 347 Madison Ave., New York, N.Y. 10017
Bailey Films, Inc., 6509 De Longpre Ave., Hollywood, Calif. 90028
Herbert E. Budek Co., 354 Union St., Hackensack, N.J. 07601
Bureau of Publications, Teachers College, Columbia University, 525 W. 120th
      St., New York, N.Y. 10027
Carousel Films, Inc., 1501 Broadway, New York, N.Y. 10036
Cenco Educational Films, 1700 Irving Park Rd., Chicago, Ill. 10013
Church-Craft Pictures, Inc., 3312 Lindell Blvd., St. Louis, Mo. 63103
Coronet Instructional Films, 65 E. South Water St., Chicago, Ill. 60601
Encyclopaedia Britannica Films, Inc., 1150 Wilmette Ave., Wilmette, Ill. 60091
Eye-Gate House, Inc., 146-01 Archer Ave., Jamaica, N.Y. 11435
Films, Inc., Subsidiary of Encyclopaedia Britannica Films, Inc., 4420 Oakton
      St., Skokie, Ill. 60076
Filmstrip House, 432 Park Ave. S., New York, N.Y. 10016
Indiana University, Audio Visual Center, Bloomington, Ind. 47401
International Film Bureau, Inc., 332 S. Michigan Ave., Chicago, Ill. 60604
The Jam Handy Organization, 2821 E. Grand Blvd., Detroit, Mich. 48211
Life Filmstrips, Time & Life Bldg., Rockefeller Center, New York, N.Y. 10020
Long Filmslide Service, 7505 Fairmont Ave., El Cerrito, Calif. 94530
McGraw-Hill Book Co., Inc., Text Film Div., 330 W. 42d St., New York, N.Y.
      10036
Modern Learning Aids, 3 E. 54th St., New York, N.Y. 10022
Official Films, 25 W. 45th St., New York, N.Y. 10036
Pathescope-Berlitz, 71 Weyman Ave., New Rochelle, N.Y.
Perceptual Development Laboratories, 6767 Southwest Ave., St. Louis, Mo.
      63117
Society for Visual Education, Inc., 1345 Diversey Pkwy., Chicago, Ill. 60614
United Nations, Film and Visual Information Div., New York, N.Y. 10017
United World Films, Inc., 1445 Park Ave., New York, N.Y. 10029
Visual Sciences, Suffern, N.Y. 10901
WaSP Filmstrips, Palmer Lane W., Pleasantville, N.Y. 10570

Selected List of Industries, Associations, and Agencies Distributing Free or Inexpensive Films, Filmstrips, and Tapes

No listing could conceivably exhaust the names of all the national and local manufacturers, industrial associations, charity organizations, foreign information offices, and the like that distribute audio-visual and other materials. This brief list, therefore, is intended merely to indicate the great variety of possible sources. Moreover, this list is not meant to indicate the author's personal preferences or recommendations; as this book has tried to suggest, every school and indeed every classroom will have its own needs and interests, and a film or other instructional device that might be suitable for one classroom inquiry might not be appropriate for another classroom inquiry, even though the general topic might be identical. Each teacher must make an individual judgment of appropriateness.

The federal government of the United States also distributes an enormous variety of instructional films. These are listed, with annotations, in the U.S. Department of Health, Education, and Welfare, Office of Education, *U.S. Government Films for Public Educational Use* (Washington: Government Printing Office, 1963).

Allis-Chalmers Mfg. Co., Tractor Photographic Group, Milwaukee, Wis. 53201

Aluminum Co. of America, Motion Picture Section, 1501 Alcoa Bldg., Pittsburgh, Pa. 15219

American Federation of Labor—Congress of Industrial Organizations, Educational Dept., 815 16th St., N.W., Washington, D.C. 20006

American Gas Assn., Film Service, 420 Lexington Ave., New York, N.Y. 10017

American Institute of Steel Construction, Inc., Dept. of Educational Services, 101 Park Ave., New York, N.Y. 10017

American Iron and Steel Institute, Teaching Aids Distribution Center, Bedford Hills, N.Y. 10507

American National Cattlemen's Assn., Director of Information, 801 E. 17th St., Denver, Colo. 80218

American Petroleum Institute, Committee on Public Affairs, 1271 Ave. of the Americas, New York, N.Y. 10020

American Red Cross (consult local chapter)

American Sheep Producers Council, Film Div., 909 17th St., Denver, Colo. 80202

American Stock Exchange, Public Affairs Div., 86 Trinity Pl., New York, N.Y. 10006

American Trucking Assns., Inc., 1616 P St., N.W., Washington, D.C. 20036

American Waterways Operators, Inc., 1025 Connecticut Ave., Washington, D.C. 20006

Anti-Defamation League of B'nai B'rith (consult local chapters in these cities: Atlanta, Ga.; Boston, Mass.; Buffalo, N.Y.; Chicago, Ill.; Columbus, Ohio; Denver, Colo.; Detroit, Mich.; Houston, Tex.; Indianapolis, Ind.; Los Angeles, Calif.; Miami, Fla.; Milwaukee, Wis.; Minneapolis, Minn.; New Haven, Conn.; New Orleans, La.; New York, N.Y.; Newark, N.J.; Omaha, Neb.; Philadelphia, Pa.; Richmond, Va.; St. Louis, Mo.; San Francisco, Calif.; Seattle, Wash.; Springfield, Ill.; Washington, D.C.)

Association of American Railroads, School and College Service, Transportation Bldg., Washington, D.C. 20006

Austrian Institute, 11 E. 52d St., New York, N.Y. 10022

Bell Telephone System (consult local business office)

The Boeing Co., Film Editor, News Bureau, Box 3707, Seattle, Wash. 98124

Boise Cascade Corp., Director of Corporate Relations, Box 200, Boise, Idaho 83710

Brazilian Government Trade Bureau, 551 Fifth Ave., New York, N.Y. 10017

Bureau of Communication Research, 267 W. 25th St., New York, N.Y. 10001

Canadian Travel Film Library, 680 Fifth Ave., New York, N.Y. 10019, or 230 N. Michigan Ave., Chicago, Ill. 60601

CARE, Inc., National Field Director, 660 First Ave., New York, N.Y. 10016

Chicago Board of Trade, Public Information and Education Dept., 141 W. Jackson Blvd., Chicago, Ill. 60604

Christian Rural Overseas Program, 117 W. Lexington Ave., Elkhart, Ind. 46515

Consulate General of Canada, Film Library, 310 S. Michigan Ave., Chicago, Ill. 60604

Consulate of the Federal Republic of Germany, 460 Park Ave., New York, N.Y. 10022

DuPont deNemours & Co., Inc., Motion Picture Section, Advertising Dept., Wilmington, Del. 19898

The Dow Chemical Co., Audio Visual Center, Abbott Road Bldg., Midland, Mich. 48640

Embassy of Finland, Press Section, 1900 24th St., N.W., Washington, D.C. 20008

Embassy of Malaysia, 2401 Massachusetts Ave., N.W., Washington, D.C. 20008

Farm Credit Banks (consult nearest bank in one of these cities: Baltimore, Md.; Berkeley, Calif.; Columbia, S.C.; Louisville, Ky.; New Orleans, La.; Omaha, Neb.; St. Louis, Mo.; St. Paul, Minn.; Spokane, Wash.; Wichita, Kan.)

Farm Film Foundation, 1425 H St., N.W., Washington, D.C. 20005

Federal Reserve Banks (consult nearest bank in one of these cities: Atlanta, Ga.; Boston, Mass.; Chicago, Ill.; Cleveland, Ohio; Dallas, Tex.; Kansas City, Mo.; Minneapolis, Minn.; New York, N.Y.; Philadelphia, Pa.; Richmond, Va.; San Francisco, Calif.)

Federation of Jewish Philanthropies of New York, Film Bureau, 130 E. 59th St., New York, N.Y. 10022

Firestone Tire & Rubber Co., Dept. of Public Relations, Akron, Ohio 44307

Ford Motor Co. (consult nearest Ford Film Library at one of these addresses: The American Road, Dearborn, Mich.; 16 E. 52d St., New York, N.Y. 10022; 4316 Telegraph Ave., Oakland, Calif. 94609)

General Mills, Inc., Film Library, 9200 Wayzata Blvd., Minneapolis, Minn. 55426

General Motors Corp. (consult nearest public relations staff at one of these addresses: General Motors Bldg., Detroit, Mich. 48202; 1775 Broadway, New York, N.Y. 10019; 405 Montgomery St., San Francisco, Calif. 94104)

Ghana Information Services, 565 Fifth Ave., New York, N.Y. 10017

B. F. Goodrich Co., Public Relations Dept., Akron, Ohio 44318

Goodyear Tire & Rubber Co., Audio-Visual Dept., Akron, Ohio 44316

Henry Ford Museum and Greenfield Village, Audio-Visual Services, Dept. of Education, Dearborn, Mich.

Illinois Central R.R., Library of Audio-Visual Aids, 135 E. 11th Pl., Chicago, Ill. 60605

Information Service of India (consult nearest office at one of these addresses: Embassy of India, 2107 Massachusetts Ave., N.W., Washington, D.C. 20008; Consulate General of India, 3 E. 64th St., New York, N.Y. 10021; Consulate General of India, 215 Market St., San Francisco, Calif. 94105)

Institute of Life Insurance, Educational Div., 488 Madison Ave., New York, N.Y. 10022

Insurance Information Institute, Film Library, 267 W. 25th St., New York, N.Y. 10001

International Business Machines Corp. (consult nearest Film Library at one of these addresses: 618 S. Michigan Ave., Chicago, Ill. 60605; 3424 Wilshire Blvd., Los Angeles, Calif. 90005; 425 Park Ave., New York, N.Y. 10022)

Investment Bankers Assn. of America, Educational Director, 425 13th St., N.W., Washington, D.C. 20004

Japan Information Service, Consulate General of Japan, 235 E. 42d St., New York, N.Y. 10017

Korean Information Office, 1828 Jefferson Pl., N.W., Washington, D.C. 20006

Lockheed-Georgia Co., Motion Picture Film Library, Zone 30, B-2 Bldg., Marietta, Ga. 30061

Metropolitan Life Insurance Co., Health and Welfare Div., 1 Madison Ave., New York, N.Y. 10010

Midland Cooperatives, Inc., Library, 739 Johnson St., N.E., Minneapolis, Minn. 55413

Minneapolis Grain Exchange, Educational Director, 150 Grain Exchange Bldg., Minneapolis, Minn. 55415

Mizrachi Women's Organization of America, 242 Park Ave. S., New York, N.Y. 10003

Modern Talking Picture Service, 3 E. 54th St., New York, N.Y. 10022

National Assn. of Manufacturers, Film Bureau, 2 E. 48th St., New York, N.Y. 10017

National Canners Assn., Information Div., 1133 20th St., N.W., Washington, D.C. 20006

National Committee for Education in Family Finance, 488 Madison Ave., New York, N.Y. 10022

National Committee for Labor Israel, Film Dept., 33 E. 67th St., New York,

N.Y. 10021

National Conference of Christians and Jews, Inc., 43 W. 57th St., New York, N.Y. 10019

National Consumer Finance Assn., Educational Services, 1000 16th St., N.W., Washington, D.C. 20036

National Lumber Manufacturers Assn., 1619 Massachusetts Ave., N.W., Washington, D.C. 20006

New Zealand Embassy, Information Office, 19 Observatory Circle, N.W., Washington, D.C. 20008

North Central Airlines, Inc., Public Relations Dept., 6201 34th Ave. S., Minneapolis, Minn. 55450

Philippine Travel Information Office, 535 Fifth Ave., New York, N.Y. 10017, *or* 212 Stockton St., San Francisco, Calif.

Phillips Petroleum Co., Advertising & Public Relations Dept., Bartlesville, Okla. 74003

Polish Embassy, 2640 16th St., N.W., Washington, D.C. 20009

Port of San Diego, 1365 Harbor Dr., San Diego, Calif. 29101

Pure Oil Co., General Office Library, 200 E. Golf Rd., Palatine, Ill. 60067

Quebec Government House, Rockefeller Center, 17 W. 50th St., New York, N.Y. 10020

Radio Free Europe Fund, Inc., Public Information Dept., 2 Park Ave., New York, N.Y. 10016

Reynolds Metals Co., Motion Picture Dept., Box 2346, Richmond, Va. 23218

Santa Fe Film Bureau, Atchison, Topeka & Santa Fe Ry., 80 E. Jackson Blvd., Chicago, Ill. 60604

Shell Oil Co., Film Library, 149-07 Northern Blvd., Flushing, N.Y. 11354

Society for Visual Education, Inc., 1345 Diversey Pkwy., Chicago, Ill. 60614

Southern Pacific Co., Public Relations Manager, 1675 Marquette Bldg., Chicago, Ill. 60603

Sterling-Movies U.S.A., Inc., 43 W. 61st St., New York, N.Y. 10023

Swedish Film Center, Dept. of Creativision, Inc., 1780 Broadway, New York, N.Y. 10019

Tea Council Film Library, 267 W. 25th St., New York, N.Y. 10016

Texaco, Inc., Sales Promotion Manager, 135 E. 42d St., New York, N.Y. 10017

Union Pacific R.R., Dept. of Livestock & Agriculture, 1416 Dodge St., Omaha, Neb. 68103

United Air Lines (consult sales offices in major cities)

United Israel Appeal, 515 Park Ave., New York, N.Y. 10022

United States Steel Corp., Film Distribution Center, 525 William Penn Pl., Pittsburgh, Pa. 15230

United World Free Film Service, 211 Park Ave. S., New York, N.Y. 10003

Washington Convention & Visitors Bureau, Metropolitan Washington Board of Trade, 1616 K St., N.W., Washington, D.C. 20006

West Coast Lumbermen's Assn., 1410 S.W. Morrison St., Portland, Ore. 97205

The Wool Bureau, Librarian, 360 Lexington Ave., New York, N.Y. 10017

INDEX